Building Corporate
AccountAbility

PRAISE FOR *BUILDING CORPORATE ACCOUNTABILITY*

'This book should be helpful to companies considering a social performance report, not only for the case studies but for the assurance that they will be in good company.'

Ralph Estes, American University and the Stakeholder Alliance

'An impressive piece of work [which] makes a real contribution to the literature... The variety of examples and perspectives is particularly valuable; there is no *one way* to do this work, but a variety of approaches, appropriate for various purposes and with diverse implications.'

Lee E Preston, Emeritus Professor of Business and Management, University of Maryland

'*Building Corporate AccountAbility* presents a clear state of affairs and a promising outlook on the future of social and ethical accounting, based as it is on practical auditing experiences and the best available thinking. It could not be more timely.'

Hank van Luijk, Professor of Business Ethics, Nijenrode University and Director of the European Institute for Business Ethics

'This book presents a radically different yet a well-documented and operational perspective on management, measurement, morals and responsibility.'

Finn Junge-Jensen, President, Copenhagen Business School

Building Corporate AccountAbility

Emerging Practices in Social and Ethical Accounting, Auditing and Reporting

edited by

Simon Zadek, Peter Pruzan and Richard Evans

Earthscan Publications Ltd, London

First published in the UK in 1997 by
Earthscan Publications Limited

Reprinted 1999

A catalogue record for this book is available from the British Library

ISBN: 1 85383 413 0 paperback / 1 85383 418 1 hardback

Typesetting and page design by PCS Mapping & DTP, Newcastle upon Tyne

Printed and bound in Great Britain by Biddles Ltd, Guildford and King's Lynn

Cover design by Andrew Corbett

For a full list of publications, please contact:
Earthscan Publications Ltd
120 Pentonville Road
London N1 9JN
Tel: (0171) 278 0433
Fax: (0171) 278 1142
Email: earthinfo@earthscan.co.uk
WWW: http://www.earthscan.co.uk

Earthscan is an editorially independent subsidiary of Kogan Page Limited
and publishes in association with WWF-UK and the International Institute
for Environment and Development.

Contents

ANNEXES

List of Illustrations

FIGURES

TABLES

BOXES

Acronyms and abbreviations

AAC	against animal testing
AGM	annual general meeting
ATMS	automated teller machines
BEST	better environmentally sound transportation
BITC	Business in the Community
BP	British Petroleum
BSI	British Standards Institute
BSR	American Business for Social Responsibility
CATI	computer-assisted telephone interviews
CBI	Confederation of British Industry
CEO	chief executive officer
CEP	Council on Economic Priorities, US
CER	Council on Economic Priorities
CERES	Coalition of Environmentally Responsible Economies
CFC	chlorofluorocarbon
CO_2	carbon dioxide
CSR	corporate social reporting
EMAS	Eco-Management and Audit Scheme
EMS	Environmental management system
EPA	Environmental Protection Act, US
ICCR	Interfaith Centre on Corporate Responsibility
IIP	Investors in People, UK
ISO	International Standards Organization
MERLIN	Medical Emergency Relief International
NAAC	National Association of Consumer Co-ops
NEF	New Economics Foundation
NGO	non-governmental organization
RPI	retail price index
SCF	staff charity fund
SEAAR	social and ethical accounting, auditing and reporting
SIS	Social Information System
SMA	Society of Management Accountants of Canada
SMAS	Sustainability Management and Audit
TQM	total quality management
UNCED	United Nations Conference on Environment and Development
UNEP	United Nations Environment Programme
UQM	University of Quebec at Montreal (Université de Quebec à Montreal)
WWF	World Wide Fund For Nature

Preface

In early 1994, the European Network for Self-Help and Local Development was launched at a major conference in Dessau in the eastern part of Germany. It was an exciting affair, with several hundred people from all over Europe sharing their experiences in the practice of business and economics working for the benefit of people and the environment.

One particular group of people attending the conference, six in all, seemed quite oblivious to the boisterous debates going on around them. They were often to be found in the café of the historic Bauhaus complex where the event was going on, sometimes seen wandering quietly around the grounds, or perched on top of the bales of straw that were strewn down one of the pathways. Wherever they were, they seemed rather separate from the rest, talking intently – and more or less exclusively – to each other.

What would not have been obvious to anyone who happened to look in on this small fellowship was that many of them were meeting for the first time. Equally obscured from the casual observer was that they all had one thing in common – a fascination for and involvement in the subject of social and ethical accounting and auditing. There was Richard Evans, then director of external affairs of the British fair trading company Traidcraft plc, one of the key people to develop the approach to social auditing that was gaining credence in the UK and elsewhere. There was Jane Press, researcher at the Italian environmental research institute, the Fondazione Eni Enrico Mattei. Third was Professor Peter Pruzan from the Copenhagen Business School, principal architect of the method that was being increasingly applied in Denmark and elsewhere in Scandinavia; the Ethical Accounting Statement. There was Maria Sillanpää, then head of social audit at The Body Shop International, deeply preoccupied with guiding the company through the complexities of its first social audit cycle. Bringing up the rear was Simon Zadek, research director of the London-based non-profit research organization, the New Economics Foundation, who had worked with Richard Evans in developing social accounting and auditing in the UK.

Two other people at the conference also had a particular fascination with and commitment to social and ethical accounting and auditing, and paid occasional visits to the group over the two days. First was Tina Liamzon, working for the two international networks: the Society for International Development headquartered in Italy and the People-Centred Development Forum based in New York. Tina's particular interest was in how non-governmental organizations in her home country, the Philippines, and elsewhere, could use social and ethical accounting and auditing as an institutional building tool as well as a means of being more accountable to their constituencies. Second was John Pearce, the founder of Community Enterprise Consultancy and Research in Scotland, who had led the way in Europe in developing social audit techniques for community enterprises.

These people had travelled to Dessau on the invitation of Simon Zadek to meet each other and to share their experiences in social and ethical accounting, auditing and reporting (SEAAR). All shared the view that SEAAR was a critical ingredient of effective social responsibility, whether for the business community, private non-profit organizations, or the state. Equally shared, however, was a concern that the proliferation of different approaches and models – whilst exciting – carried the dangers of confusion, misrepresentation and ultimately deterioration in the quality of practice.

That meeting in Dessau proved to be a watershed in the development of contemporary SEAAR. The recognition of the many common elements of practice of the various methods, combined with a shared sense of the importance of some convergence of these methods towards an agreed set of standards, precipitated a veritable explosion in networking of people working in this area.

The second important event that has marked the path to the publication of this book was a major conference organized by the New Economics Foundation on SEAAR in March 1995 in Edinburgh, Scotland. The conference was attended by practitioners from all over Europe and the US. Workshops were run mapping out experiences drawn from business, academic, non-profit, and government bodies from such diverse places as Russia and South Africa. Through this and other meetings in the UK, other key individuals and organizations began or continued to make critical inputs into the discussion about standards, notably John Elkington and Andrea Spencer-Cooke from the innovative corporate environmental consultancy SustainAbility; Rob Gray, Professor of Accountancy and Head of the Centre for Environmental and Social Accounting Research at the University of Dundee, Scotland; and Charles Medawar, Director of Social Audit Ltd.

In April of the same year, the developments in SEAAR were debated at a major meeting of ethical businesses hosted by the Social Venture Network in Tuscany, Italy. At this meeting, the importance of the field was once again debated and confirmed with vigour. All of the companies present were actively exploring how best to build clear social and ethical principles into their business practice. In this task, they all felt a lack of concrete methods, tools and techniques to assist them. Furthermore, it became clear in discussions that most of them had at one time or other been challenged as to the underlying ethos and practical social effects of their businesses. In most cases, companies had found it difficult, if not impossible, to respond adequately to these challenges, not having any objective, systematic basis for identifying and reporting on their social and ethical performance. In this context, the prospect of an agreed set of standards for SEAAR received welcome applause and encouragement.

Agreement was finally reached at this meeting that it would be necessary to establish a professional body if we really wanted to secure appropriate standards in SEAAR. It was also at this meeting that the original Dessau group joined with other key people in forming a working group to establish such an institute, including Henk van Luijk, Professor of Business Ethics at Nijenrode Business School in the Netherlands and President of the European Business Ethics Network; Alice Tepper Marlin, director of the New York-based corporate responsibility organization the Council on Economic Priorities; and David Wheeler, then head of ethical audit at The Body Shop International.

So the stage was set. Many of the key people, organizations and networks had reinforced our original sense of the need for standards. To varying degrees they had joined forces in commiting themselves to working together in agreeing such standards. The institute, which later was named the Institute of Social and Ethical AccountAbility, would be the vehicle for ensuring that the dialogue needed to underpin any agreed standards took place.

A key element of demonstrating the relevance of SEAAR to the corporate community is to show how it is already being done. From this came the decision to write a book about what people and organizations had achieved to date. This was not to be a book with a dry academic face – it was to be a book that lived through the practical experience of the editors and contributors in SEAAR. It was not to be a textbook or a manual, but neither was it to be principally about an issue in search of a solution. It was to be a book that offered practical guidance through the demonstration and analysis of experience. In that sense, its aim was to speak to people in the business community, those consultants servicing that community, and students planning to enter into the world of business, with a voice that supported the emerging social and ethical agenda for business.

This book is one result of that evolving history and ambitious aims. It provides the reasons why this agenda is important. It offers an overview of how the practice of SEAAR has got to where it is now, and where it is likely to go in the coming years. Finally, it provides a set of case studies of experiences in social and ethical accounting, auditing and reporting. *Building Corporate AccountAbility* presents 'work in progress'. It is incomplete because the story of social and ethical accounting and auditing continues to unfold with increasing vigour and effect. The experiences discussed in the following chapters have already influenced many other companies around the world, which are in turn examining and changing their own practice. The Institute of Social and Ethical AccountAbility has also grown over the course of the writing of this book, and its description in the following chapter will be out of date by the time of publication. Being a work in progress, for these reasons, is indeed a delight.

In a venture of this kind, the editors have drawn on the experience, insight, and energies of many individuals and organizations around the world. Most important have been the organizations that have experimented in SEAAR, and the individuals who have taken the time to document these experiences in ways that are accessible and meaningful to a wider audience*. Particular thanks are due to the organizations at which the editors are based – the Copenhagen Business School (Peter Pruzan), the New Economics Foundation (Simon Zadek), and Traidcraft (Richard Evans). These organizations, and specifically the colleagues working within them, have indulged the editors in the time they have been given to prepare this book, and have assisted by commenting on various chapters. Particular thanks in this regard go to Maya Forstater, Claudia Gonella, Ann-Marie Sheppard and Peter Raynard of the New Economics Foundation. Then there are those people who have supported the work of preparing this book through their general contribution to the field of SEAAR. We would particularly wish to thank many of those involved in the Institute of Social and Ethical AccountAbility, especially Henk van Luijk, Katherine Howard, Patrice van Reimsdijk and Vernon Jennings.

Simon Zadek
Peter Pruzan
Richard Evans
London, February 1997

* The editors are therefore particularly grateful to all of the contributors to this book, particularly Rob Gray, Alan Parker, Maria Sillanpää and David Wheeler.

PART 1

Why, How and Where To

1

Introduction

This book is about the evolution of social and ethical accounting, auditing and reporting (SEAAR), and its implications for the practice of corporate responsibility. We examine why and how increasing numbers of companies are measuring and reporting on their social and ethical behaviour and impact. We throw light on some of the methodological difficulties in achieving rigour and objectivity by examining how it has been done in practice, rather than how it might be done in theory. Finally, we explore what is likely to happen in this area over the coming years, in particular the basis on which standards are going to be set for SEAAR, and the people and institutions involved in these activities.

We have focused here on the emerging practice of SEAAR within the business community. However, there are two senses in which this book also speaks to the wider community of organizations, including public and private non-profit organizations.[1] Firstly, these latter types of organizations are just as, if not more, concerned about their social and ethical impact and behaviour. Secondly, the methods described in this book have also been widely applied to non-profit organizations.[2] It is largely because of the need to demonstrate this point that we have included two public sector case studies in Part 2 of this book.

This book is for people facing the practical task of handling, developing and implementing corporate, social and ethical responsibility agendas. These are the managers who have been given the job of 'making it happen'. These managers come from diverse backgrounds and locations within their companies, including corporate affairs and reputation management, marketing, environmental management, human resources and personnel, strategic planning, and community affairs. They have an understanding of *one* particular area of corporate responsibility. They therefore know what constitutes good practice in dealing with staff, in terms of environmental performance or in the area of corporate philanthropy. The quandary they face, however, is that the concerns they find themselves grappling with cannot be contained within these narrow boxes. Environmental issues turn out to have as much to do with the social and ethical concerns of the communities in which the company works as, say, the biophysical effects of production. Meeting the needs of the market increasingly means going beyond the delivery of technically superior products and services as consumers show a growing concern with the social and ethical dimensions of production – such as in relation to the use of child labour, senior citizens or the handicapped.

As these many dimensions of social and ethical responsibility pervade an increasing proportion of a company's activities, those nominally responsible for 'the social and ethical responsibility' of the company find themselves outflanked and often quite overcome by their own company's numerous and fragmented initiatives. The purchasing department may be developing an ethical supplier relations policy, whilst the human resource department is establishing whistleblowing systems for staff, and the reputation team is trying to cope with the latest environmental campaign by non-governmental organizations (NGOs). This decentralized approach might be acceptable if there were not so many unavoidable linkages between the different initiatives. Most large companies do indeed have a corporate-level ethical code of conduct that is intended to embrace their entire operations: but do these different initiatives add up to their overall ethical claims and postures? Who is to know, and who is responsible for finding out? This occurs amidst the realities of downsizing, delayering, and more generally stripping to the bone people, systems, and procedures that do not seem to contribute directly to the financial bottom line.

Faced with the new challenge of handling a complex and often volatile blend of social and ethical issues, responsible managers turn to the outside to seek information, expertise and guidance. What they find is a sea of information generated by communication consultants, business ethicists, and campaigning organizations. Just keeping up with the proliferation of literature, and dealing with people offering a myriad of related services, can entirely absorb a manager's time and energy. Far from providing a sound foundation for developing coherent initiatives that meet best practice industry standards, this information often leaves the manager confused and more likely irritated, despondent or outright cynical.

These managers need to implement a change process that addresses both expected short- and long-term needs and can handle unexpected external pressures and events as they develop. At the same time, an approach is required that remains rooted in the prevailing organizational culture and imperatives. Without finding a way of achieving this juggling act, managers are likely to fail – buried under their colleagues' resistance and ineffective in dealing with the ever-changing and more complex environment within which the company exists.

The challenge taken up by this book is to assist these managers in their difficult task by providing a window onto the one essential element of *any* change process – a mechanism for learning as a basis for improvement. *An organization without a systematic way of understanding what it has or has not achieved is unlikely to succeed, irrespective of its aims or determination.* This is obvious to anyone focused on financial success, who would walk away from a company that had inadequate financial accounting systems. Similarly, anyone interested in social and ethical performance would first look to see how an organization records, interprets and acts on its understanding of its previous actions as a basis for improving its social and ethical performance in the future.

What this book, therefore, offers managers is an insight into how their organization can develop processes that enable them to understand what has and is likely to happen, what key people think about it all, and what might be done to improve social and ethical performance. While writing principally for corporate managers, the editors are aware of the burgeoning interest in the subject of SEAAR to people in other institutional settings. The natural counterpart of the manager's concern in social and ethical responsibility is the interest of other corporate stakeholders: notably, staff and workers' organizations, shareholders, consumer groups, the ethical investment community, regulators, consultants and accountants, and community and campaigning organizations. Each of these groups has an interest in knowing more about companies' social and ethical performance, as well as wishing to make their views better known and have them taken into account. These corporate stakeholders, who need to distinguish public relations hype from sound relationship-building through social and ethical accounting, auditing and reporting constitute the second target audience for this book.

The third audience are the stakeholders of other types of organizations (including their managers), particularly public and private non-profit organizations with overt commitments to pursuing non-financial goals. These organizations – often given statutory rights on the basis of their commitment to address non-financial goals (eg tax exemption) – are in many ways under even more pressure than the commercial sector to demonstrate their social and ethical performance.

Lastly, this book anticipates an audience of students and researchers. We make no conscious attempt to review the deeper theoretical dimensions of the subject. In this sense, students and researchers with an interest in the area will need to look at the literature that is more deeply rooted within the academic tradition, some of which is referred to in the following chapters and the concluding annotated bibliography. At the same time, students and researchers alike would do well to be aware of the emerging *practice* of SEAAR that is described in this book, since it is this practice which is likely to form the basis of those conventional wisdoms in the future on which strong theoretical foundations will certainly be built. In this sense, *Building Corporate AccountAbility* offers students and researchers a unique source of information, such as case studies produced by the people involved in them, or with a close involvement in the processes they describe.

THE BASIC DILEMMA

One common concern arises from the increased disclosure of corporate social and ethical performance; there is a need to establish methods for assessment, verification and disclosure that meet the requirements of both companies and outside parties. 'Glossy' social reporting no longer satisfies the demands of groups that have the power to support or undermine a company's market position, through organizing consumer boycotts or blocking planning permission. Nor does a gloss over a company's ethics help in attracting creative, dedicated and responsible employees who feel a strong sense of identity with the company and whose commitment is vital for overall business success. Shareholders themselves are also demanding to know more about social and ethical performance as an increasing number of high-profile cases highlight the financial consequences of unethical business behaviour. So, whether in response to the needs of single-issue groups, actual and prospective staff, or shareholders, glossy offerings are failing to build good reputations and relationships. Something else is needed if social and ethical reporting is to effectively consolidate a company's viability, whilst at the same time edging it towards improved standards of social and ethical performance.

Recognizing the need to go further in assessing and reporting on social and ethical performance is a critical step that most companies have now taken, if only to secure their licence to operate. With the recent experiences of such leading companies as Shell, Texaco, Nike and others, there is a growing acceptance that reputation cannot be sustained through a culture of secrecy. Rather, there is a recognition that relationships in the future will rely more on balanced, systematic sharing of information as a basis for dialogue. This is what lies at the heart of SEAAR. As a senior executive of a major multinational declared in discussing whether the company he worked for would move towards a rigorous approach to social auditing: 'It is no longer a matter of *whether*, but of *when*, and *how*'.

Knowing that you need to move forward is one thing: knowing *how* to move forward is an altogether different matter. There are many issues to resolve before it becomes possible to report on social and ethical performance in a way that is accurate, complete, understandable, and useful. Firstly is the matter of measurement. It is reasonably straightforward to report on how much a company gave away through its charitable programmes and philanthropic activities. In the UK, for example, British Telecom is the largest corporate giver, donating at a rate of £15 million per annum at the last count. It even makes some sense to compare the performance of different companies, usually by ranking their charitable donations as a percentage of some measure of net income or profit before tax.

But such input indicators tell us little more than that some monies have been spent or profits used. They do not tell us the effect of that expenditure, whether on the recipients or on the company itself. Should philanthropic spending be valued by its financial volume? Or should its value take account of whether, for example, the donation contributed to the company obtaining critical planning permission for a new petrol station or supermarket; or whether it went to sponsoring a photographic exhibition or to training youths for future employment; or whether it provided out-of-date produce to community functions that were of little real value to the company? Is a million dollars of 'giving' to be valued the same way irrespective of its use or its effectiveness for the intended beneficiaries and the company itself? Clearly not.

The question of what to measure, and how to measure it, is therefore not straightforward. Our *simple* example in the previous paragraph easily illustrates the magnitude of the dilemma. Input data (such as financial costs or time) have absolute and relative dimensions; there is a difference between input and output data (the costs of training unemployed youths as opposed to its results); output data can be measured in different ways depending on what is seen to be important. Different outputs are not really comparable. Measuring in an accurate and useful way is clearly not straightforward.

The question of *how* to produce social or ethical assessments is not only a matter of finding some objective form of measurement, but also concerns how measures are understood and responded to by their intended audiences.

It is one thing to report on the staff wages and the employment of women and people from disadvantaged minority groups. Despite controversies, there are more or less accepted approaches to measuring these aspects of a company's performance, and acceptable approaches to comparing between companies and against local, regional and national norms. Beyond this, however, lies an ocean of issues where neither the basis for measurement or judging the resulting performance report can be agreed upon. The heated debate about the use and treatment of child labour in Third World countries – or the South – provides a good case in point. Consumers in industrialized countries may be horrified to hear that young children have stitched the shoes they wear, or have woven the carpets they walk on. But easy judgements are confounded by the fact that voices from those countries where child labour is used highlight the need for children to work to support the very lives of their families.

Which view is correct – the concern for children, their role in supporting their families, or both? Similarly, it is one thing to compare wages between similar companies in the same geographical locality, but what of the financial *needs* of employees? Is it acceptable that a company pays low wages because they are comparable to those paid by other companies? The short-term commercial view of this question is likely to be a straightforward 'yes'. However, the consumer response to information about the measly wages being paid by companies from which they buy their bedlinen or their children's schoolbooks may be very different. If people who buy a company's produce are concerned about the nature of the production and trading process, then business survival may depend on whether and how the company is seen to respond to these concerns.[3]

So the problem with SEAAR is not merely a question of measurement but of how those measures are viewed by stakeholders who can determine a company's future. The values of key stakeholders cannot be ignored, even when they conflict with the company's social, ethical and environmental mission and aims. Whilst a company clearly cannot take account of everyone's views all of the time – let alone respond to these views – equally they are ignored at the company's peril. Some mechanism is needed to measure and report on performance in relation to different views and interests.

The extent and type of SEAAR is itself a function of how the particular company sees itself and its relationship with the outside world. Many companies have a culture of secrecy that extends well beyond any grounded rationale of commercial confidentiality.[4] There is often a presumption that any disclosure which takes the company beyond compliance is an unnecessary risk. Equally, there is often an assumption that the disclosure of what appears to be relatively harmless information can lead to a company being pressurized to release potentially more damaging information. 'Why should we', companies argue, 'stick our heads above the parapet and risk being shot at?'. Underlying this is a view that any news which is not positive is bad; a company's key audiences – such as government and consumers – will always punish companies for admitting that they have not performed as well as they might in social or ethical terms.

The question of *how* to proceed in SEAAR is not, therefore, merely a technical matter of getting the mechanics right. There is a set of qualitative questions that any company considering an extension of their social and ethical assessment and reporting needs to answer. Interestingly, these questions are not only answered *before* any work begins, but are key 'hot points' around which SEAAR exercises pivot. A company, for example, may well seek to establish what it means by 'fair trade' and set it out in a policy document or a set of guidance notes. A good illustration of this is in what Levi Strauss calls its *Terms of Engagement*, which are intended to guide the company in its relationships with its suppliers. At the same time, the *practical* basis for this engagement is not dictated only by such terms, which can do no more than guide the process of engagement that is meant to balance ethical and commercial needs. This means that the process of measurement itself throws up new perspectives on the question of how a particular company understands fair trade, and does not only provide a set of compliance-oriented results.

THE THREE BASIC QUESTIONS

SEAAR therefore underpins a process of continual assessment. It not only offers a view of what has happened in the past, but drives the creative challenge to the company's mission and to the means by which the mission is addressed. In exploring this emerging phenomenon, the book's editors and contributors have sought to answer three basic questions: *why*, *how* and *where*.

First is the question of *why*: why do companies seek to understand, report on and improve their social and ethical performance? The polar views – that companies merely project a social or ethical image behind which lies a cynical foundation of exploitation, or that companies see the moral light and seek to mend their ways by doing good – are wholly inadequate. There is a need to explore the more complex and diverse reasons why the people who own, manage and work for companies adopt ethical practices that exceed what is legally required of them. Second is the matter of *how*: what have companies done to understand their social and ethical 'footprint'? Here is the opportunity to review some exciting and important contemporary developments in corporate SEAAR. Third is the speculative matter of where to: where is the practice of corporate SEAAR heading; what are the standards that need to be set to avoid a degeneration of quality and legitimacy of the practice; and what is the likelihood of those standards being established?

THE STRUCTURE OF THE BOOK

This book has been divided into two parts. In the first part, Chapter 2 explores the question of *why* companies have moved towards increased assessment of, and disclosure about, social and ethical performance. The chapter offers a brief historical overview of some of the key developments in SEAAR as a means of highlighting how the '*why*' can be understood. It identifies and explores some of the key dimensions of why that are relevant to the contemporary corporate scene.

Chapter 3 explores what common patterns have emerged in *how* SEAAR is carried out. A brief historical overview again seeks to identify in what ways the contemporary approaches have emerged from previous generations of practice and theory. The chapter then sets out a framework for assessing the quality of any particular SEAAR exercise, and outlines a five-stage model for social and ethical reporting that allows reports to be rated and ranked over time and in relation to each other.

The fourth and final chapter of Part 1 explores possible directions for SEAAR – the question of *where to*. Central is how accounting, auditing and reporting will extend beyond the innovative companies illustrated into the mainstream of the corporate community. In this chapter the need for professionalization and standardization is considered through an initiative to set up an international institute of standards for SEAAR, and to establish accreditation procedures for external auditors and verifiers. This is the Institute of Social and Ethical AccountAbility.

Part 2 comprises a set of nine case studies of contemporary initiatives in SEAAR. Most of the case studies are written by people directly involved in the practice they describe. These authors speak from the insights gained in facing the challenge of turning principles into practice, rather than from the green pastures of theory. Each reveals a fascinating case of social and ethical responsibility in action. Together, they provide a striking view of emerging practice, and therefore act as a reference point for those who are feeling their way towards SEAAR as a basis for strengthening their practice of social and ethical responsibility.

The cases span a number of different types of organizations in various contexts as well as several approaches. Three Scandinavian cases – Sbn Bank and the municipality of Aarhus from Denmark, and Wøyen Mølle from Norway – cover applications of the Ethical Accounting Statement developed at the Copenhagen Business School and now used extensively in Scandanavia. Two British cases –Traidcraft plc, and The Body Shop International – illustrate the evolution of the approach originally developed by the New Economics Foundation and Traidcraft, which is now being taken up by other companies and NGOs in the UK and elsewhere. As will be clear, there are considerable similarities between the methods and perspectives characterizing the first five cases. The final four cases illustrate a more varied group of experiences. The Coop in Italy has worked along quite different lines in developing and using their Social Balance in quantifying benefits and costs in financial terms. VanCity Savings and Credit Union have also drawn on and used a quite different approach developed in Canada for scoring organizations against measures of the quality of disclosure of information about social, ethical and environmental performance. Ben & Jerry's Homemade, Inc has pursued its own path of how best to account for and disclose its social and ethical performance for many years, whilst more recently adopting the standards developed in the British context. Finally, the case offered by Professor Rob Gray is of the 'compiled' social and ethical report of a major multinational, Glaxo Holdings plc.

These cases, taken in conjunction with Part 1, are intended to illustrate what the editors consider to be some of the most important developments in SEAAR. They provide a basis for understanding many of the underlying conceptual and methodological issues, as well as pointing the way towards the future.

BEYOND THE MAGIC BULLET

This book takes the view that there is no magic bullet waiting to be discovered and applied in addressing social and ethical concerns. Every part of civil society today – including business, the state and the NGOs – is changing with extraordinary speed, and yet simultaneously seems constrained in its scope for meaningful shifts towards a more ethical stance in practice. It is in this context that the cases and the associated moves to promote the take-up of SEAAR need to be understood.

Underlying the positions taken in this book is a sense of the need for, and the possibility of, change: a sense that shifts in consciousness and behaviour, even if they come at rare moments or arise from the ground swell of preceding and often marginal processes and initiatives do occur, and have in this critical area. SEAAR – particularly in the corporate context – seek to bring radical change through the gradual introduction of new approaches to securing accountability. For this to work, a form of accountability that is consistent with market survival will be required; such accountability should enhance organizational productivity in its broadest sense and initiate deeper, longer-term changes by influencing social, ethical and personal norms, expectations and practices.

For some, this approach is too uncomfortable to live and work with, often involving a painfully slow process of change. To others, it is an important wedge in the powerful armoury of an economic ideology that sees people's inspiration and efforts as human capital, their income as no more than costs, and the natural environment as little more than material inputs, at best associated with certain contingent liabilities.

Like all social innovations, the progress of SEAAR is likely to be a difficult one. It will be buffeted by both those who feel imposed upon, and those who feel that it does not adequately reflect or effect a radical agenda. Like environmental auditing, it will ultimately be judged on the basis of whether it has encouraged a serious move towards a broader understanding of and approach to accountability.

Whatever perspective the reader may bring to this book, one thing is clear. The experiences described and analyzed comprise serious attempts to find new ways to do business at a time of intensification of the combined effects of globalization and technological change. The experiences and views offered in this book are a contribution to squaring this particular circle by offering practical means whereby businesses and other organizations can strengthen their accountability to all stakeholders and the natural environment within the context of today's political economy.

ENDNOTES

1   By public organizations, we refer to those organizations owned and/or controlled directly by governments or multilateral institutions (such as the World Trade Organisation) By private, non-profit organizations, we include here so-called non-governmental organizations, voluntary organizations, citizens' groups, community-based organizations, charities, community enterprises, and co-operatives.

2   See, for example, the cases described in J Pearce, P Raynard, and S
     Zadek (1996) *Workbook on Social Auditing for Small Organizations*, New
     Economics Foundation, London Also see E Mayo (1996) *Social Auditing
     for Voluntary Organizations* City University, London, and J Pearce (1996)
     *Measuring Social Wealth: A Study of Social Audit Practice for Community
     and Cooperative Enterprises* New Economics Foundation, London. See
     too the discussions in U Hjelmar (ed) (1997) Ethical Accountability: A
     New Approach to User Influence and Quality in the Public Sector (in
     Danish), Fryalund, Copenhagen. It should be noted that within a
     Scandinavian context, social and ethical accounting, auditing and
     reporting are most often implemented in non-profit organizations
     (schools, universities, hospitals, government departments, communities
     and local governments, etc).
3   See, for example, New Economics Foundation and the Catholic Institute
     for International Relations (1997), *Open Trading: Options for Effective
     Monitoring of Corporate Codes of Conduct* NEF/CIIR, London.
4   This culture of secrecy, and its unintended costs, is elegantly described
     in J Stack (1992) *The Great Game of Business* Doubleday, New York.

2

Why Count Social Performance?

To understand the emerging pattern of SEAAR requires first that one understands *why* there is a burgeoning interest in the field. What may be burdensome procedures and processes should not be taken on lightly by any organization. Companies will not take on such burdens merely because it seems like a logical extension of financial and environmental accounting and auditing. Companies faced with the pressures of showing healthy financial returns will want to see new activities contributing to their overall viability.

WHY ETHICS?

An exploration of the question of *why* can be broken down into two (closely related) parts: why should companies be ethical, and why should they bother to account for their ethics? On the first part, Professor Henk van Luijk and others from the European Institute for Business Ethics (EIBE) sums up the essential business case as follows:

> *High ethics companies such as Texas Instruments, IBM, or Marks and Spencer ... know that behaving ethically is integral to their success. They know that their reputation - a reputation for fair dealing, which gains them the trust of their customers, suppliers, and the community at large - is crucial to their bottom line.*[1]

This view conforms with the findings of an increasing number of studies into the foundations of successful business, whether for the multinational or the corner shop: reputation counts.[2] Relationships matter in seeking business success, and such values as trust, integrity and commitment are integral to long-term relationships that work.

What is not clear in Henk van Luijk's quote is what exactly is meant by ethics. It is certainly appropriate if a company does not discriminate against women to have a law against such discrimination - but that has little to do with the ethics of the company or its managers. Similarly, we cannot count a company as ethical if it stops employing child labour because of the threat of a consumer boycott. A company may assist people previously disadvantaged in the market, or protect the environment, in ways that may be good for both.

However, we cannot deem this to be ethical if the company really had little choice or acted merely to sustain its level of financial success.

Conversely, is a company unethical if it seeks to offer a fairer deal to community producers in the South, but makes a complete mess of it and ends up doing more harm than good? Is a company unethical if it makes some of its staff redundant because it believes it has no choice if it wants to stay in business; and what if it turns out that there was a choice, albeit a risky one?

Ethics is therefore not merely a matter of result or impact, but turns out to have much to do with *intention* and *choice*. This then raises the question: should we be concerned with *why* companies choose to behave in particular ways, or should we focus pragmatically on the *effect* of their decisions – or perhaps both? Our answer to this question has profound implications for what we choose to measure and how.

Ethics is therefore an illusive term. Everyone uses it and yet few people are clear about what it means. Henk van Luijk does, however, seem to use it in a particular way. He is arguing that ethics is, effectively, about a company's *reputation* for being fair and trustworthy. Ethics from this perspective is about whether stakeholders understand and can broadly agree with why a company is doing something not so much whether they think it is a good thing. For example, a company that has an honest and fair reputation decides to stop using a long-term supplier, who will suffer badly as a result. There is little chance of the supplier thinking this is a good idea. But it may well be that the supplier appreciates that the company had little choice, given its own market conditions; perhaps the company sought to work with the supplier in bringing changes that would have allowed the relationship to continue, and gave reasonable warning to the supplier of its forthcoming loss of business. The supplier may well in this situation consider the company to be ethical or at least fair in its approach, whilst not in any way approving of the outcome.

Important, then, is Henk van Luijk's recognition of the significance of reputation and its links to stakeholder perceptions of a company's intentions, decisions and practices in the face of particular options, as well the outcomes of those practices. What is reasonable is what stakeholders deem acceptable behaviour. Which stakeholders, and how they decide on what *is* reasonable, is a subject we will return to below.

So why should companies be concerned about ethics? Henk van Luijk's statement points the way to the simplest reason – it is good for business. This argument suggests that companies who demonstrate an arrogant disregard for what stakeholders – or society at large – consider to be acceptable behaviour will pay the cost in terms of profit and, ultimately, survival.

Unfortunately, this argument has some major limitations. Firstly, companies seek to profit from doing things that are deemed negative by society, such as making people unemployed or damaging the environment. As the Institute for Policy Studies reports, while annual worker layoffs across the US corporate sector increased by 39 per cent between 1990 and 1995, corporate profits over the same period increased by 75 per cent.[3] As the editors of the magazine *Business Week* concluded, 'It doesn't take a brain surgeon to see why millions of people who worked hard to make their companies competitive feel shafted'.[4]

So, being unethical *can* pay, at least in the short run, if stakeholders do not penalize the company through lower staff productivity, lower consumer interest, or investment realignments. The link between ethics and success is not, therefore, as straightforward as Henk van Luijk's statement suggests. Failing to live up to key stakeholders' expectations does not necessarily lead to a company being penalized where it hurts – at the bottom line. Even Shell's experience of dramatic and unexpected stakeholder action in response to its plan to sink the *Brent Spar* platform in the North Sea resulted in only a very minor and temporary dip in earnings and share prices, at least so far.

What is equally apparent is that a failure to behave ethically in the eyes of key stakeholders *can* pose a threat to a company's long-term financial health. The clothing retail chain, Gap, understood this when it agreed to adopt a code of conduct covering the factories in the South from which it purchases the products it sells. It understood that its customer base could be influenced by the growing number of non-profit organizations campaigning around labour conditions in these factories, particularly those focused on the emotive issue of child labour. This threat of a consumer boycott has led, at the time of writing this book, to a number of companies throughout the clothing, sportswear and toy industries to accept the need to adopt codes of conduct and to allow for external verification of performance against these codes.[5]

WHY COUNT ETHICS?

Companies need to know the views of key stakeholders with regard to social, ethical and environmental issues. They also need to know how these views are changing over time, and how their views will underpin responses by stakeholders towards the company.

Is this just a question of more market surveys covering a wider range of issues? Apparently not. Shell has been supporting environmental initiatives for several decades, and until the *Brent Spar* fiasco was seen by most of its customers as a reasonably green company. No amount of traditional market research would have been likely to predict the public response to Greenpeace's call not to sink the *Brent Spar*. Similarly, it is very unlikely that the managers of toy, sportswear and textiles companies in the late 1980s would have believed that the consumer would respond to concerns about the labour conditions of Southern suppliers.

Companies are increasingly realizing that merely asking people their opinion about things does not reveal the dynamic process of how and in what directions people develop their ideas. Counting in the traditional sense of polling people's views may work in choosing between different flavours of ice-cream, but it is unlikely to be helpful in understanding how people develop a sense of moral concern, and how this concern is voiced. So understanding stakeholders' views requires much more than simple survey work. Some deeper social contract is needed to go beyond inaccurate counting to a point where stakeholders become more open because they begin to feel that their views can count.

In moving away from the conventions of traditional market surveying, companies are faced with a far more interactive set of relationships. For stakeholders to be willing to offer insights into their own interests and concerns, they need an environment of trust and honesty. This in turn means that companies have to think quite differently about what they need to reveal about their own operations and practices. It is not possible to demand commitment from employees if the future of their own jobs is shrouded in secrecy. Suppliers are less likely to comply with codes of conduct imposed by their prime clients if they sense that these companies are less than concerned, and even less open, about their own behaviour. Consumers will simply not believe any more the claims of companies without a more systematic, rigorous approach to disclosure.

Companies are finding, in a growing number of cases, that they need to respond to stakeholder concerns not only by changing their practices, but by being more open in reporting how they have performed against key social, ethical and environmental dimensions of their behaviour and impact. It is a short step from accepting the growing need of companies to account for their social, ethical and environmental performance to recognizing the need for rigorous, comprehensive, and externally verified SEAAR. Companies are, of course, accustomed to adopting an extensive array of procedures, including a range of accounting and auditing forms. Financial accounting, for example, started originally because of the need for managers to have some basic records of cash flows, to provide a means whereby shareholders could hold the stewards of their investments to account, and as a means of working out how to divide the profits at the end of the day. It was only subsequently that the requirement to audit accounts became enshrined in law, principally as a means of protecting shareholders against unscrupulous managers and directors of the companies that they had bankrolled.[6] Financial accounting was (and still is), therefore, seen as a tool for identifying how the organization was doing, for being accountable to one particular stakeholder group – the shareholders – and for working out who should get what share of the financial surpluses generated by the company. Auditing was similarly seen as a means of ensuring that the financial accounts reported to shareholders (and, subsequently, other sources of funding and the government for regulatory and tax purposes) were accurate.

Environmental assessment was extremely rare only a decade ago but now is common practice by increasing numbers of companies. A recent survey carried out by the International Institute for Industrial Environmental Economics at Lund University, Sweden, concluded that 23 per cent of Europe's largest companies in 1995 produced some sort of environmental report, compared to 15 per cent in 1993.[7] The reasons for companies being willing to undergo such exercises varies to a considerable degree, as does the content and form of environmental assessment. In the early stages, the principle reasons concerned acquiring knowledge to avoid legal liability, and in some cases to avoid confrontation with increasingly assertive and effective environmental campaigning organizations. Over time, the more positive business case for environmental auditing has, for many industries and contexts, been proven many times over, particularly the 'win–win' arguments for cost-savings through eco-efficiency measures.[8] Unlike in the financial sphere, statutory regulations guiding environmental accounting and auditing are not yet common. In Europe the Eco-Management and Audit Scheme (EMAS) has been adopted and advocated as a best practice standard by the

European Commission, and is being taken up by an increasing number of companies operating in Europe.[9] At the same time, the ISO 14000 series has emerged as a competitive standard and, although many in Europe and elsewhere view it as a considerable dilution of what had been achieved in the negotiations that led to the adoption of EMAS.[10]

A range of quality assurance systems have been developed over the last two decades to meet the needs of large organizations to organize and rationalize their change processes to achieve the maximum possible quality throughout their operations. Possibly the most well-known of these has been total quality management (TQM), arguably (as its name suggests) the most comprehensive approach developed to date. What matters here is not so much the details of how or whether TQM works in practice, but that it is an entirely voluntary process completely devoid of any external pressure, such as campaigning organizations in the case of environmental reporting. That is, the widespread adoption of TQM and other system-level quality assurance systems (such as ISO 9000 and BS 5750) by parts of the corporate sector, illustrates the fact that companies *will* commit considerable resources to securing better, more effective management systems and procedures. It is worth noting, furthermore, that approaches such as TQM include not only quantitative output data, such as the technical failure rate of a particular product or process, but also subjective outcome data, such as the views of staff or indeed of the wider public.

It therefore turns out that companies invest heavily in procedures and processes that yield complex sets of quantitative and qualitative, and objective and subjective, data covering issues both within and outside of the organization. This should, of course, hardly be surprising, since it is precisely these combinations of views and facts that make or break a company at the end of the day. Indeed, it turns out that a major reason for mainstream companies' increased interest in SEAAR is exactly to cope with the increasing complexity of their situation and associated management processes. As one senior manager of a major oil company said during an internal seminar introducing the topic:

> We are having to cope with so many different quality issues at the same time, some technical, but many of them dealing with 'soft' issues. If social auditing helps us to deal with them more rationally, then we really could use it.

So, while companies love to hate procedures because of their time and financial costs, the most sophisticated and widespread systems have been developed for use principally by the business community, particularly larger-scale corporations. The key issue is more than a question of 'how much does it cost' to do some form of SEAAR, but rather a matter of 'is it worthwhile?'.

A BRIEF HISTORY OF 'WHY'[11]

One of the first recorded use of the term *social audit* was by the US-based academic Theodore J Kreps in 1940. In the context of the severe economic depression in the US in the 1930s, Kreps argued that companies needed to take on, and report against, wider societal responsibilities. The response to this call appears to have been very marginal, with no recorded cases of mainstream companies undertaking, let alone disclosing, social audits.

In the early 1950s, Howard Bowen reinvigorated the idea of *social auditing* by arguing that companies should better understand their social impact, and that there was a need for *social auditors* to produce unbiased views of corporate social and ethical performance.[12] Of particular importance was that Bowen advocated social auditing for internal purposes only, essentially as a management tool. This rationale was quite at odds with Kreps, who saw the process as being managed and reported to external interests.

This difference in view of social auditing as a *management tool* or as an *accountability mechanism* has remained a critical frontline of both theory and practice, a subject to which we will return to again below.

George Goyder, writing in the UK with considerable foresight in the early 1960s about 'corporate responsibility' as an alternative to nationalization, summed up the need for what he termed corporate 'social auditing' as follows:

> ... [financial auditing] is a one-sided state of affairs and belongs to the days when companies were small and public accountability was secured. ...In an economy of big business ... there is clearly as much need for a social as for a financial audit.[13]

Goyder listed what the social audit would need to cover and some of the reasons for companies undertaking one:

> ...it is an obvious way by which the public may be informed of the manner in which a large business with a position bordering on monopoly is discharging its social responsibilities in the fields of labour relations, pricing policy, and local interests.... In the case of big companies it would provide a useful safety-valve for criticism. But it is essential that the social audit, when it comes, be made not only in the area of work and human relations, but also in that of the company's dealings with its customers, suppliers and the community.[14]

Goyder, writing over three decades ago, captured with eerie accuracy the issues facing contemporary approaches to SEAAR. Seeking a balance between Kreps and Bowen (although without any reference to, or perhaps knowledge of, their work), Goyder argued that social auditing could provide management with a useful tool, *and* the stakeholder with a basis to challenge and influence corporate practices.

The social unrest and changes in Europe and the US in the 1960s provided a boost to SEAAR. A new wave of writings and practice emerged advocating SEAAR in the corporate sector as 'a vision that at some future time corporations will assess their "social and ethical" performance in as systematic a manner as they now assess their financial performance'.[15] Influenced by the work of Ralph Nader, the Public Interest Research Centre in the UK established a company, Social Audit Ltd, with the aim of exploring and publishing information about the social and ethical performance of business.[16] The Company Affairs Committee of the Confederation of British

Industry (CBI) at that time recommended that there should be changes in company law aimed to encourage companies:

> ...to recognise duties and obligations (within the context of the objects for which the company was established) arising from the company's relationships with creditors, suppliers, customers, employees and society at large.[17]

This was the period when the stakeholder concept emerged in academic literature and policy debate in relation to the responsibilities of business. The US Chamber of Commerce, for example, noted:

> ...a fundamental shift from the principle that all business is essentially private and accountable to stockholders and the free marketplace, to legal doctrines that make large enterprises and, in particular, more and more accountable to the general public.[18]

A report by the US Department of Commerce summarized the reasons why social and ethical reporting was of increasing interest to companies and the public alike:

> Many firms have taken the view that self-generating efforts to improve corporate social performance lead to positive perceptions of their products.... And given the enormous costs of regulation, some argue that the short-term costs of greater corporate concern for the social consequences of business activities will result in greater profitability in the longer term.[19]

Similar developments were taking place all over Europe and the US during this period. In the Netherlands, a major steel producer, Hoogovens, initiated a social audit in 1969 as part of a collective agreement with the trade unions. The report was distributed to all employees and formed a key basis for negotiations about wages and working conditions. In Sweden, an account was published in 1977 of a project to develop social accounting procedures in two major Swedish manufacturing companies.[20] In Germany, a survey was published by Dierkes in 1979 of how social reports were being used by German business.[21] Dierkes, like Bowen before him, argued that social reporting was a necessary tool for effective management.

The 1980s in some ways did not provide a conducive environment for the development of social auditing. It was a period when business was arguably given more of a 'green light' to set its own terms for engagement with society than at any other time in this century, certainly in the industrial world. The view that business had responsibilities beyond the pursuit of profit was subject to attack and ridicule at the highest levels. As the Nobel Prize-winning economist, Milton Friedman, argued:

> Few trends could so thoroughly undermine the very foundation of our free society as the acceptance by corporate officials of a social responsibility other than to make as much money for their shareholders as possible.[22]

Yet, by the end of that decade there were clear signs of a renaissance in the practice of SEAAR. Several trends informed this development. Of particular importance was the emergence of environmental auditing as a respectable quality assurance process within the corporate sector and elsewhere. This established a critical precedent for non-financial auditing systems, verification processes and reporting responsibilities.[23] Of equal importance was the emergence – particularly in the US and Europe – of 'screening' corporate social and environmental impacts and intentions as a foundation for the emerging ethical consumerism and investment funds.[24]

The 1990s has seen a continuation of the historical tradition of social and ethical accounting, auditing and reporting, building particularly on emerging techniques and practices in the 1980s. The last decade has been an immensely fertile period; it has seen intense experimentation in the development and application of many different approaches to corporate SEAAR. Some of the most visible experiments involving the development of regular, systematic, disclosed processes have been in Denmark, the UK and the US. However, with the strengthening of international information networks, it has become increasingly apparent just how much is going on around the world. The cases in Part 2 of this book offer one of the first published windows into the wealth of this recent experience.

SEAAR has had a volatile history to date. There have been periods of much debate when much has been published amidst calls for greater corporate accountability – such as following the end of World War II in the early 1940s and again in the 1960s in Europe and the US. However, this heated debate resulted in little by way of practical action. Similarly, there have been periods of intensive activity – such as during the 1970s – that disappeared almost without trace within a matter of a few years following a change in the political and economic climate.

Whether the current surge in interest and practice of SEAAR will be sustained *and meaningful* will depend on whether there are deeply rooted changes taking place that will require different models of business success from those of the 1980s. This question is considered further in the final section of this chapter and in Chapter 4 of this book. It is important to highlight at this stage that a combination of different factors contribute to making it very likely that SEAAR will take a more permanant place in the corporate landscape. These factors were highlighted at a recent Business Roundtable at Windsor Castle, and include the very process of globalization of markets itself, technological changes, associated shifts in the nature of organizations, and, finally, radical changes in the patterns of public action by diverse forms of civil institutions and groups.[25]

THE RATIONALE TRIANGLE

This thumbnail historical sketch provides some ready clues to the question of why companies have began to engage in SEAAR. Three principal reasons emerge.

The first is essentially managerialist: to survive and prosper in society, management needs to know what is happening, what people think about the organization and how best to influence those perspectives. At the simplest level, this addresses the need for good market research and public relations. At the more sophisticated level, this highlights the need for managers to have a broader understanding and appreciation of stakeholder requirements and views, and the patterns of demands on business that are likely to arise in the future.

Secondly, society must make business respond to changing interests and needs. This is the *public interest* perspective that emerged in the 1970s but has deepened over recent years through the growth of the ethical consumer and investment movements. Here, businesses are not merely *choosing* to undertake some form of SEAAR as a means of understanding and manipulating their social environment, but are being forced to respond to demands from the actors that make up that environment.

Thirdly, there has been a *value-shift* in business which may, contentiously, replace a compliance or managerialist-based response to new pressures. Here lies the view that business can evolve and take on a different historic role in society, at the same time as the roles traditionally taken on by the state are increasingly under threat. Leaders tend to question the *raison d'être* of their company's and their own activities and are searching for an expanded repertoire of explanations and measures of success provided by the bottom line.[26]

Why perform social and ethical accounting and auditing?

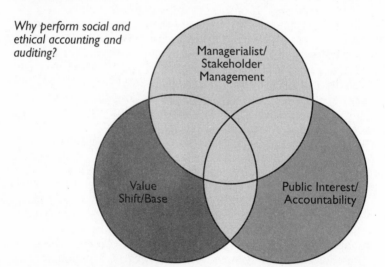

Figure 2.1: *The Rationale Triangle*

This overview provides a picture of why companies have historically been interested in SEAAR. However, what it does not tell us is what companies *are actually doing today*. The case studies in Part 2 of this book do just that. In the following pages we summarize and analyze the specific reasons set out in the case studies, and compare these reasons to those more generalised reasonings highlighted above.

The Body Shop is a good place to start in our quest for understanding the 'why' of social and ethical accounting, auditing and reporting.[27] More than any other multinational today, The Body Shop has generated a fierce debate as to whether ethics is a meaningful term in relation to business. This is at least in part because the company, whilst evangalizing the need for a value shift in business, has also benefited financially from being able to position itself in the market as a company with ethics that span social, environmental and animal spheres. It was in 1991 that one of the founders of The Body Shop, Anita Roddick, spelt out her interest in developing the company's practice in social auditing.

> *I would love it if every shareholder of every company wrote a letter every time they received a company's annual report and accounts. I would like them to say something like, 'OK, that's fine, very good. But where are the details of our environmental audit? Where are the details of your accounting to the community? Where is your social audit?'*[28]

There is no doubt that Anita Roddick's statement was intended to place The Body Shop towards the bottom left-hand side of the Rationale Triangle: the company was a living demonstration of a value shift in business towards a broader sense of social, environmental and ethical responsibility. However, whereas Anita Roddick intended to highlight the voluntary concern of The Body Shop in public accountability, she was also advocating a more pressured approach to encouraging the realignment of business values away from a narrow financial focus. That is, her statement goes further in actively encouraging public interest pressure in bringing companies in line with these new values: the bottom right side of the Rationale Triangle.

The degree to which The Body Shop's decision to undergo a social audit has its roots at the top of the triangle – rooted in an interest in manipulating the market for financial gain – is difficult to determine from outside the company, since it concerns the intangible matter of *intentions*, particularly those of its senior managers and founders. Two interlinked sources of information do, however, provide information relevant to this question. First is the extensive stakeholder dialogue embedded within the company's social audit process that explores (amongst other things) the stakeholders' perceptions of the organization's values. It might be expected, for example, that if the moral posture of the company was a cynical ploy to exploit the naive idealism of its customers, this would come through from some stakeholders, particularly those closest to the company: the staff. The information contained within the company's Social Statement for 1995 indicates that the majority of staff are of the view that the company broadly 'means what it says it wants to do', even if it does not always achieve it.[29]

A second way of exploring the question of intention is to challenge whether the company's social audit is indeed an accurate and adequate form of external verification and disclosure.[30] An approach aligned with a managerialist rationale would be expected to have weak or incomplete information, disclosure or verification (or some combination of these). For example, a managerialist rationale would probably be linked to an approach that minimized real transparency and accountability to maximum effect in terms of the company's image. From this perspective, full and accurate disclosure is almost by definition aligned with some combination of the value shift and/or public interest rationale.[31]

The social audit process of The Body Shop was verified by an external body, the non-profit organization the New Economics Foundation (NEF).[32] The approach to verification adopted by NEF included involving a 'stakeholder council' of eminent and skilled people who had the opportunity to publically challenge the report (this approach is discussed further below).[33] Also of note is that The Body Shop simultaneously commissioned an evaluation of its operations by a business ethicist based at Stanford University.[34]

Finally, what was the extent to which the company's commitment to social auditing arose as a result of the pressures placed on it in the market through the work of investigative journalists – the bottom right hand of the Rationale Triangle advocated as important by Anita Roddick in the statement quoted above?[35] It is certainly the case that the social audit process initiated by The Body Shop began in 1992–93. This was two years before the company was faced with a series of allegations in the public media regarding their ethical behaviour. It does not follow from this, of course, that The Body Shop was not responding to the 'public interest/accountability' reason for undertaking social audits. Indeed, the original quote from Anita Roddick seems to confirm that this is a core reason for companies undertaking some form of social and ethical audit. However, the timings do suggest that The Body Shop moved towards social auditing in large part as a result of its vision of business accountability rather than as a result of direct pressure on itself.

The Body Shop is clearly a company with a difference, in that a key part of its market image is its ethical position on a range of issues. It is as well, therefore, to look carefully at companies that operate in the market with a less than unique ethical image. The case of Sbn Bank in Denmark offers a very different perspective on why 'Ethical Accounting' should be introduced as a regular process in an otherwise quite normal bank. Professor Peter Pruzan, in Chapter 5 of this book, summarizes his understanding of why the Sbn Bank invited him to trial the process. The bank, he explains, was seeking to develop its own leadership processes towards one that built the company's success on shared values within the organization and with key external stakeholders. But, according to Pruzan, the process they had adopted prior to instigating ethical accounting:

> ...was 'top-down'; although it spoke of employee commitment, it was for all intents and purposes developed by top managment with the aid of outside consultants. In addition, the emphasis was more on the 'product' (the code) than on the 'process' of integrating values and ethics into the organization. Not only were the employees not involved in designing the code, neither were the other major parties who are affected by the bank's actions and whose behavior in turn affects the bank, ie the 'stakeholders'. Thus, there was no way of determining whether the values formulated were relevant, were in fact lived up to and whether the commitments listed were not just good intentions formulated by managment. In other words, the Code of Values by itself could not provide a means for the values to be integrated into the organization so that it could identify itself, reflect upon itself, and evaluate itself from a value-based perspective.

At a meeting between Pruzan and the bank's senior staff, it became clear that the bank recognized the deficiencies in its internal processes, and from that point the ethical accounting method was taken on as a means of overcoming them and building the company on a strong base of shared values.

For Sbn Bank, therefore, the underlying reason for taking on the practice of ethical accounting lay particularly along the line spanning from the value shift at the bottom left of the Rationale Triangle through to the managerialist view at the top of the triangle: a better management of the 'values process' would enhance the efficiency of the bank. There is little evidence in this case that the adoption of ethical accounting arose as a result of pubic interest pressure. This latter point is perhaps most easily highlighted by the fact that the ethical accounting of Sbn Bank is not, and was never intended to be, externally verified.

The case of the giant retail chain, Coop Italia, offers a similar picture of the reasons for engaging in the building of a Social Balance. Like Pruzan, Alessandra Vaccari describes in Chapter 11 the early stage of the process as involving discussions between the organization and interested academics:

> *More than six years ago, the Coop initiated discussions about the need to give an account of its social performance in relation to its mission. It was predominantly an internal discussion, stimulated more by studious university people than by other organizations or individuals.*

Beyond this, however, the decision to move forward was based on a view of several levels of benefits that might acrue to the Coop. First and foremost was a recognition and wish to assert publically, as well as internally, their identity as a co-operative. As Vaccari argues:

> *Underlying the Coop's decision to develop its social accounting practice has been its belief in the need to give an account of the relationship that exists between a company's values and mission, and the actions that it carries out on a daily basis. From this perspective, the 'social accounts' of an ordinary company reports on its performance in relation to the interests of its shareholders in maximizing profit, or more generally the financial market value of invested capital. This is, after all, its central mission or aim. The fundamental difference between the Coop and ordinary companies is therefore reflected in a different emphasis on social accounting. The Coop's social accounts are the means of quantifying the effectiveness of the Coop in fulfilling its institutional function of acting in its member-consumers' interests, acting to the social benefit of all its stakeholders whilst being a non-profit organization, and at the same time demonstrating its ability to compete effectively in the market.*

Vacarri therefore sees traditional financial accounting as one form of social accounting oriented more or less exclusively towards shareholder interests. Being a cooperative, Coop Italia needed to extend this social accounting in order to become relevant to the wider groups of stakeholders to which it is accountable. This was not the end of the story, however. Coop Italia also saw the social balance as a way of engaging and increasing the level of participation of its members: 'By providing meaningful and comprehensive information, the social accounts provide an instrument that allows members and different parts of society to participate in the Coop.'

As with Sbn Bank and The Body Shop, the Coop Italia saw a central role for management in interpreting and acting on the results of the SEAAR process: 'Central to this is the role of management. The social accounts are a means of enabling co-operative management to combine efficiency and social stategy, values and actions, into an integrated approach that reflects the holistic Coop identity, and also its specific entrepreneurial and social culture.' One further underlying reason for undertaking social accounting marks the Coop Italia out from all of the other cases.

> ...new legislation (L 59/92) concerning co-operative companies says that each one of them must include in the annual balance the 'criteria followed to reach the social mission'. It is necessary to underline the main co-operative legislation is the 'Basevi Law' of 1948 that defines the principle of mutualism and the role of the National League of Cooperatives.

The case of Coop Italia reveals a complex pattern of reasons for engaging in SEAAR. At the heart of the Coop's concern is the need to satisfy the public interest of their key stakeholders and their members. That is, their decision to produce an annual Social Balance lies first and foremost in their sense of accountability towards their members. This accountability agenda is, in this case, further strengthened through the existence of legislation requiring that Coops demonstrate that their practice complies with the principles of mutualism which afford them preferential treatment under the law.[36] The Coop's reasoning does not, however, stop there. It is also clear that they see the possibility of improving their efficiency and their market position through the Social Balance process. Thus, the Coop lies along the right-hand line of the triangle, moving from its core rationale of public interest to a more instrumental view of how the organization can gain from this approach to accountability.

The case of VanCity Savings and Credit Union (VanCity), based in Vancover in Canada, reveals a further rationale for engaging in social accounting. In 1992, the University of Quebec reported on the results of their first assessment of the quality of corporate disclosure by Canadian financial institutions. To the dismay of VanCity, known for its community programmes, it ranked sixtieth out of 127 financial institutions.

> As a relatively small, locally owned financial institution, with no offshore assets and a long history of strong community reinvestment and support, VanCity had expected to excel in this area. The rating of VanCity's social information as inferior to the 'big banks', especially the Royal Bank, surprised and disappointed both VanCity's executive and the board.

As a direct result of this finding, VanCity decided to invest in improving their performance in the area of disclosure. Within one year they had developed and trialed a more comprehensive approach, which led to them being ranked eighth out of 134 financial institutions in the next round of comparative assessments.

At the heart of this experience was a sense by the senior managers of VanCity that the organization reflected a different way of thinking about and practising business, and that transparency was a key element of this difference. This then placed the core of the rationale in the bottom left part of the Rationale Triangle, concerning centrally the value base that VanCity saw itself as representing. Interestingly, however, it was through public interest research and reporting that VanCity was encouraged to question the adequacy of its social reporting, although it is not clear from the available material whether the organization was in practice vulnerable as a result of its low ranking on the social reporting scorecard. Beyond this, however, lay a perspective of how best to differentiate the credit union from its more traditional banking rivals, particularly with respect to the manner in which VanCity traded on its ethical image in the market. This interest then placed the experience particularly along the line spanning a value shift with a managerialist view and rationale.

Finally, we return, by example, to the most obvious reason for wanting to undertake some form of SEAAR: the need to know what had happened. Traidcraft plc is a company that buys goods from community producers in the South and sells them to consumers under the umbrella term 'fairly traded goods'. Traidcraft, with deep-rooted Christian origins, aspires to give a fair deal to its suppliers, particularly in terms of the price paid for goods purchased from community-based organizations. Traidcraft is a commercial company, but most of the voting shares are held by a NGO: the Traidcraft Foundation. The role of the foundation is to ensure that the company fulfils both its financial and social and ethical goals.

It was through this unusual structure of ownership and associated goals that the company embarked on a process of social accounting. As the then external affairs director of the company, Richard Evans, summarizes in Chapter 6 of this book:

> The trustees of the Traidcraft Foundation, who hold the voting shares in the company, asked the directors to develop a process of accounting for the company's social impact and to carry out an annual audit of its performance against non-financial criteria. Early in 1992 the board agreed to publish its first externally audited account, with its annual statutory accounts, the following year.

A careful examination of Evans's paper reveals several other reasons for Traidcraft electing to undergo an annual social accounting and audit exercise. In common with most of the other cases, it sees social accounting as providing a management tool for supporting better decision-making, as well as a means for differentiating the company in a competitive market. Similarly to The Body Shop and Sbn Bank (as well as others using the UK and Danish models, which are described further in Chapter 3), Traidcraft saw the process as enabling the greater engagement of its stakeholders, particularly those who had less direct power, such as the Southern producers themselves. What is finally spelt out is Traidcraft's interest in providing a model of how responsible business can behave, much like The Body Shop and Ben & Jerry's Homemade, Inc.

In conclusion, then, the Rationale Triangle offers one way of organizing and analyzing information about why companies say they are interested in engaging in levels of social and ethical accounting, auditing and, in particular, reporting that extend beyond statutory compliance. What is clear from the examples given is that in no case was the reason singular. Rather, in each case, companies had many reasons which spanned the tough needs of the market, particularly where public interest challenges to the companies' claims were at stake, to the more visionary and in some ways less tangible claims of seeking to build business on values that embrace broader conceptions of responsibility.

REASONING FOR THE MAINSTREAM

The companies referred to above and explored in more detail in Part 2 of this book are on the surface quite distinct from the mainstream corporate community. They are organizations that are, in the main, consciously seeking to mix business with broader values and related aims and activities. There are few companies, after all, which engage in the kinds of high-profile campaigns for which Ben & Jerry's Homemade, Inc and The Body Shop are renowned. Traidcraft's core aim to give a fair price to its suppliers in the South is not exactly a commonplace vision within the corporate community. The membership-based structure and associated obligations of Coop Italia and VanCity Savings and Credit Union is an unusual ownership model for either the retail or financial services industries.

These cases clearly involve unusual organizations. This is not a problem unless we are seeking to make points about the future direction of the main part of the corporate community. In this case there is a need to ask the question: is social and ethical performance relevant to the mainstream, and does this mean that SEAAR is also a forthcoming imperative or at least a need for healthy business?

The basic answer to these questions appears to be that the mainstream business community is increasingly concerned with its social and ethical performance. It is as well to begin exploring this question by reporting on what business says on the subject. The Royal Society for the Arts in the UK, for example, completed a major consultative study entitled *Tomorrow's Company* that drew extensively on the experience and expertise of the management of major companies operating in the UK, and on researchers and consultants.[37] The study examined, as its name suggests, what kind of companies are likely to be successful in tomorrow's business climate. In the study report, a number of chief executives set out a vision of their own companies. Typical of these visions is that of the group chief executive of Grand Metropolitan, George Bull:

Increasingly, business people are recognizing that their prosperity is directly linked to the prosperity of the whole community. The community is the source of their customers, employees, their suppliers and, with the wider spread of share ownership, their investors.[38]

Here, then, is the 'stakeholder economy' espoused by the British journalist and economist Will Hutton, and the leader of the British Labour Party and current British Prime Minister Tony Blair.[39]

So what exactly does a statement such as this mean? The answer at an organizational level appears to lie firmly along the axis that spans from the bottom right of our Rationale Triangle, that of public interest pressure, through to the top of the triangle, that of managerialist approaches to stakeholder management. A recent study commissioned by the Co-operative Wholesale Services in the UK highlighted the rise in 'ethical' or 'vigilante' consumerism'.[40] The survey of a sample of 30,000 food retail customers found that:

- 35 per cent answered yes to the question: 'Have you boycotted any product because you are concerned about animal rights, the environment, or human rights?'
- 60 per cent answered yes to the question: 'In the future, would you boycott a shop or product because you are concerned with these issues?'

In another survey asking more broadly about the public's view of the importance of business ethics, and as to whether the sampled interviewees felt that business was indeed ethical, the results emerged that:

- 73 per cent answered yes to the question: 'How important is it that the public view British businesses as ethical?'
- 27 per cent viewed British business as 'unethical', and a further 31 per cent were 'undecided' or neutral on the question.

Business ethics matter because the public says it does. Attempts by companies to 'keep their heads down' have met with plummeting returns in recent years, as corporate responsibility initiatives, and the sophistication of the organizations managing such processes, have increased. As Shell discovered to its cost via first the *Brent Spar* fiasco, and then through the disclosures over its approach to business in the Ogoni region of Nigeria, the views either that social and ethical performance can remain private or that the public do not care about what happens beyond their backyards have proved to be misguided. Furthermore, companies are finding themselves victim to the excesses of their competitors. Shell's revealed performance in Nigeria led quickly to a far higher profile of the campaigns against the activities, for example, of the French oil company Total in Burma, and of British Petroleum (BP) in relation to its operation of a massive on-shore exploration site in Colombia. The consumer campaigns launched at particular textile and toy companies regarding the labour standards of their suppliers in the South has now cascaded right across the five key sectors that sell retail products produced in the South: textiles, sportwear, toys, food, and flowers.[41]

Market profile is a critical – but not the only – factor in the equation that makes social and ethical performance relevant to business. In a recent seminar held for a major oil company by one of this book's editors, a senior staff representative offered the following view:

> The company has downsized in recent years with massive redundancies. You have to understand that people are disillusioned and frustrated. They cannot be driven to work harder through fear alone – they need to know that the company does care, and does hear what they are saying, even though we all know about business imperatives. The view that staff are disposable will eventually make for a disposable company.

The British standards organization Investors in People (IIP) has for long argued that high productivity requires committed staff, which in turn requires a company that can earn that commitment. In offering evidence to support this assertion, IIP has shown that companies who have gone through the IIP process of staff consultation, staff-related systems and procedures development, as well as improved staff training, simply perform better financially, whether measured in terms of return on capital or pre-tax profit.

The corporate sector, therefore, has good reason to show concern for its social, ethical and environmental performance. Beyond any possible personal views held by managers and investors that companies *do* indeed have a social and ethical responsibility, there is the more hard-bitten view that social and ethical responsibility is good for business. It consolidates market positions, or at least protects the business from public-interest campaigning, and it can strengthen the solidarity, commitment and productivity of a company's key assets: its relationship with its staff (and also, by extension, the productivity and quality of its suppliers and advisers) and other key stakeholders.

The need for companies to convince the public of their ethical integrity is, however, only the first step in demonstrating a fundamental need for some form of SEAAR. As companies focus increasing attention and resources on public relations, reputation management, marketing, and just plain selling, there is an inevitable inclination on their part to seek ways to fake it as a cheaper approach to building a sound reputation for corporate citizenship. There may appear to be good reasons for this. The commercial environment of the last two decades has convinced companies of the need to cut costs as they have never done before. A major part of the burden of this drive for competitiveness and profitability has fallen on workers or, in many cases, ex-workers.

So why would companies disclose their social and ethical performance in an environment of this kind, where many of them have found themselves active participants in a painful downsizing process? The answer to this lies in the basic need for companies:

- to understand what they are trying to achieve and how best to measure performance against their aims;
- to know what they are doing;

- to understand the implications of what they are doing;
- to understand in what ways, if any, they can explain their actions to an increasingly sceptical and aggressive consuming and voting public; and
- to understand whether there are practical options for improving on their social performance in ways that will not harm their business performance and may in many cases improve it.

Surely, you might argue, senior managers at least *know* what they are doing? The worrying answer to this is: not always, and often not in critical areas where 'soft' information is required. In one recent internal seminar run for a major multinational, a copy of an article about people demonstrating against US companies' use of child labour was projected onto a screen. The seminar's facilitator laughingly said, 'Of course, you don't do this sort of thing'. A nervous silence was followed by one of the more outspoken participants blurting out: 'But that is the whole point. We don't know. This whole downsizing and decentralization has meant that we no longer get information about these sorts of things. And even if we did, we would never get a chance to look at it, analyze it, or check if it is accurate.' This proved a prescient statement. Just a few months later, the company was subjected to an aggressive challenge in the national press over its social, ethical and environmental record in and around one of its major facilities, a facility that had the reputation within the company of having best practice community relations and environmental programmes.

Beyond the basic information about what is going on is the question of its relevance to the company's current and long-term performance. On the day that Shell reversed its own decision to sink the *Brent Spar* oil platform, a small meeting was taking place in London by senior managers to talk about measures of non-financial performance. Amongst the participants was a Shell manager. On being asked by his peers from other companies about the events of the day, he declared solemnly:

> Today we have learnt a serious lesson, and one that may cost the company a great deal for many years to come. We have learnt that we must take the views of the public into account, even where they have been influenced by single-issue organizations to the point where they are thinking and behaving entirely irrationally.

The quote, if at all representative of the thinking of Shell senior management, reveals a great deal about that company's fortress – and arguably arrogant – culture. Important here, however, is a simpler point; this manager's recognition that a company's reputation depends on what people *think* is true and *feel* is important. The fact that scientists may view things differently, or that managers may not consider the issue to be relevant or central to the company's strategy, may prove entirely irrelevant if the public decides otherwise.

Companies seek to influence public perception about their social, ethical and environmental performance. While this is a task that all companies take to with considerable relish and vigour, the ways in which they have done this has generated considerable scepticism and indeed cynicism towards corporate claims of good behaviour. Despite a veritable outpouring of information from companies about their good social, ethical and environmental performance, there is ample evidence to suggest that the public rarely believes what they are told by companies, certainly not beyond basic technical product-related information.

It is for this reason that standards covering social, ethical and environmental performance have emerged and have been increasingly embraced by the corporate community in recent years. The most advanced non-financial standards in terms of their take-up by the corporate community are certainly environmental standards and basic staff-related information. Many other social, ethical and environmental standards have come into common practice over the same period, including staff-related standards – such as IIP in the UK – green and organic product standards, and more recently 'fair trade' product labels covering labour standards and related issues in relation to trade with developing countries.[42]

From this perspective, SEAAR is not a future proposition, but a current reality. As Professor Rob Gray points out in his discussion of 'silent accounting' in Chapter 14, all companies today, *particularly* the larger corporations, are already offering ever-increasing volumes of information about their social, ethical and environmental performance, albeit in a fragmented form, of varying quality, and often with quite inadequate or at least unclear levels of external verification.

This emerging profusion of standards, accounting, auditing, and verification systems, and reporting mechanisms and formats, has underpinned an interest in systematic SEAAR for an altogether different reason: *the management of complexity*. This proved to be a central issue for companies attending the first formal, business-related training course on social and ethical accounting, auditing and reporting staged by the New Academy of Business in conjunction with the New Economics Foundation and the Institute of Social and Ethical AccountAbility in early 1996. As one senior manager of a food retailer bemoaned:

> *If I have to respond to one more ethical standard, I am going to explode. What I need is a way of putting them all in one pot. That way I can understand their relationship, make better decisions, and generally do my job better. Its not that I mind ethical standards, it is that there are too many of them being used throughout the company without an understanding of their linkages.*

This, then, calls not merely for *some* form of SEAAR, but for one that helps put the whole puzzle of business ethics together. Companies, particularly large ones, are in general very keen on developing integrating systems, all the more so if the company is very decentralized and yet has common brand images and products. There are well-established approaches to this integration process when dealing, for example, with product and service quality. However, there are no adequate systems when it comes to integrating the complex dynamics at the interface between financial, and social and ethical spheres of action.

ADDING IT ALL UP

Companies are having to cope with an increasingly complex business environment, with the need to maintain staff commitment and productivity in the face of downsizing and redundancies; they must cope with people, markets and communities that respond to and are concerned about a rapidly changing range of social, ethical and environmental issues. Coping can mean being forced to respond to issues beyond legal compliance through public interest campaigning; or it can mean a more proactive process of evolving outstanding performance as a corporate citizen. From either extreme, or for the many intermediate places in which most companies find themselves, there is a need for companies to know what is happening and what to expect, to understand what people feel is important today and in the future, and to be able to respond to previous mistakes and successes in seeking to improve corporate social and ethical performance and reputation. Amidst all of this is a need to communicate more effectively with key stakeholders; to ensure that they know what you are trying to do, and believe in what they hear; and to ensure that the communication is a two-way process that not only is effective in acquiring information, but is able to strengthen key relationships.

We have covered a range of possible reasons that businesses might have for undertaking some form of SEAAR, ranging from the clarification of values identifying possible risks, to the company's survival, as summarized below.[43]

BOX 2.1: WHY ENGAGE IN SEAAR?

- Clarify and strengthen values.
- Establish a baseline to judge change.
- Learn about societal expectations.
- Identify specific problems.
- Understand what motivates staff.
- Identify areas of vulnerability.

Source: based on EIBE, 1995

In exploring the reasons for undertaking some form of SEAAR, this chapter has pointed out a range of possible concrete business gains from the practice, as summarized below.

There is a need, in short, for SEAAR. This need is not abstract or ideological. It does not arise from an unnecessary obsession with measurement, systems or reporting. The need is concrete, rooted in today's experience and the expectation of what tomorrow will bring. As one manager of a major oil company concluded, 'It is no longer a matter of whether, it is a matter of when, and how.' It is to the matter of 'how' that we now turn.

BOX 2.2: THE BUSINESS GAINS OF SEAAR?

Increases should occur in the following:
- staff total loyalty/productivity;
- customer sales/loyalty;
- decision-making effectiveness;
- effective risk management;
- community receptivity;
- government assistance/support;
- share price/price stability.

ENDNOTES

1 H J L van Luijk, S M Carmichael, G J A Hummels & A C ten Klooster (1995) *The Technology of Ethical Auditing* Nijenrode University, The Netherlands Business School, and the European Institute of Business Ethics, Breukelen: pp1.
2 See, for example, a discussion of this in the the Royal Society for the Encouragement of Arts Manufacture & Commerce (1996) *Tomorrow's Company: The Role of Business in a Changing World* RSA, London.
3 S Anderson and J Cavanagh (1996) *Top 200: A Profile of Global Corporate Power* Institute for Policy Studies, Washington, DC.
4 *Business Week*, 22 April, 1996.
5 NEF/CIIR (1997) *Open Trading: Options for Effective Monitoring of Corporate Codes of Conduct* NEF/CIIR, London.
6 Thanks to Professor Rob Gray for this simplified but cogent summary of the origins of financial accounting.
7 *International Survey of Environmental Reporting: Results Presented at Press Conference September 10, 1996*, International Institute for Industrial Environmental Economics.
8 F Cairncross (1995) *Green Inc: A Guide to Business and the Environment* Earthscan, London.
9 R Hilliary (1996).
10 Environmental Benchmarks.
11 We are grateful to Kim Davenport for her making an early draft of her PhD available to us.
12 Carroll and Beiler, 1975.
13 G Goyder (1961) *The Responsible Company* Blackwell, Oxford: pp109.
14 *ibid* : pp110–111.
15 Dierkes and Bauer, 1973.
16 C Medawar (1978) *The Social Audit Consumer Handbook* Social Audit Ltd, London
17 Confederation of British Industry (1973) *The Responsibilities of the British Public Company* CBI, London.
18 US Chamber of Commerce, 1970.
19 US Department of Commerce (1979) *Corporate Social Reporting in the United States and Western Europe: Report of the Task Force on Corporate*

Social Performance US Department of Commerce, Washington, DC, ppvii.

20 J E Grojer and A Stark (1977) "Social Accounting: A Swedish Attempt" in *Accounting, Organisation and Society* Vol 2 No 4, Pergamon Press, Oxford.

21 M Dierkes (1979) "Corporate Social Responsibility in Germany: Conceptual Developments and Practical Experiences", in *Accounting, Organisation and Society* Vol 4 No 1/2, Pergamon Press, Oxford.

22 M Freidman (1962) *Capitalism and Freedom* University of Chicago Press, Chicago.

23 For a cogent summary of this development, see R Gray, J Bebbington et al (1993) *Accounting for the Environment* Paul Chapman, London.

24 Of particular significance was the work of the Council on Economic Priorities based in New York, which has since provided a model for non-governmental corporate monitoring in other countries and contexts See a recent Canadian version of screening in EthicScan Canada (1996) *Shopping with a Conscience: the Informed Shopper's Guide to Retailers, Suppliers, and Service Providers in Canada*, John Wiley and Sons, Toronto For the UK, see R Adams, J Carruthers, and S Hamil (1991) *Changing Corporate Values: A Guide to Social and Environmental Policy and Practice in Britain's Top Companies* Kogan Page, London.

25 See, in particular the summary of the keynote address by David Grayson of Business in the Community (BITC) in Institute of Social and Ethical Accounting/NEF (editor) (1997) *Sixth Environment Foundation Windsor Roundtable on Social and Ethical Accounting and Auditing: Summary of Proceedings* Institute of Social and Ethical AccountAbility, London.

26 An alternative name for this offered has been *value-base*, indicating a greater focus on the revealing of existing values of key stakeholders, rather than a *shift* in those values.

27 D Wheeler and M Gallajan (1997) *The Stakeholder Company* Pitman, London.

28 A Roddick (1992) *Body and Soul* Ebury Press, London (emphasis in italics added).

29 The Body Shop International (1996) *The Body Shop Social Statement 1995* The Body Shop, Littlehampton.

30 Taken in conjunction with the company's environmental and animal testing audits, the relationship between which are described in the paper by Maria Sillapää and David Wheeler on The Body Shop International in this book.

31 There is, of course, the possibility of a mangerialist rationale with full and accurate disclosure where the company's performance is in any case fully aligned with the interests of the key stakeholder groups In this case of shared values across and between stakeholders and the company, the distinction between the three different reasons for undertaking social auditing more or less collapses into one.

32 For further information on the New Economics Foundation, it is worth reviewing its externally verified social audit, New Economics Foundation (1996) *Social Statement 1994–95* New Economics Foundation, London.

33 There is no external verification process that can be fully guaranteed to be accurate and complete, as is shown by the high-profile cases of

failure of well-developed financial audit methods to pick up in practice complex and wide-ranging financial irregularities The point made here is not that the external verification process was of a high quality, but rather that the process adopted gave it a high likelihood of being meaningful.

34 Kirk Hanson (1996) *Social Evaluation of The Body Shop* The Body Shop, Littlehampton For a discussion of this work, see also Curtis Vershoor and Jon Entine (1996) *Advancing Social Auditing: A Critique of Body Shop's 1995 Social Assessments* DePaul School of Accountancy Working Paper, Chicago.

35 We refer here particularly to the work of Jon Entine, a journalist who has specialized since the early 1990s in publishing 'challenge articles' aimed at the 'ethical business community', particularly The Body Shop International and Ben & Jerry's Homemade, Inc. See, for example, his article with Roger Cowe in the UK newspaper *The Guardian* on the 14 December 1996.

36 Although at a seminar organized by Co-op Italia on social auditing in Florence in early 1996 it was made clear by members of Co-op Italia that they had enormous scope in interpreting the existing legislation, and could – had they wished to – have got away with a considerably lower level of disclosure.

37 Royal Society for the Encouragement of Arts Manufacture & Commerce (1996) *Tomorrow's Company: The Role of Business in a Changing World* RSA, London.

38 ibid.

39 Will Hutton (1995) *The State We're In*, Jonathan Cape, London.

40 Co-operative Wholesale Society (1995) *Responsible Retailing* CWS, Manchester.

41 See, for example, the International Monitoring Working Group (1997) ibid.

42 NEF and CIIR (1997) *Open Trading: Options for Effective Monitoring of Corporate Codes of Conduct* NEF/CIIR, London.

43 Based on H J L van Luijk, S M Carmichael, G J A Hummels & A C ten Klooster (1995) *The Technology of Ethical Auditing* Nijenrode University, The Netherlands Business School, and the European Institute of Business Ethics, Breukelen: pp1.

3

How to Do It

There is a growing body of experiences in corporate SEAAR, particularly across Europe and North America.[1] Associated with this development has been the emergence of varied terminology and differing approaches. There are ethical accounts, social audits, ethical audits, social performance reports, and social reviews, just to name a few. In some cases these methodologies appear very similar. The ethical audit advocated by the European Institute for Business Ethics and the Nijenrode Business School,[2] for example, is similar in many respects to the social accounts method developed, adopted, and applied by Traidcraft plc and the New Economics Foundation.[3] The Body Shop International's ethical audit is, on the other hand, quite different since it represents a combination of social, environmental and animal testing audits.[4] This in turn is only comparable in parts to the 'ethical accounting' developed at the Copenhagen Business School and adopted by Sbn Bank and other companies and public sector organizations across Scandinavia.[5]

Much of the diversity in practice can be attributed to at least four significant differences in:

*   interests on the part of those initiating the process;
*   types of organizations;
*   contexts; and
*   theoretical and philosophical roots.

Many of these differences are entirely acceptable in that they reflect varied needs for which different methods are required. For example, organizations such as Sbn Bank in Denmark and Wøyen Mølle in Norway start with an emphasis on the evolution of shared values through ethical accounting. Not surprisingly, they focus on dialogue with key stakeholders rather than third-party verification. On the other hand, a company concerned with meeting the challenge of public accountability may well place far greater emphasis on securing adequate comparison with other companies or accepted social norms and benchmarks. For example, the move by companies in the textile, sportswear and toy sectors to adopt and comply with labour codes of conduct in their production in, and purchases from, the South, will focus on external verification precisely because the pressure comes from public consumer campaigns.[6] Similarly, a company principally concerned with public accountability may focus exclusively on the production of a report for external publication, whereas a company with an interest in SEAAR as a tool to facilitate internal change may have little or no interest in the published document, but may instead focus on the process of accounting, and the reports generated for internal use.

Identifying the right approach to SEAAR is therefore intimately related to *why* the particular organization engages in the exercise. This implies that there is no single approach that is correct for all situations: there is strength in diversity for diverse needs.

At the same time, there are variations between methods and practices that are not justified by any objective difference in circumstance and need. These are variations that may be rooted in two possible reasons for poor practices:

• an underspecification of the accounting, auditing and reporting process because of insufficient knowledge, skills, experience and/or resources applied to the process; and/or
• a deliberate attempt to underspecify the accounts and/or the verification process in order to report in a less than accurate, incomplete or unintelligible, manner.

For example, a company may undertake an externally verified exploration of the social impact of one area of its operations knowing full well that there is a critical problem associated with an area of work that they have chosen to omit from the assessment. An SEAAR exercise undertaken by a bank that did not deal with the nature of its investment portfolio, or an exercise by an advertizing company that did not consider with care the nature of the images they were promoting and their effect, could not really be seen as being of adequate quality. Similarly, a company may forgo a dialogue with staff to determine key issues of concern because of inadequate resources, and as a result develop a survey that omits a range of critical issues that would profile the company in a negative light, or that are important for the staff and therefore for their propensity to be responsible, committed and creative employees. It would not be appropriate, for example, for a fair trade organization (eg one seeking to offer a better deal to community suppliers in the South by offering such added benefits as a better price) to carry out an SEAAR exercise without adequate consultation with Southern suppliers.[7]

The challenge is to be able to distinguish between acceptable and unacceptable reasons for methodological (and terminological) differences. The failure to meet this challenge effectively will allow the 'bad to chase out the good', as companies and consultants alike find good reason to cut corners to save costs and to omit difficult areas from accounting, auditing and reporting. The ability to distinguish good from bad practice therefore provides a foundation on which standards can be set, a subject to which we return in Chapter 4.

A BRIEF HISTORY OF 'HOW'

An extensive array of methods has been offered up over the years for assessing and reporting on corporate social and ethical performance. This is not the place to attempt a scholarly exposition of this history, which has been achieved more effectively elsewhere.[8] Of interest here is not so much the history of how social and ethical accounting and auditing have been talked about and practiced for their own sake. Rather, the intention is to show how today's emerging practice is informed by both the theoretical literature and earlier practical experience.

One of earliest proposed approaches to social auditing was that of the *cost or outlay audit*.[9] The basic idea, as the name suggests, was to specify the financial costs associated with social activities, and to set these out as an account of the social contribution made by the organization. The major disadvantage of this approach is that financial costs give little idea of the outcome's value. As one assessment of this method concluded: 'since the cost approach makes no effort to measure benefits to the corporation and others associated with the expenditures, it provides little evaluative information to the public.'[10]

Despite this very real limitation, the ready availability of financial data from conventional financial accounts and management systems has made this approach a durable one over the years. Many companies, for example, report on the amount of money that they donate to charitable causes, often expressed both as an absolute amount and as a percentage of pretax profits or gross earnings.[11] The cost or outlay approach has been formalized into a method also known as the *social balance*, effectively a record of financial costs based on a reanalysis of the audited financial accounts associated with actions that can be attributed to the company's social rather than its financial mission. This approach, for example, is currently being used by the Italian retail co-operative movement as the core of its *social balance* accounting, as described in the case study of Coop Italia by Alessandra Vaccari in Part 2.

A second methodological strand that has found its way into modern usage is *constituency accounting*, named by Grey in 1973.[12] Grey argued that traditional financial accounting could simply not accommodate the needs of SEAAR. Instead, an entirely new calculus was required. What he proposed was that companies should examine and report against the demands of key constituencies, whether inside or outside of the company concerned.[13]

There is little evidence of this 'constituency-based' approach having been taken up at the time that it was established at a theoretical level. As the US Department of Commerce commented at the time:

> While this approach attempts to assess benefits as well as costs, some critics believe that it does not state benefits in terms that are meaningful to constituencies outside the corporation. It has not been widely used in corporate social reporting.[14]

The concern raised about the accuracy and usefulness of benefits defined by constituents is one that warrants careful examination. However, such concerns have not prevented this form of consultation becoming a core part of many of the contemporary approaches to SEAAR in the guise of 'stakeholder consultation and dialogue'. As one senior corporate executive remarked at the time: 'All...[corporations]...must...be visibly attentive to public interest – to the public interest as the *public* views it.'[15] Consultation has not only become a vital means by which the views of key stakeholders can be elicited, it has also become a way of legitimizing a company's social and ethical accounting process. Very recently, for example, the financial services company Allied Dunbar produced a publicly available report covering some of its philanthropic activities. Rather than report the financial costs of its contribution following the *outlay approach* described above, Allied Dunbar chose to follow more closely the *constituency* or *stakeholder approach*. In its summary of its *Stakeholder Accountability Report* for 1996, the company declares:

> *1996 marks the twenty-first anniversary of the Staff Charity Fund [SCF]. What better time to study the views of those with most interest in its work. The future will hold new challenges and the way the SCF develops the relationship it enjoys with its stakeholders lies at the heart of what happens next.*[16]

Stakeholders' views have been increasingly seen as a critical part of any thorough accounting, auditing and reporting process. However, it has also also been clear from an early stage that even the most accurate reporting of these perceptions may not be adequate. For example, in one social accounting and auditing exercise with a British company, staff repeatedly highlighted the view that they were being paid too little. In considering the wage data, it became clear to the auditors that they were in fact being paid just as much as people working for other companies that required broadly the same 'job of work' in the same region of the country. Eventually, the external auditor understood that since the company declared itself to have unusually high moral and ethical codes and values, staff expected to be paid what they saw as a *decent* rather than a *comparable* wage. What needed to be highlighted in this case was the tension revealed by examining the relationship between normal comparative financial indicators and staff perceptions. To omit either would have been to miss the point (or at least *this* point).

The limitations of using financial data is not therefore seen as a reason for rejecting all manner of quantification. Similarly, the limitations in working with people's subjective views is not a reason to ignore or marginalize them.

Financial data, furthermore, has only been one element of the quantified information about social and ethical performance that has been publicly available. What has emerged from the early 1970s has been the practice of *corporate rating* against key social and ethical performance criteria. While many different approaches to this have been adopted, the essence of the practice has been to rate companies in one or both of two possible ways: against predetermined 'binary' criteria that seek the answer to the question: 'Is this company doing this?'; and against scaled criteria that seek to answer the question: 'How is the company doing in this area?'

One of the earliest documented users of this approach was the Interfaith Centre on Corporate Responsibility (ICCR), which took a particular interest _ for example, in the practices of companies doing business in South Africa. Probably the most well-known contemporary practitioner in this area is the Council on Economic Priorities (CEP), a public-interest organization based in New York. CEP has been producing corporate ratings against social and environmental criteria for over 25 years, with a particular focus on retail companies and the education of consumers in their purchasing decisions through its annually produced *Shopping for a Better World*.[17] Corporate rating has developed rapidly since the mid 1980s, with a host of public interest NGOs entering the field with their own rating systems aimed at feeding the consumer public, and/or the growing number of ethical investment funds, with information.[18] Most recently, a group of these organizations from North America and Europe have come together in an effort to share information and to move towards some level of convergence in the manner in which screening is being undertaken.

A related development emerged in the 1970s on the back of the so-called *social indicators* movement.[19] Whereas *corporate rating* was an exclusively external activity undertaken by public interest, non-profit organizations and researchers, companies became more involved in the development and application of social performance indicators. The drive towards defining social indicators was closely intertwined with the growing interest in what we would now call stakeholder dialogue. For example, the US Department of Commerce saw some form of community consultation process as initiating the development or selection of relevant social indicators.

> *For example, in establishing annual objectives for a corporate community affairs program, a firm would first attempt to develop a quality of life profile for the community, using social indicators regarding unemployment, environmental quality, education, health, and so on. Thereafter a firm could establish performance indicators for some or all of its own activities in relation to these indicators, establish priorities in relation to each other and then measure performance in relation to objectives and their assigned importance.[20]*

Community-based approaches to selecting indicators of social and environmental development have emerged as a major theme of community development in the 1990s, particularly following the historic signing of the so-called Local Agenda 21 at the Earth Summit in Rio in 1992.[21] While certainly intended as an empowering process, these approaches can equally suffer from identifying what is important and how best to measure it. As Kim Davenport comments:

> *[An] objection is that the catalogue of social indicators is not truly comprehensive, but simply reflects the concerns of the most active or organized constituencies. Also, establishing a fixed catalogue of social indicators might give corporations permission to ignore those issues outside of the catalogue. Moreover, the fixed catalogue could also prove a hindrance to the development and adoption of new, more effective, indicators.[22]*

These perceived shortfalls of the pure constituency-based approach to selecting social indicators have opened the door to a complementary approach to the selection process: through identifying best practice or conventionally used indicators and benchmarks. For example, any report on the issue of gender within an organization would today be quickly ridiculed and dismissed if it omitted to report the number of men and women in different positions within the organization, or failed to provide data regarding wages and salaries to allow the proposition 'equal pay for equal work' to be tested. Similarly, any corporate environmental report found to have omitted information on the company's failure to comply with statutory regulations of self-imposed standards would be challenged in today's environmental-compliance sensitized world. At any time there are key issues for which there exist performance indicators that are widely acknowledged as an appropriate and essential part of any performance assessment and disclosure process.

Contemporary forms of SEAAR have drawn inspiration from many earlier approaches and initiatives, such as those highlighted in this section. For example, the Ethical Accounting Statement approach that emerged in Denmark in the late 1980s, through the work of Peter Pruzan and Ole Thyssen at the Copenhagen Business School, has focused exclusively on what might in earlier times have been called constituency accounting, rather than stakeholder dialogue.[23] Similarly, the approach developed by Traidcraft and the New Economics Foundation has drawn on the inspiration and calculus of the social indicators movement, as well as the lessons gained through the development of environmental auditing in the 1980s.[24] More generally, the cases described in this book, and the analytic framework offered in the following paragraphs, certainly arise from the rich and complex history of SEAAR.[25]

UNDERSTANDING QUALITY

This historical thumbnail sketch of how SEAAR has evolved highlights some of the key methodological strands, and their possible relationships with differing reasons for the implementation of specific practices. However, despite the need for continued sensitivity towards the needs of diversity, there are also good reasons for establishing methods to compare different approaches.

In short, we need to find ways to be able to tell if a specific exercise in social and ethical accounting, auditing and reporting is worth the candle?

We have developed for this purpose an analytic framework for exploring the quality of a particular experience or initiative in SEAAR. In doing so, we have been painfully aware of the sheer scale of experimentation in this area, and of its increasing quality across many different contexts. In this light, we offer the tool not as a finished product, but as a first stab at what needs to be continued over the coming period. The framework is a means of categorizing experiences or initiatives through:

- *principles* of 'good practice' in SEAAR;
- the *elements* into which the principles can be subdivided to enable more detailed analysis, and
- the *level and quality* of reporting.

Each of these elements of the framework are discussed below, first at a general level, and then by applying them to the case studies contained in Part 2 of this

Table 3.1: *Typology*

Type	Name	Cases	Description
A	Corporate-Led Reporting	Glaxo Holdings plc	Statutory disclosure plus additional internally generated, non-verified discretionary disclosure
B	Ethical accounting	Aarhus Municipality Sbn Bank Wøyen Mølle	Non-statutory disclosure of unverified stakeholder perceptions based on stakeholder-selected issues and questions
C	Social evaluation	Ben & Jerry's Homemade, Inc	Non-statutory disclosure of stakeholder views and social indicators based on exploration and views of external assessor
D	Social accounting & auditing	The Body Shop International plc Traidcraft plc	Statutory and non-statutory disclosure of stakeholder views, indicators and benchmarks with external verification of process
E	Outlay audit (social balance)	Co-op Italia	Non-statutory disclosure of reanalysis of audited financial data to reveal social costs
F	Disclosure ranking	VanCity Savings and Credit Union	Non-statutory disclosure by external body of extent of public disclosure

book. The aim here has not been to judge the relative quality of the cases. At any rate each has been chosen for inclusion on the basis of representing good practice. Rather, the aim has been to use the case studies to demonstrate how the tool can be employed in assessing the relative merits of different approaches.

BOX 3.1: THE EIGHT PRINCIPLES OF QUALITY

- Inclusivity
- Comparability
- Completeness
- Evolution
- Management Policies and Systems
- Disclosure
- Externally Verified
- Continuous Improvement

AN INITIAL TYPOLOGY OF CASES

We begin by offering a simple typology for the nine cases contained in Part 2. The six different types (A to F) set out in Table 3.1 are not intended to be exhaustive, but rather to illustrate some of the key dimensions of the cases in their respective clusters.

THE 'QUALITY' PRINCIPLES

By voicing the history of different approaches to SEAAR, we are provided with a ready list of hints as to what are some of the key dimensions against which quality needs to be assessed. these have been formalised into eight key principles of quality.

Inclusivity

The principle of *inclusivity* means that the social and ethical accounting and auditing must reflect the views and accounts of all principal stakeholders, not only the particular stakeholders who have historically had the most influence over the evolution of the organization's formal mission statement. What this means, furthermore, is that the assessment cannot be based on a single set of values or a single set of objectives. While over time the various stakeholder groups *may* come to agree on many things, the assessment process cannot assume this to be the case and must therefore accommodate such diversity.[26] It is important to distinguish between consultation in the form of one-way surveying – ie essentially market research – and dialogue, which can be understood as a two-way process that brings the views and interests of all parties to the table.[27]

Comparability

The principle of *comparability* is quite simply that SEAAR enables the performance of the organization to be compared as a basis of assessment. Comparison may be based on the organization's performance in different periods, or on external benchmarks drawn from the experience of other organizations, statutory regulations or non-statutory norms. It is important that external benchmarks are selected for their relevance and legitimacy, not only for their accuracy. For example, comparisons of wage rates with outside organizations need to select the appropriate types of organizations, and also need to draw the comparative data from sources that would be considered legitimate (such as government statistics, or labour-research bodies).[28]

Completeness

The principle of *completeness* means that no area of the company's activities can be deliberately and systematically excluded from the assessment. This principle is important to ensure that the company does not 'cherry-pick' the areas of its activities which will show – on inspection – the most positive social and ethical performance.

Comprehensiveness in combination with the principle of inclusivity raises major practical problems, given the potential magnitude of the assessment process. A major manufacturing company may have thousands of products produced and marketed in a large number of contexts and cultures. What this means in practice is that not everything can be covered at once, or more specifically during any one cycle. The essence of this principle is therefore that no area of the organization's activities are necessarily excluded from any particular cycle because of any unwillingness on the part of the organization _ ie no 'malicious exclusion'. Over several cycles, furthermore, all of the principle stakeholder groups would be covered through an exploration of all the effects of all of the organization's activities.[29]

Evolution

It is not be possible, as we have here noted, to cover an entire company's 'social footprint' at one time; furthermore, it is likely that this footprint will vary over time. Furthermore, the impact and meaning given to its footprint will also vary, as the composition and expectations of key stakeholder groups change over time. The implication of this is that one-off accounting exercises are not sufficient for the needs of management – in seeking to understand what is happening – or in terms of the company's accountability to the wider public. A key principle against which the practice of SEAAR needs to be judged is therefore whether the exercise is repeated in a manner that demonstrates learning and continual challenge. That is, the process must follow an *evolutionary* path over time.

Management Policies and Systems

As with both financial and environmental auditing, it is not enough for an organization to get a snapshot of its performance in order to secure its learning processes. It is essential for any systematic process that the organization develops clear policies covering each accounting area, and systems and procedures that allow the accounting process itself to be controlled and evaluated and the organization's awareness and operation of policies and commitments to be assessed through an audit process.

Disclosure

The question of whether the social and ethical accounting and auditing processes are intended primarily for an internal audience, ie as a management tool, or whether they are a means of contributing to organizational learning or of strengthening public accountability, is a conflict that has figured in both the reasons *why* companies engage in the process and the *means by which* the accounting is undertaken. Clearly the focus on an internal audience obviates any need to disclose the results to the public, or even perhaps within the organization beyond the management and board. At the same time, an interest in establishing and maintaining organizational learning and a dialogue culture as well as in strengthening the company's legitimacy in the public domain would require some sort of disclosure. Where a disclosure route is chosen, the matter of quality concerns the extent to which disclosure is a formality or an active means of communication with key stakeholders and the wider public. Merely publishing a document – however comprehensive – does not constitute good practice if the document is difficult to obtain, costly, misleading, or unintelligible to key stakeholders.

Externally Verified

The need for external verification concerns, again, the relative emphasis between SEAAR as a management tool and as a means of organizational learning; or as a means of strengthening accountability and legitimacy. Clearly, an emphasis towards the latter implies the need for external verification of some kind. The challenge is, of course, what kind of external verification process will be of a sufficiently high professional quality and independence for it to validate the published material.

Continuous Improvement

The aim of any SEAAR system must be to assess progress rather than merely retrospective performance. That is, any relevant system must be able to identify whether the organization's performance has improved over time in relation to the values, missions and objectives set by the organization and its stakeholders, as well as by those established through broader social norms. Moreover, beyond the measurement of progress is the need for a method that actively encourages 'raising the floor' of social and ethical performance.

These eight principles seem to represent the most basic dimensions of quality against which any social and ethical accounting, auditing and reporting process can and should be judged. That does not mean to say that a case where several principles are not being adhered to is necessarily 'poor' in quality. For example, the Scandinavian applications of Ethical Accounting do not include external verification (principle seven), yet this may well be because it is not required given the societal context or the particular applications. So the principles cannot, in isolation, be a basis for intercase judgement, although they *can* provide a checklist of things to look for in any assessment or selection process.

SCORING QUALITY

The eight principles are relevant in offering an initial basis for assessing the quality of any exercise in SEAAR. They are, however, too general to be of use in anything but the most basic assessment process. For example, how can one distinguish between stakeholder consultation (essentially limited and one way) and an approach to stakeholder dialogue that is intended to be more deeply participative? Similarly, there are clearly many different ways in which external verification, comprehensiveness, and disclosure can be interpreted in practice.

The approach taken here has been to consider in more depth the possible elements that define the quality of each principle set out above. Specifically, the principles have been broken down into 45 elements against which any particular social and ethical accounting and auditing process can be judged. These elements have been derived from the experience of the case studies, the broader experience of the editors and an analysis of the literature.[30] These elements are detailed in Annex 1.

The cases in the next section have been 'approximately rated' by these elements. The rating is approximate in that there has been no attempt to construct a numerical scoring system. To do so would imply, amongst other things, that there was some *a priori* basis on which these principles and elements can be seen to be more or less important. For example, it would be problematic to add up the smiling or gloomy faces in the table to determine which organization or method had proved more successful. This stage would require comparisons between organizations with similar aims and comparable contexts.

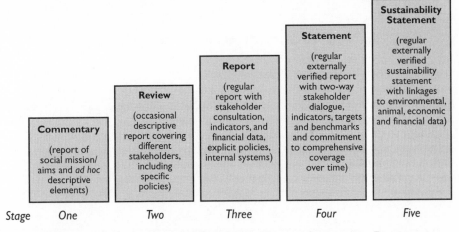

Commentary	Review	Report	Statement	Sustainability Statement
(report of social mission/ aims and *ad hoc* descriptive elements)	(occasional descriptive report covering different stakeholders, including specific policies)	(regular report with stakeholder consultation, indicators, and financial data, explicit policies, internal systems)	(regular externally verified report with two-way stakeholder dialogue, indicators, targets and benchmarks and commitment to comprehensive coverage over time)	(regular externally verified sustainability statement with linkages to environmental, animal, economic and financial data)

Stage	One	Two	Three	Four	Five

Figure 3.1: *Social and Ethical Disclosure: Assessing Progress*

ASSESSING THE QUALITY OF DISCLOSURE

The problems of *ranking* through such scoring and weighting have already been highlighted and concern, in particular, the need to recognize legitimate differences in SEAAR processes. At the same time, there is a demand by all stakeholders to be able to assess the quality of any *disclosure* of social performance, and therefore by implication of the accounting and auditing underlying the 'discovery process' (for reasons discussed further in the next chapter). Drawing inspiration and method from work undertaken by the United Nations Environment Programme (UNEP) and the environmental consultancy SustainAbility Ltd, we have constructed a five-stage developmental model for social and ethical reporting.

Table 3.2: Quality Rating Against Basic Principles and Elements

Case	Inclusivity	Comparability	Completeness	Evolution	Policies/ Systems	External Verification	Disclosure	Continuous Improvement
Aarhus	●	○	●	●	●	□	●	●
Ben & Jerry's Homemade, Inc	●	○	●	●	□	●	●	○
The Body Shop International	●	○	●	●	●	●	●	●
Coop Italia	□	●	□	□	□	□	●	□
Glaxo Holdings plc	□	○	□	□	○	□	○	○
Sbn Bank	●	○	●	●	●	□	●	●
Traidcraft plc	●	●	●	●	●	●	●	●
VanCity	○	●	○	○	○	○	●	○
Wøyen Mølle	●	○	●	●	●	□	●	●

● = method seeks to address principle
○ = method partially seeks to address principle
□ = method does not adequately seek to address principle

46

The basis of scoring an organization against the five developmental stages of social and ethical reporting is, in the main, drawn from the principles set out above and the elements in the annex to this chapter. An analysis of Glaxo's experience, for example, would place it in stage one, although the availability of some financial data would give it elements of stage three characteristics. Similarly, a major difference between Sbn Bank and Traidcraft's experience, that of external verification, would separate them into stages three and four respectively.

This five-stage model clearly does take the step of defining, to a large degree, what principles and elements are more important than others. While this is a step cautioned against by the editors themselves in earlier sections, the model does illustrate where the whole assessment of the quality of SEAAR should go in the future. Specifically, *if* there is a need to be able to judge accounting, auditing and reporting against each other, some form of developmental model will almost inevitably be used, whether formally or implicitly.

Of course, the 'inevitability' of the need for some developmental model depends, in large part, whether or not some form of certification of quality is necessary, either now or in the future, a subject to which we turn in the next chapter.

ENDNOTES

1   Published information on corporate social and ethical accounting and auditing almost exclusively covers Western Europe and the US Research has revealed, however, that other experiences exist. One of the most important of these is probably the ground-breaking work of the Indian industrial conglomerate Tata Industries, which is covered in Institute of Social and Ethical Accountability (1997) *Sixth Environment Foundation Windsor Cattle Roundtable on Social and Ethical Accounting* Auditing and Reporting Accountability Works 1, Institute of Social and Ethical Accountability, London.

2   Nijenrode University, The Netherlands Business School/European Institute for Business Ethics (1995) *The Technology of Ethical Auditing: An Outline* Nijenrode University, Breukelen.

3   S Zadek and R Evans (1993) *Auditing the Market: the Practice of Social Auditing* Traidcraft/New Economics Foundation, Gateshead.

4   *The Body Shop Approach to Ethical Auditing* The Body Shop International, Littlehampton, 1996. See also the entire *Values Report* (1996) which contains all three audits.

5   P Pruzan (1995) 'The Ethical Accounting Statement', *World Business Academy Perspectives* Vol 9, No 2, 1995: pp35–46.

6   See for example, the paper prepared on this subject by a group of Northern non-governmental organizations, Corporate Monitoring Working Group (1996) *Monitoring Codes of Conduct*, prepared by the New Economics Foundation and the Catholic Institute for International Relations, London.

7   See, for some discussion of this, S Zadek and P Tiffen (1996), 'Fair Trade: Business or Campaign' *Development* Autumn 1996: 3: pp48–53.

8   For those interested in some of the historical background that is at best only alluded to in this section, we would suggest R Estes (1992) 'Social

Accounting Past and Future: Should the Profession Lead, Follow – or Just Get Out of the Way?' *Advances in Management Accounting*, 1: pp97–108; R Estes (1995) *Tyranny of the Bottom Line: Why Corporations Make Good People Do Bad Things* Berrett-Koehler, San Francisco; R H Gray, D L Owen & K T Maunders (1996) *Accounting and Accountability: Social and Environmental Accounting in a Changing World* Prentice Hall International, Hemel Hempstead; C Medawar (1976) 'The Social Audit: A Political View', *Accounting, Organizations, and Society*, 1(4) pp389–394; and S Zadek and P Raynard (1995) 'Accounting Works: A Comparative Review of Contemporary Approaches to Social and Ethical Accounting', *Accounting Forum* 19 (2/3) Sept/Dec.

9   D H Blake, W C Frederick and M S Myers (1976) *Social Auditing: Evaluating the Impact of Corporate Programs* Praeger, New York.

10 US Department of Commerce (1979) *Corporate Social Reporting in the United States and Western Europe: Report of the Task Force on Corporate Social Performance* US Department of Commerce, Washington, DC: pp6.

11 See, for example, D Logan (1993) *Transnational Giving: An Introduction to the Corporate Citizenship Activity of International Companies Operating in Europe* The Directory of Social Change, London.

12 Discussed in M Dierkes and R A Bauer (eds) (1973) *Corporate Social Accounting* Praeger, New York.

13 A related method, known as *human asset evaluation*, sought to measure the value of productive capability of the firm's human organisation, and simultaneously the loyalty of the firm's employees and other constituencies affected by the organisation. There is a very interesting development in this approach being trialed by the Swedish insurance company, Skandia, under the title intellectual capital valuation. See Skandia (1994) *Visualising Intellectual Capital in Skandia: Supplement to Skandia's 1994 Annual Report* Skandia, Sweden.

14 US Department of Commerce (1979), op cit: pp6.

15 John W Filer, CEO of Aetna Life and Casualty, quoted in US Department of Commerce (1979), *op cit*: ppvi.

16 Allied Dunbar (1996) *The Big Picture: A Summary of the Allied Dunbar Staff Charity Fund Stakeholder Accountability Report for 1996* Allied Dunbar, Swindon: pp2 Based on the full report, *Staff Charity Fund Review & Stakeholder Accountability Report* Allied Dunbar, Swindon.

17 See also the British equivalent of this, A Adams, J Carruthers, and S Hamil (1991) *Changing Corporate Culture: a Guide to Social and Environmental Policy and Practice in Britain's Top Companies* Kogan Page, London.

18 For example, Ethibel in Belgium, and EthicScan in Canada.

19 For a brief description of this movement and related references, see A MacGillivray and S Zadek (1995) *Accounting for Change: Indicators for Sustainable Development* New Economics Foundation, London.

20 US Department of Commerce (1979) *op cit*: pp8.

21 See, for example, P Walker (1995) 'Turning Dreams into Concrete Reality', *New Economics* Winter 1995: pp5–9; and J Morris (1995) 'Indicators of Local Sustainability' *Town and Country Planning*, April 1995, Vol 64 No 4: pp113–119. For a review of some of the historical and contemporary strands of work in this area, see A MacGillivray and S Zadek (1995) 'Accounting for Change: Indicators for Sustainable Development WEF, London.

22 K Davenport (1996) *Corporate Social Auditing* draft of unpublished thesis, Chapter two, p26.

23 P Pruzan and O Thyssen (1990), 'Conflict and Consensus: Ethics as a Shared Value Horizon for Strategic Planning', *Human Systems Development* 9 1990: pp134–152.

24 S Zadek and P Raynard (1995), 'Accounting Works: A Comparative Review of Contemporary Approaches to Social and Ethical Accounting', *Accounting Forum*, 19 (2/3) Sept/Dec.

25 For a more extensive description of some of the historical patterns that have been briefly alluded to in this section, see, for example, R H Gray, D L Owen, & K T Maunders (1996) *Accounting and Accountability: Social and Environmental Accounting in a Changing World* Prentice Hall International, Hemel Hempstead.

26 The principle of inclusivity can also be understood as the equivalent of the standard accounting principle of *materiality*. That is, the rights of stakeholders to choose performance indicators associated with their interests – in conjunction with the right of the organization to measure its performance against its own mission statement – is part of what secures information that is not only accurate but relevant or material.
    There is an interesting connection with Fourth Generation Evaluation here, which suffers from the methodological defect of requiring balanced power conditions from the outset of the evaluation process See S Zadek (1995) *Beyond Fourth Generation Evaluation* unpublished paper, New Economics Foundation, London.

27 There have been enormous strides forward in the last decade in developing more participative approaches to dialogue between institutions and their stakeholders. Some of the most interesting work has been in the development field, where participative learning methods have been developed to cope with gross imbalances of power between the dialoguing partners, for example, those that exist between development agencies and village communities in the South See, for example, J Pretty, I Guijt, J Thompson and I Scoones (1995) *Participatory Learning and Action: A Trainer's Guide* International Institute for Environment and Development, London.

28 There has been intense activity in the area of social indicator development over the last decade, particularly since the Rio Summit under *Local Agenda 21*. A good review of some of this material is provided by A MacGillivray and S Zadek (1995) *Accounting for Change: Indicators for Sustainable Development* New Economics Foundation, London.

29 Note, too, that this may mean it is more realistic and relevant for a large, diversified company to develop different social and ethical accounts for different subunits instead of trying to develop one single accounting, auditing and reporting system for the whole organization.

30 A considerable debt is due to John Elkington and Andrea Spencer-Cooke for their work in benchmarking environmental reports See in particular United Nations Environment Programme (1994) *Company Environmental Reporting: A Measure of the Progress of Business & Industry Towards Sustainable Development* Technical Report 24, UNEP, Paris, and UNEP/SustainAbility (1996) *The Benchmark Survey: The Second International Progress Report on Company Environmental Reporting* UNEP, Paris.

4

Accountable Futures

The social audit does not have to wait for legislation. Any company could establish one voluntarily...It requires a new profession and a new outlook.

(George Goyder, 1961)[1]

THE WAVES OF PRACTICE

At the *heart* of this book is a set of stories about experiments in social and ethical accounting, auditing, and reporting. At the *head* of this book's agenda, however, is an enquiry into what is both the preferred and possible futures of the practice. What the historical thumbnail sketches in the previous chapters did not highlight were the 'waves' of interest and practice that have taken place. A wave of corporate social reporting emerged during the 1970s, particularly in the US and parts of Europe. The accountancy firm Ernst and Ernst produced annual reports on the emerging practice from 1971, covering the reporting practice of the Fortune 500. In 1978, the report highlighted the confident growth in both the quantity and quality of corporate social reporting.[2] Just two years later, however, the trend had entirely reversed, with a collapse in corporate social reporting. The reasons most commentators give in explaining this collapse is generally the hike in oil prices in 1979 and the resulting economic recession, and the (arguably linked) change in political climate with its more explicit, exclusive focus on short term financial results for business. The glowing shadow of the post-war boom had ended, as had the confidence of the period of nationalization in Europe. The strong political shift to the Right reasserted the right of business to focus on profits at a time of economic turmoil and downturn.

The 1980s was a difficult, but by no means fallow, period for SEAAR. Of particular importance was the emergence and consolidation of several somewhat separate strands of corporate or business-related practice.[3] The first was corporate environmental accounting, auditing, and reporting, which developed with remarkable speed in the second half of the 1980s.[4] This consolidated the precedent of systematic, non-financial accounting, auditing and reporting as a response to a combination of regulatory shifts and public concerns. Related to this was the emergence of external social, ethical and environmental screening of corporate performance for the purposes of informing consumers and the 'ethical investment' community. These screening activities were once again a response to – and a catalyst for – the emerging power in the late 1980s of consumer actions to challenge corporate social and environmental performance, also reflected in the growth in ethical investment funds. These two developments – SEAAR and screening – formed a part of a broader debate that emerged particularly towards the end of the 1980s concerning the role of business in society. The third – and largely unrelated – development was the growth of quality assurance systems within and for the business community, such as total quality management (TQM), BS 7750 and ISO 9000. Together, these trends combined to establish a base for the practice of SEAAR.

The last two chapters have described the emergence of this second powerful wave of SEAAR during the late 1980s. This second wave has drawn its energy from the growth in high-profile ethical business communities in Europe and North America, the evolution of 'consumer concern', and the specific success of the environmental lobby in the 1980s. At the same time, the wave has drawn on the longer-term developments in the mainstream corporate sector, all of which have encouraged companies to audit non-financial processes and outcomes, and in some cases to report on them as a part of their standard annual reporting (as summarised by Rob Gray in Chapter 14).

The strength of this second wave to date does not, however, guarantee the long-term survival of the practice of social and ethical accounting, auditing, and reporting, as the fate of the optimistic first wave illustrates.[5] Even the continuation of the practice of corporate environmental auditing – which has been institutionalized to a high degree – cannot be taken for granted. As one senior corporate environmental manager declared at a recent UNEP-sponsored meeting on the future of environmental reporting:

> *A small number of companies have led the way in corporate environmental accounting and reporting. But we cannot take this leadership for granted, particularly if others don't follow. Sooner or later our directors are going to ask what we are getting for the cost of being leaders in this field – and I'm not sure what I'm going to tell them.*[6]

Some events and trends will tend to reinforce the practice of SEAAR. In particular are such experiences as the consumer responses to Shell's behaviour in Nigeria, actual and threatened consumer boycotts of sportswear and garment companies because of their use of child labour in the South, the increasingly public drive to identify and root out corporate corrupt practices by non-profit organizations such as Transparency International, and the increasing number of specific social issues that need to be understood and reported on, such as gender equality in the workplace.

Other trends do, however, threaten the long term prospects for corporate SEAAR. Market pressures appear to force companies to downsize, to take advantage of the lowering of the legislative floor in the areas of labour protection, to cut corners in the treatment of suppliers, or to delay investment in environmentally friendly equipment or processes. These pressures can make it hard for companies to excel in social and environmental performance unless it can simultaneously bring short-term financial gains to shareholders.[7] Similarly, pressures on stakeholders themselves – particularly staff and consumers – make them less willing to use any influence they have to challenge overall corporate social and ethical performance; instead they understandably look for specific gains, such as employment rights or cheaper prices respectively. In these situations, companies are less inclined to see the gains from comprehensive SEAAR, and will see disadvantages in public disclosure rather than confidential management reports.

THE NEED FOR STANDARDS?

Economic downturns and other potential routes, where corporate SEAAR might be undermined, will not go away. Thus, the consolidation of the practice in a manner that will be effective in both improving corporate social and ethical performance, as well as making them more transparent and accountable, requires a mechanism for protection against such potentially undermining forces. It is not adequate for corporate SEAAR to be only a 'fair weather' practice. For it to be meaningful, it needs to be a practice in which a company engages as necessarily as it would a financial audit, irrespective of the level of profits. Neither is the practice going to give any reliable indication of corporate social performance if a company or their consultants can design the process entirely to their needs and interests, and name it and the results in any way they choose. The quality of a company's practice of SEAAR must be as clear to all interested parties as is the technical quality of the goods and services they produce.

There is, therefore, a need for agreed standards of corporate SEAAR. While experimentation can continue to yield a wealth of experiences, there is equally a need to limit the danger of fragmentation of efforts and directions leading to considerable confusion as to what different methods are being used and to what effect. As Rob Gray explains: 'The long history of social and ethical accounting has been characterised by a *disturbing* variety of approaches and standards'.[8] Although there are clearly dangers in determining standards for social and ethical accounting, auditing and reporting, there are also clear potential gains. First, divergent terminology and method can be a sign of flourishing creativity in the early stages of the life cycle of an innovation of any kind. For the innovation to mature in terms of more widespread use or take-up, however, it must become less dynamic, more stable and more recognizable. There is already evidence of resistance to take-up that is associated with a confusion as to which approach is more effective, or more generally which will win-out in the end. Second, one of the reasons that organizations undertake some kind of social and ethical accounting and auditing is that it allows them to make claims about their openness, and hopefully about their sound social practice. Such claims can only be made on a basis that is seen to be legitimate in the eyes of the intended audience. We have seen that there is little or no challenge when organizations prepare Ethical Accounting Statements, possibly because of the more open culture of Scandinavian countries or the (perhaps associated) lower level of social conflict. In the UK and the US, on the other hand, organizations have invested heavily in securing some form of explicit legitimizing process in the form of an external audit or verification.

There is ample evidence that a strong assurance label aids take-up where it is underpinned by robust standards that are widely acceptable, such as in the area of financial and environmental auditing, or in the case of product labels for organic, safety or fair trade qualities. As the CEO of one major commercial bank stated quite bluntly: 'Come back to talk to me about social auditing when you have a quality label that is recognisable in the market that I can put on all of our literature.' Experience has clearly shown that the value of social and ethical accounting and auditing in building an organization's public profile is an important factor in determining take-up, and an agreed set of standards is an essential element of making this factor count.

By far the most important reason for standards, however, is to *ensure quality* in the process of accounting, auditing and reporting to support improved corporate social responsibility. This is not merely a question of what gives a method respectability, or what gives an organization some market gain from adopting such a method. This is about what methods seem to work best in achieving the underlying aim of assisting organizations in achieving continual improvement against agreed social and ethical aims, and indeed of challenging and raising the aspirations of those aims themselves.

ROUTES TO STANDARDS

Standards can be achieved in a number of different ways. At one extreme is the *benchmark of practice*, which others must follow if they want their attempts to be taken seriously. Many of the case studies have to varying degrees succeeded in establishing at least temporary standards in this manner. Sbn Bank's annual Ethical Accounting Statement has certainly come to be seen as a benchmark against which corporate social reporting in Denmark and elsewhere in Scandinavia is judged. Traidcraft's Social Accounts have similarly set a standard in the British context, as evidenced by the companies that have sought to draw from and be measured against Traidcraft's standards of quality. This latter case is interesting in the way it has precipitated an escalation of standards. The Body Shop International has drawn from both Traidcraft's and Sbn Bank's example, but has also sought to set new and higher standards. Ben & Jerry's Homemade, Inc is a further case in point, having undertaken some kind of social reporting for seven years. As the United States Trust Corporation, a socially responsive investment firm, stated in the August 1995 edition of its newsletter *Values*: 'Ben & Jerry's, which publishes unedited conclusions of its independent social auditor, remains the "gold standard" in open, self-critical evaluation.' Interestingly, the company is now seeking to consolidate and further strengthen its own performance in social reporting by taking on some of the lessons learnt in Denmark and the UK.

Leadership benchmarking has a critical role to play in the take-up of any innovation, and is a major reason for adopting the sort of five-stage corporate social reporting model outlined in the last chapter.[9] Several of the case studies described in Part 2 of this book are classic examples of leadership benchmarking. Such standard setting has, however, its limitations. A prolif-

- mandatory legislation
- non-mandatory legislation
- private external screening
- voluntary codes
- leadership benchmarking

Figure 4.1: *The Standards Spectrum*

eration of different approaches, for example, can undermine the quality push of leadership benchmarking. It is possible, furthermore, for a concerted effort on the part of reluctant 'followers' to marginalize the example set by the leader. A few of the representatives of large, mainstream corporations attending seminars on social and ethical accounting and auditing, for example, have argued that it is only relevant for 'wierd companies that try to mix ethics with business'. The more radical the innovation in question, the more likely is it that a serious attempt to marginalize it will occur. So leadership benchmarking is important at the early stages of innovation, but can be of less use at the critical stage where serious mainstream adoption is being sought.

At the other extreme are standards established through the force of legislation. Clearly the advantage of legislation is that the associated standards cannot be simply ignored. This is most obviously the case with financial accounting and auditing, where extensive legislation exists. Over recent years, this has also increasingly been the case for standards in environmental auditing, although still to a far less extent than financial auditing, and with far greater variation between countries. Some countries have legislation covering some aspects of SEAAR. In the UK, for example, corporations over a particular size are obliged to report on their charitable giving, and must provide certain information regarding staff conditions and employment practices, such as the proportion of staff who are registered disabled. This extent of *de facto* mandatory social reporting in the UK is illustrated in Table 4.1, reproduced from Rob Gray's chapter on silent accounting.

There are, however, serious disadvantages to relying on the law to secure standards. First and foremost is the sheer time involved in getting to the point of legislation. Clearly a part of this process is very productive, involving an iterative path of distilling the required standards into a form that can be reasonably expected to apply to many different organizations in different situations. Much of the process, however, is decidedly unproductive time spent in endless, bureaucratic and extremely costly debates. Underlying this is a potentially far more serious objection to seeking legislation in order to secure standards. This is the danger of downgrading under pressure from

Table 4.1 *Typical Social and Ethical Areas Covered in UK Company Annual Reports*

Voluntary	Required/Mandatory
• environmental protection; • energy saving; • consumer protection; • product safety; • community involvement; • value-added statement; • health and safety; • racial and sexual equality; • redundancies; • employee training; • mission statement/statement of social responsibility.	• charitable donations; • employment data; • pension fund adequacy; • consultation with employees; • employee share-ownership schemes; • employment in South Africa; • employment of the disabled; • contingent liabilities and provisions for health and safety or environmental remediation.

Source: adapted from R H Gray (1991b) *Trends in Corporate Social and Environmental Accounting* British Institute of Management, London, pp3.

strong vested interests. There is little doubt, for example, that any attempt to enshrine key principles of social and ethical accounting and auditing in law would elicit serious objection from many parts of the corporate sector. It is very likely, furthermore, that any legislation that was agreed would represent a watered-down compromise compared to the original vision. It is this weak legislation that would then become the basis for standards. The question is, then, whether weak legislation is better or worse than no legislation.

Between the extremes of leadership benchmarking and legislation is a range of other means through which standards can be set, including, for example, voluntary codes and external screening by private, often non-profit, organizations. Those options that tend towards voluntarism and have the danger of becoming confused over time, and also of degrading in the face of pressure from the main body of organizations which do not wish to follow the set examples. Those options that tend towards statutory enforcement suffer from the disadvantage that the time-frame for accepted standards tends to extend into the distant future, and the end result is often painfully weakened through the negotiation process.

The most productive approach to standards is to see the various options as complementary rather than exclusive. It is necessary to set quality standards through leadership in practice as well as in theory. These standards then need to form the basis for negotiation on voluntary codes, and ultimately for legislation of some kind. Leadership standards create pressure for codes and legislation, and can help in resisting any watering down of what those standards might be. Voluntary codes and legislation ultimately help in preventing a gradual erosion of standards through the abuse of method and its use for crude public relations exercises.

The development of standards must therefore be skillfully managed by those wishing them to count. There is no reason to assume *a priori* that formal standards are better than no standards, whether set through voluntary codes or embedded in legislation. A key determining factor of whether the formalization of standards helps or hinders in building real quality (and in this case, real accountability) is who is at the negotiating table where standards are agreed and their relative strengths. The more open and public the debate, the more likely it is that the watering-down process can be avoided or at least minimized. The more the process is driven by professionalized interest groups – unfortunately often where the corporate sector is involved – the more likely is it that the standards will be positioned close to floor level. At the same time, negotiation-by-confrontation is an inadequate route to agreeing standards that need to be both relevant and feasible, particularly in the business context.

TOWARDS CONVERGENCE

There are clear signs of a convergence of standards taking place in the practice of SEAAR. The relevance of both external benchmarks and stakeholder dialogue is confirmed in most current practice, albeit to differing degrees. Even those approaches which have focused exclusively on one or other element are now moving towards some combination. The originators of the Ethical Accounting Statement, for example, are actively exploring how external benchmarks might be used where the approach has, to date, focused exclusively on stakeholder dialogue. At the other extreme, both VanCity and the Co-op are now examining how greater stakeholder participation in the accounting process might best be achieved.

A similar convergence is taking place in the the need for the external agent, although again with different emphases. Ben & Jerry's Homemade, Inc, for example, has in its recent history of social performance reports seen the external agent essentially as an evaluator who is asked to pass personal judgement on the company's social performance. More recently, however, they have been experimenting with a move away from this personalized judgement process towards a view of the external agent as auditor, charged with the duty of ensuring that the published statement is a correct description of what happened over the period, rather than his or her view of those events.

There is, then, the gradual emergence of a consensus about what constitutes some of the key principles of good practice. Far from closing the door to further experimentation, this convergence allows for a more systematic assessment of different approaches, a clearer dialogue between those who are trialling and using these different approaches, and a deeper appreciation of what skills and experience are required to make any process effective. This approach to the organization, including the assessment of experience, can be understood as the basis upon which a profession is built. This, in turn, implies a number of things. First, SEAAR is an increasingly bounded and hence defined set of activities; it becomes less and less possible for anyone to describe just anything as being the practice of social and ethical accounting and auditing. Second, *quality* – in addition to activities and their outcomes – is subject to assessment as a part of the 'professionalization' process. Third, the skills and experiences required to support the process of SEAAR are more and more specified.

It is in the context of these issues and experiences that a decision was made to establish an institute that would seek to promote a convergence of standards in SEAAR. The possibility of such an institute was first discussed by a group from business schools, non-profit corporate responsibility organizations, consultancies, and business ethicists meeting together in early 1994, as outlined in the preface to this book. A decision in principle was made at the Social Venture Network conference in Tuscany, Italy, in early 1995.

THE INSTITUTE OF SOCIAL AND ETHICAL ACCOUNTABILITY

The Institute of Social and Ethical AccountAbility has been established to develop consensus on a set of standards that, in turn, can form the basis for securing a recognisable and assessible level of quality in social and ethical accounting and auditing. In this sense, *'AccountAbility'* will encourage the emergence of a professional approach with agreed standards not only in the method, but also in the quality of accounting and auditing in practice.

For such an institute to play a useful role in developing standards and securing quality in SEAAR requires a legitimacy that goes beyond professional skills and experiences. It would simply not work if such an institute was established unilaterally by the business establishment. The reports and statements arising from practical social and ethical accounting and auditing, blessed by such an institute, would not be considered legitimate by community groups, the corporate responsibility movement, or many of the other organizations representing key stakeholders. It is these constituencies

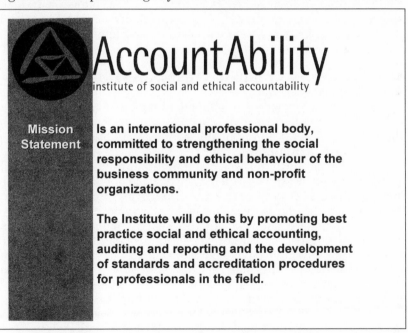

AccountAbility
institute of social and ethical accountability

Mission Statement Is an international professional body, committed to strengthening the social responsibility and ethical behaviour of the business community and non-profit organizations.

The Institute will do this by promoting best practice social and ethical accounting, auditing and reporting and the development of standards and accreditation procedures for professionals in the field.

Figure 4.2: *The Mission Statement of AccountAbility*

that need to legitimize the appropriate standards if social and ethical accounting and auditing are to have any real role to play in forging new directions for the corporate sector. Furthermore, it is not only those outside of the corporate sector that need to be involved in the development of appropriate standards. It is critical that skills and insights from within the business community are applied to the development of meaningful and practical standards.

AccountAbility appreciates the need for a broad set of constituencies to be adequately represented. For this reason, the executive board which manages the early stages of the institute includes representatives from the non-profit corporate responsibility movement, consultancies wishing to deliver services associated with SEAAR, business schools, and a mixture of types of businesses which are likely to be audited at some stage in the future. From the corporate responsibility movement, the Council for Economic Priorities (US), Ethibel (Belgium) and the New Economics Foundation (UK) are represented. A number of consultancies have joined the board who offer a range of relevant and linked services, including business ethics, financial and environmental auditing and advice. Two major European business schools sit on the board: the Copenhagen Business School (Denmark) and the Nijenrode Business School (the Netherlands). As well as one major accountancy research unit, the Centre for Environmental and Social Accountancy Research in Scotland, is also included. Major companies who have agreed to become founding members include the Avina Group (Switzerland), Ben & Jerry's Homemade, Inc (US), British Telecom (UK), KPMG (US), the Link Group (Belgium), and The Body Shop International (UK). The challenge that AccountAbility has to meet is to establish a framework of standards, training and accreditation that will allow SEAAR to move beyond the experimental end of the corporate sector and into the mainstream.

ENTERING THE MAINSTREAM

To enter the mainstream means to successfully encourage companies – who have historically been oriented primarily towards financial gain – to engage in the process of social and ethical accounting, auditing and reporting as a practical demonstration of their commitment to – and move towards – improved social and ethical accountability and practices. Many of these companies produce and sell the branded goods and services that appear on our high streets. They offer the financial services that many of us rely on. They include the companies that make the vehicles we travel in and the telephones that we use. Beyond these large companies are the smaller businesses that also play a key role in influencing the quality of our lives. Here are the private hospitals and care centres, the bus companies and the local newspapers.[10] Beyond this still are those organizations who are publically owned or controlled: the research units, the national health systems, and the administrative services. There is certainly nothing about SEAAR that makes it suitable only for private businesses.[11] All organizations have social 'footprints' and face ethical dilemmas that they must address daily.

ACCOUNTABLE FUTURES

There are, and always have been, fine examples of organizations that go beyond the norm in seeking to demonstrate social and environmental responsibility in their practices. Some are small, such as Wøyen Mølle, some are not so small, such as The Body Shop International. These organizations, often with their driving mission statements and visonary leaders, show that it is possible for businesses to be socially responsible as well as financially viable and rewarding. Those that are companies find the spaces in the pipeline between investors and consumers where some choice in behaviour is possible. Furthermore, they take on the far more ambitious agenda of shifting the basic boundaries by raising public awareness towards social, ethical and environmental agendas, and supporting the emergence of new forms of investors that take non-financial criteria into account.

These organizations are the experimental laboratories of the future. Just as Nissan or Ford invest billions in the search for the most marketable car for the millenium, other organizations choose to invest in the design of ethical aspects of 'tomorrow's company'. SEAAR has been nurtured and developed in these laboratories in recognition of the need for *conscious, mindful* action to ensure that the corporate sector plays a positive role in securing our future. Measurement is not a passive, neutral activity. If we want social and ethical dimensions of business activity to be taken more seriously in decision-making, we must work out how to count them as one part of a complex and often difficult process of making them count.

ENDNOTES

1   G Goyder (1961) *The Responsible Company* Blackwell, Oxford: pp110–111.
2   US Department of Commerce (1979) *Corporate Social Reporting in the United States and Western Europe: Report of the Task Force on Corporate Social Performance* US Department of Commerce, Washington, DC: pp10–12.
3   The question of 'why' companies choose to engage in the practice has already been discussed in detail in Chapter 2.
4   United Nations Environment Programme (1994) *Company Environmental Reporting: A Measure of the Progress of Business & Industry Towards Sustainable Development* Technical Report No 24, UNEP/SustainAbility Ltd, Paris.
5   R Gray, C Dey, D Owen, R Evans and S Zadek (1996) *Struggling with the Praxis of Social Accounting: Stakeholders, Accountability, Audits, and Procedures* discussion paper, Centre for Social and Environmental Accountancy Research, University of Dundee, Dundee.
6   Quote from discussions at a meeting hosted by the United Nations Environment Programme in Paris in October 1996 to discuss the progress of corporate environmental reporting.
7   For a particularly bleak picture of the extent of this pressure, see D Korten (1995) *When Corporations Rule the World* Earthscan, London.

8 *AccountAbility Quarterly*, No 1 Summer 1996: pp5. Italics added.

9 The first volume of the UNEP/SustainAbility report *Engaging Stakeholders* offers a benchmark survey that seeks to set out what the leaders are doing in environmental reporting, and in this manner encourages others to follow.

10 There is an increasing body of work dealing with small-scale social and ethical accounting, auditing, and reporting See, for example, J Pearce, P Raynard and S Zadek (1996) *Social Auditing for Small Organizations: A Workbook* New Economics Foundation, London.

11 The literature on social and ethical accounting for the non-profit, non-governmental sector is also expanding rapidly See, for example, E Mayo (1996) *Social Auditing for the Voluntary Sector* City University, London, and J Pearce (1994) *At the Heart of the Community* Gulbenkian Foundation, London.

PART 2

The Briefings

5

The Ethical Dimensions of Banking: Sbn Bank, Denmark

Professor Peter Pruzan
(Copenhagen Business School)

BANKING AS SERVING

The history of Ethical Accounting at Sbn Bank is really the history of Ethical Accounting.[1] Although its development at the bank could be explained in rational and logical terms, there is more to it. Looking back on how things developed, it appears to have been more a case of the right idea at the right time and place than of careful analysis and economic rationality. Spontaneous combustion is a better metaphor than a carefully lit fire.

In a Danish article of 1988 my colleague Ole Thyssen and I proposed the development of Ethical Accounting as a means of operationalizing ethics and value-based leadership in an organization. The article, now available in English,[2] was based on our work with ethics in organizations and with decision-making contexts characterized by multiple criteria. Our proposal was brought to the attention of the management of Denmark's seventh largest bank, Sbn Bank, or 'Sparekassen Nordjylland' as it is known in Denmark. The bank is a regional bank primarily serving Northern Jutland with 71 branches in 19 regional areas and with roughly 1300 employees, 200,000 customers and 60,000 shareholders, most of whom are customers. The bank's market share of private customers in North Jutland is roughly 35 per cent, and 25 per cent with respect to corporate customers. A year earlier the bank had begun to develop its 'code of values' based on certain psychological theories regarding people's basic needs. The code provided a long list of so-called shared values and the commitments facing employees and management if these values are to be promoted.

When we wrote our article we were unaware of the bank's work on explicitly introducing values as a leadership perspective – and of the problems it was facing in implementing the code. Our article pointed out several pitfalls of the approach that the bank had taken. For example, it was 'top-down'; although it spoke of employee commitment, it was for all intents and purposes developed by top management with the aid of outside consultants. In addition, the emphasis was more on the product (the code) than on the process of integrating values and ethics into the organization. Not only were the employees uninvolved in designing the code, but neither were the other major parties who are affected by the bank's actions and whose behaviour in turn affects the bank, ie the stakeholders. Thus, there was no way of determining whether the values formulated were relevant, were lived up to, and whether the commitments listed were just good intentions formulated by management. In other words, the Code of Values by itself could not provide a means for the values to be integrated into the organization so that it could identify itself, reflect upon itself, and evaluate itself from a value-based perspective.

'Ethical Accounting is not for softies or funks. It takes guts to hang your dirty linen in public and to walk your talk.' (Jørgen Giversen, former CEO of Sbn Bank)

Not only did our article ring a bell at the bank's head office by making the problems it was facing explicit; it also suggested a methodology for overcoming just these deficiencies. We were therefore invited to present our ideas to several hundred employees at a meeting in the bank's headquarters in autumn 1988. Immediately following our presentation, the Chief Executive Officer, Mr. Jørgen Giversen, invited us to have a glass of wine together with other members of the top-management team and several employee representatives. We noticed that an animated discussion was taking place – and before the first 'skål' was pronounced. Mr Giversen turned to us and said: 'If you will help us develop Ethical Accounting at the bank, we will turn it over to you for the next three years as a laboratory where you can experiment in applying your theories.' For professors accustomed to university decision processes characterized by inertia, petty jealousies and non-decisions, this was a rather remarkable and daring statement. We replied spontaneously that this was a deal. Without any of us really reflecting on the possible consequences of our impulsiveness, the bank and a small group from the Copenhagen Business School launched an applied research project which was to lead to the development of a methodology now being employed at roughly 50 Danish private and public enterprises, and which is currently being implemented in Norwegian and Japanese companies as well. The project also led indirectly to the development of radically new teaching and research perspectives at the Copenhagen Business School as well as the development of an international teamwork to promote and establish standards for social and ethical accounting.

'The ethical accounting statement measures how well we live up to the values we have commited ourselves to follow.' (Sbn Bank's ethical accounting statement, 1993.)

Since 1990 (covering the year 1989) the bank has published Ethical Accounting Statements each year. Furthermore, based upon the experience gained, the bank's Code of Values has regularly and interactively been modified so as to represent the values of the customers, employees, shareholders and local community in their relationships with the bank – and to keep these values in focus. The project of implementing Ethical Accounting was originally led by Dr Thorbjörn Meyer at the Copenhagen Business School as action research in connection with his doctoral thesis on the ethical learning process. Since 1992, however, it has been the responsibility of the bank's chief economist, Mr Keld Gammelgaard, who is also responsible for its financial statement. It should be mentioned that while Mr Gammelgaard originally (like so many other of his peers) was sceptical about this new approach with its rather strange name, he is now a warm supporter of it – so much so, that in his spare time he has worked on a PhD thesis based upon the bank's experiences with Ethical Accounting. According to Mr Gammelgaard, 'Ethical Accounting provides the bank with a significant supplement to its traditional financial accounts – a supplement that constitutes a richer repertoire of measures and perspectives than that provided via economics.'

Not only have Ethical Accounting and value-based leadership provided the bank with new tools, they have provided it with a new vocabulary, a new frame of reference for self-evaluation and a new perspective on leadership. This has been evident in the way that members of management speak in the arguments they have used to justify their plans, decisions and behavior, in the signals they have sent out to the stockholders, and in the way they have lead their daily lives. A transition has been made from banking as facilitating monetary transactions to banking as serving those parties who are affected by its actions. According to the former CEO: 'The Annual Report and Accounts tell us how much we have earned or lost and how much we own. But they do not tell us how the company functions, whether our employees are satisfied, if the customers respect the quality of the service we provide, how our shareholders evaluate our performance or how the local society we are a part of reacts to our behaviour.'

WHAT IS ETHICAL ACCOUNTING AT SBN BANK?

The underlying idea is simple: it is vital for the bank to know its major stakeholders – its employees, private and corporate customers, shareholders and local community.[3] But to 'know' necessitates dialogues where a shared language develops and interests become explicit. Therefore, at a pragmatic level, the bank considers its Ethical Accounting Statement as measuring the extent to which it lives up to its values.

On a deeper level, however, there is far more to the process than just identifying stakeholder values and measuring how well the bank supports these values. In fact, one might say that although Ethical Accounting Statements are important sources of information, the real impact of Ethical Accounting at Sbn Bank is the *learning process* it has instigated and the significant changes in self-reflection it has contributed to. According to the Ethical Accounting Statement for 1991:

> *Ethical Accounting contributes to a process where the bank continually develops itself via an on-going conversation with itself and its surroundings – and where its goal is not just to earn money but to contribute to its own and its stakeholder's capacities for developing themselves.*

In that process money is considered to be a *means* – a condition for business survival and for development – and not an end in itself. However, this may give too romantic a picture of what has transpired. It should therefore be noted that the bank's management still considers economic viability to be its major ethical responsibility.

'Ethics concerns shared values which people accept as the basis for commitment, action and trust.' (Sbn Bank's ethical accounting statement, 1993.)

Compared to an ordinary financial statement, the Ethical Accounting Statement includes a multiple of qualitative values while its financial accounting statement only focuses on measures of financial performance and profits, and only expresses itself via the narrow language of money. In addition, the bank's Ethical Accounting is not only aimed at its roughly 60,000 shareholders but is targeted at all its stakeholders. And a third major distinction is that while the bank's yearly operating statement is designed and developed by a small group of experts in accountancy and finance, its Ethical Accounting Statement can be said to be designed, developed, interpreted and used by all the stakeholders. Therefore, Ethical Accounting provides the bank with a much richer picture of its relationship with its stakeholders – and therefore of its potentials for surviving, thriving and developing in the long run.

IS IT ETHICAL? IS IT ACCOUNTING?

When we first presented the concept there were two groups of professionals who criticized us: philosophers/theologians and economists/accountants. The first group challenged the use of the word ethics in connection with an enterprise's evaluation. They felt that they had a patent on its usage and that it was reserved for considerations of moral principles in interpersonal relations; speaking of ethics in connection with a company's evaluation and strategic orientation appeared to sully the term. It should be noted that at present the term 'Ethical Accounting' is so widely used – also by philosophers – that it can be said to be part of the modern Danish vernacular. In the bank's first Ethical Accounting Statement (for 1989, published in spring 1990) Ole Thyssen and I provided a brief explanation as to why we called it *Ethical* Accounting.

BOX 5.1: WHY WE CALL IT THE ETHICAL ACCOUNTING STATEMENT

'Many people think of ethics as a personal matter that really cannot be discussed. Others regard ethics as some kind of checklist that can be used to determine right and wrong. We have a different perspective. The idea behind the concept of Ethical Accounting is that ethics is socially constructive and it can and should be discussed. A discussion of ethics does not elicit any unambiguous answers, but rather initiates a process in which the parties involved, each with their own values, must determine what they can agree is right and wrong.

Ideally, a decision is ethical if the parties influenced by it agree. Therefore, ethics deals with values which are strong enough to be shared and with conflict resolution via attunement of these values. The Ethical Accounting statement is based on the values that are shared by the company and its stakeholders. It demonstrates that there are other values to be promoted than power and money. The Ethical Accounting Statement measures the degree to which the company lives up to these shared values and thus supplements the financial statement's bottom line.'

The second group of critics, the accountants and economists, took exception to the use of the term accounting, which they argued only had to do with evaluating the financial position and operating results of an enterprise in monetary terms. Our response was that an organization is *accountable* or answerable to its stakeholders; there are other stakeholders than the owners who have an interest in how well an organization promotes their values, and 'there are other values to be promoted than power and money'. Once again it is noteworthy that within just a few years, the concept of Ethical Accounting has become part of the vocabulary of many Danish economists, accountants and businessmen and women.

The following – slightly modified – excerpt from the introduction to the bank's Ethical Accounting Statement for 1991 elaborates on these issues and provides as well a concise summary of the underlying concepts:[4]

'Ideally speaking, a decision is ethical if all parties affected by it give their agreement. Therefore ethics deals with values which are strong enough to be shared and with conflict resolution via the attunement of these values.'

HOW IS THE PROCESS CARRIED OUT AT SBN BANK?

The procedures employed today are far more structured than when the process commenced in 1989. The first year's procedures were characterized by considerable experimenting – as well as by uncertainty amongst the employees as to what was going on and why. With this reservation, the

BOX 5.2: INTRODUCTION TO SBN'S ETHICAL ACCOUNTING STATEMENT, 1991

What is ethics in an organizational context? Ethics is not a list of commandments as to right and wrong. Neither is it a strong, personal feeling as to what is right and what is wrong. It is, of course, important that people have strong, personal convictions. But in an organizational context these cannot be expected to be shared by everyone, nor can they be proved right. An action is not necessarily ethical just because I can accept it. It is ethical if *the parties affected by it* can accept it. Ethics refers both to a conversation process and to the action which is the product of the conversation.

What is a conversation process? In an organization, consensus as to right or wrong cannot be presupposed. Therefore, co-ordination of action calls for agreement via an ongoing conversation which defines who can participate, what is to be discussed, how to communicate, how deep to go, and how the conversation should begin and end.

What are shared values? A value is a primary goal and not just a means of achieving another goal. Shared values are the evaluation standards which crystallize out of a conversation process and which an organization and its stakeholders agree to use to evaluate whether or not the organization's actions are acceptable. Since values not only concern conduct, but also motives, they are neither visible nor precise measuring rods.

What is a code of values? A code of values is an inclusive expression of the values which an organization has agreed with its stakeholders to follow. It is not an expression of a single stakeholder's values, no matter how powerful that party may be; all stakeholders must be involved. In order to be operational, a code of values must not be banal, self-contradictory or confusing.

What is an Ethical Accounting Statement? An Ethical Accounting Statement provides measures of how well an organization lives up to the shared values to which it has committed itself. It contributes to a dialogue process where values become integrated into the organization. It provides an extensive picture of the organization's relationships with its stakeholders, and thus of its chances for long-term development and survival. But it encompasses more than just a snapshot at a particular time; its design, development and interpretation contribute to an ongoing dialogue culture where values become vital for the organization's self-reference. Compared to traditional accounting statements, an Ethical Accounting Statement comprises more values, addresses more stakeholders, and is developed, interpreted and employed by the stakeholders.

Which minimum requirements must an Ethical Accounting Statement satisfy? An Ethical Accounting Statement:

- is based upon the shared values which the stakeholders have defined in a conversation process;
- employs questionnaires based on concrete expressions of the shared values;
- is developed at regular intervals by representatives of the stakeholders;
- is published even if the results are unpleasant for the management;
- is designed so that it is impossible to identify individual respondents;
- gives no stakeholder a monopoly on interpreting the results – interpretation takes place in an ongoing dialogue between the stakeholders;
- provides the starting point for new dialogues aimed at proposing concrete actions in areas where the organization should improve its support of the shared values – and for the development of the next Ethical Accounting Statement.

What are the limits for an Ethical Accounting Statement? An Ethical Accounting Statement cannot secure agreement. It is based upon confidence and responsibility, and over time it may contribute to confidence and responsibility. An Ethical Accounting Statement is not objective. Its results must be interpreted and reinterpreted. It does not prove anything, but draws a rich and informative picture of how stakeholders perceive their relationships with the organization.

following gives a rather terse structured account of the major activities which constitute the ethical learning process at Sbn Bank, as well as a series of observations on these activities.

- The identification of the bank's *stakeholders* and of representatives of these stakeholders. The stakeholders are at present chosen to be the bank's employees, shareholders, private and corporate customers, and the local community (citizens who are neither shareholders or customers). It should be noted that the identification of the stakeholders was by no means a straightforward matter and that the list has been modified twice since 1989.

- The identification of those *values* which the various stakeholders share with the bank and the operationalization of these shared values in the form of a series of *test statements*. These values and the statements, which express what is meant by the values, were originally determined – and are now periodically re-examined – via group interviews with representatives of the various stakeholders. This was a rather demanding activity requiring considerable paedagogical skills, sensitivity and patience. A facilitator was required to get the discussions going and to keep them focused. Considerable learning took place as the members of the organization were not used to thinking and speaking about values – and certainly not with respect to the bank.

The bank's top management feels that the identification of values, and the operationalization of these values via test statements by the stakeholders themselves, is one of the fundamental ways in which the Ethical Accounting Statement distinguishes itself from traditional ethical codes as well as from market surveys and public opinion studies. This participative approach to value-based management has been of crucial importance at Sbn Bank. It has significantly affected stakeholder attitudes to the resulting questionnaire (see the next bullet). Furthermore, it appears to have contributed to stakeholder confidence in the whole process – and in particular to the employees' experience of identity and responsibility with respect to the organization.

The values and statements serve as the content of a questionnaire designed to determine how well the organization promotes the values its stakeholders share with the organization. The respondees may answer by chosing one of the following responses to each statement: strongly agree, slightly agree, slightly disagree, strongly disagree, no opinion. See Figures 5.1 and 5.2 for customer and employee questionnaires. It should be noted that the bank's management feels that it is important to be able to make intertemporal comparisons so as to see how stakeholder responses change over time. Therefore it is relatively seldom that the values and test statements are modified.

- The collection of stakeholder responses to the *questionnaires* is now carried out via computer-assisted telephone interviews (CATI-method). Originally questionnaires were sent out by mail. Anonymity is guaranteed; independent interviewers are employed with no recording of the interviewee's identity. At Sbn Bank, 97 per cent of the 1166 employees contacted participated in 1994, while representatives of the customers (1208 private and corporate customers were contacted, 78 per cent participated), shareholders (607 contacted, 82 per cent participated) and local citizens who are neither customers nor shareholders (547 contacted, 71 per cent participated) were chosen at random. These response rates are in contrast to the 1989 statement where the response rates were extremely more modest, varying between 10 per cent and 15 per cent; the idea was new, people were sceptical and the questionnaire technique was underdeveloped. The extremely high participation percentages today reflect confidence in the procedure and in the integrity of the bank.

'It is not a sign of weakness that the Ethical Accounting Statement includes interpretation and discussion. It is a strength. If there was only one right interpretation, all dialogue would cease. Ethical Accounting invites discussion and brings conflicts into the open so that they can be used constructively. It is via discussion and conflict that the organization learns and progresses.' (Report from Sbn management, 1994)

- The *presentation and interpretation* of the stakeholders' responses as well as management's statement: these constitute the organization's Ethical Accounting Statement for the preceeding period. No matter how hard one tries to be objective, interpretation will always be subject to discussion. This is the reason why all results, negative as well as positive, are made public. In this way everyone can reach his or her own conclusions. This is another way in which the bank feels that the Ethical Accounting Statement distinguishes itself from 'market surveys' and public opinion studies.

- The information collected can be sorted according to a series of basic data supplied by each respondent. These can include gender, age, job, private/commercial customer, etc, depending upon which stakeholder category the respondent belongs to. This information can therefore be used for analyses of the responses of particular subsets of – for instance – employees (men vs women, management vs white collar workers) or customers (private vs commercial).

  These data also serve as the starting point for more detailed *internal* statements for the bank's 19 geographical regions and two centralized administrative departments. While the official Ethical Accounting Statement provides an overall impression of the results of the bank's value-based management, top management particularly emphasizes the importance of the internal statements as providing results which are practically meaningful at more local levels. Stakeholder evaluations at regional and branch levels permit the management of decentralized units to react forcefully when there is a need for special measures with regards to customers or staff. And the individual employees can see for themselves how the evaluations have been in their own areas.

  The internal accounting statements also are the focus of inter-organizational comparisons which serve as the basis for dialogues between each decentralized management and the bank's top management, as well as with the local stakeholders, particuarly the employees. According to the management report of the bank's 1993 Ethical Accounting Statement:

  > The Ethical Accounting Statement also improves management options within the bank. The information collected provides us with the opportunity to see the results of each individual organizational unit. It allows us to initiate a dialogue and to act promptly should we become aware of developments which are contrary to the values shared by the stakeholders and Sbn Bank.

  Earlier, discussions with decentralized units were initiated based on economic key figures. Today these discussions are to a great extent based upon the results of the internal statements, which, according to the bank's chief economist, provide an extra dimension and a richer basis for discussion.

  Management emphasizes the importance of these internal statements for integrating values into the local organizations on a practical, daily level. The results are discussed at personnel meetings, at meetings of branch managers, in connection with each employee's periodic evaluations – and are used to justify new initiatives at the local levels, in particular changes in operating procedures. According to one of the bank's employee representatives:

> It is always exciting for the workers in a decentralized unit to see how it shapes up in comparison with the other departments – and with its own results a year earlier. All the employee representatives are invited to participate when the official and the internal ethical accounting statements are available in the spring.... During the fall the internal statements are discussed by all the personnel of a decentralized unit and by the regional management, together with employee representatives.

And according to a member of the bank's top management, Ethical Accounting has survived and thrived because both employees and management find it useful.

• The instigation of on-going dialogues based on the internal Ethical Accounting Statements in so-called *dialogue circles* consisting of representatives of stakeholder groups (for example, customers or employees in a certain area): these dialogues treat the year's results in detail. They identify areas where it is felt that improvement is required and make proposals to management. Proposals are initially brought to the attention of the bank's regional management, which is obliged to reach concrete decisions as to which proposals will be carried out and which should or should not be implemented. Any proposals which will affect overall policy and which must be decided upon centrally are brought before the bank's top management, which deals with these proposals in collaboration with the bank's liaison committee. In addition, the dialogue circles consider the present content of the Ethical Accounting Statement and provide suggestions as to whether any of the test statements should be changed.

For each of the last few years, roughly 30 such dialogue-circle meetings were held involving about 300 participants: employees, customers and shareholders. A dialogue circle usually consists of 12 participants from a stakeholder group. In addition, two bank employees act as process consultants.

Dialogue circles have proven to play an extremely constructive and creative role in the ethical learning process at Sbn Bank. They have served as vehicles for generating specific proposals to management and for bringing management in closer contact with the bank's stakeholders. They have also contributed to the participants' identification with the bank via their active participation in the decision-making process as *decision receivers*.

Recently, they have also proven to be of value for the important task of mediating diverse and, on occasion, conflicting stakeholder interests. A primary task in an organization which emphasizes value-based management is the identification of conflicting interests and the solution or dissolution of such conflicts. The following example illustrates the central role to be played here by dialogue circles. Information from a group of private customers indicated that they emphasized personal treatment, and that they felt it to be important for them as good customers of the bank to be a familiar person: someone who could be greeted with a 'Hello Mrs Jensen, what should we talk about today? The savings account you have established for your grandchild? Your mortgage? Your line of credit?' On the other hand, the group of employees who were tellers emphasized how important it was for their personal and professional development to participate in job rotation schemes – and also to work in different geographical locations. Apparently, customer expectations and employee expectations were diametrically opposed.

- The combination of Ethical Accounting and dialogue circles played two significant roles here. The first was in bringing this value-conflict into the open. The second was its dissolution, not via a managerial decision, but via the creative activity of the customer and employee representatives themselves. They proposed a procedure whereby employees who were to change jobs invited those customers with whom they had a close profes-sional relationship to a confidential meeting where they were 'turned over' to a colleague. The procedure was heartily approved of by customer and employee representatives – and by the bank's management.

> 'Value-based management is a leadership perspective where the promotion of stakeholder values is in focus instead of money, rules and power.' (Sbn Bank's ethical accounting statement, 1993)

- Based upon the proposals from the dialogue circles and management's responses to these proposals, ethical budgets are developed for the coming year. These commitments to action, together with the ensuing, results are presented under the Results and Plans section of the following year's Ethical Accounting Statement.

> 'Our departments pay just as much attention to our ethical performance as measured in the Ethical Accounting Statement as to purely financial matters.' (Report from the Management, Sbn Bank 1994.)

- According to the 1994 statement:

    All our regions have for many years been used to developing economic budgets and plans for the coming year's marketing activities. What is new is that they now have to develop plans for what is to be improved and what is to be maintained with respect to the Ethical Accounting Statement.

Customers

*Figures are in percentages**

Quality and Competence

1. Your branch of Sbn Bank stands for quality.

	1993
Strongly agree	61
Slightly agree	22
Slightly disagree	5
Strongly disagree	3
No opinion	9

2. You are served by well-qualified employees.

	1993
Strongly agree	72
Slightly agree	17
Slightly disagree	4
Strongly disagree	2
No opinion	4

3. Sbn Bank provides the sort of special offers and services you need.

	1993
Strongly agree	58
Slightly agree	22
Slightly disagree	7
Strongly disagree	6
No opinion	7

Confidence and Respect

4. The employee who serves you can make independent decisions regarding your needs.

	1993
Strongly agree	42
Slightly agree	22
Slightly disagree	10
Strongly disagree	11
No opinion	15

5. You are confident that the fees you pay are reasonable considering the service you get.

	1993
Strongly agree	38
Slightly agree	22
Slightly disagree	13
Strongly disagree	17
No opinion	10

6. You get sound advice.

	1993
Strongly agree	64
Slightly agree	18
Slightly disagree	5
Strongly disagree	4
No opinion	9

7. You get active counselling that suit your pocket.

	1993
Strongly agree	55
Slightly agree	19
Slightly disagree	6
Strongly disagree	6
No opinion	15

* As the figures are rounded, the total will not always amount to 100.

22

8. Sbn Bank advises against investments which, in its opinion, are too risky.

	1993
Strongly agree	29
Slightly agree	8
Slightly disagree	5
Strongly disagree	6
No opinion	52

9. You feel confident when using Sbn as your bank.

	1993
Strongly agree	76
Slightly agree	15
Slightly disagree	4
Strongly disagree	3
No opinion	2

10. Sbn Bank spends sufficient time on serving you.

	1993
Strongly agree	82
Slightly agree	11
Slightly disagree	3
Strongly disagree	1
No opinion	2

11. Sbn Bank knows you and your background.

	1993
Strongly agree	71
Slightly agree	13
Slightly disagree	5
Strongly disagree	6
No opinion	5

12. You get friendly service.

	1993
Strongly agree	90
Slightly agree	6
Slightly disagree	2
Strongly disagree	1
No opinion	2

13. You get fast service.

	1993
Strongly agree	77
Slightly agree	13
Slightly disagree	4
Strongly disagree	2
No opinion	3

Communication

14. Sbn Bank gives its customers sufficient information on special offers and services.

	1993
Strongly agree	48
Slightly agree	21
Slightly disagree	10
Strongly disagree	7
No opinion	15

15. You are given all the relevant information you need.

	1993
Strongly agree	62
Slightly agree	19
Slightly disagree	8
Strongly disagree	4
No opinion	6

16. Sbn Bank acts on criticism and proposals from its customers.

	1993
Strongly agree	21
Slightly agree	14
Slightly disagree	4
Strongly disagree	3
No opinion	57

Commitment to the community

17. The local community trusts Sbn Bank.

	1993
Strongly agree	57
Slightly agree	22
Slightly disagree	4
Strongly disagree	3
No opinion	14

18. You are confident that Sbn Bank will remain a regional bank.

	1993
Strongly agree	77
Slightly agree	13
Slightly disagree	2
Strongly disagree	2
No opinion	5

19. Sbn Bank influences developments in the local community.

	1993
Strongly agree	58
Slightly agree	19
Slightly disagree	3
Strongly disagree	3
No opinion	18

20. Sbn takes an active part in developing the region of North Jutland.

	1993
Strongly agree	51
Slightly agree	20
Slightly disagree	3
Strongly disagree	1
No opinion	24

Communication

21. You know why Sbn Bank contributes to activities in North Jutland.

	1993
Strongly agree	35
Slightly agree	20
Slightly disagree	8
Strongly disagree	9
No opinion	28

22. Sbn Bank expresses its opinion on important local and societal matters.

	1993
Strongly agree	32
Slightly agree	21
Slightly disagree	6
Strongly disagree	8
No opinion	32

Figure 5.1: *Sbn Customer Questionnaire (from Sbn's 1993 Ethical Accounting Statement)*

Employees

Independence

1. It is accepted that jobs can be done in different ways.

	1992	1993
Strongly agree	59	56
Slightly agree	35	39
Slightly disagree	5	2
Strongly disagree	0	1
No opinion	1	1

2. You believe your job is meaningful.

	1992	1993
Strongly agree	79	78
Slightly agree	17	19
Slightly disagree	2	2
Strongly disagree	0	0
No opinion	1	1

3. Customers get sound advice.

	1992	1993
Strongly agree		67
Slightly agree		23
Slightly disagree		2
Strongly disagree		0
No opinion		8

Appreciation

4. You have influence on decisions regarding your work team when they affect your own situation at work.

	1992	1993
Strongly agree	53	48
Slightly agree	38	39
Slightly disagree	7	8
Strongly disagree	1	2
No opinion	2	3

5. Your superiors listen to your suggestions.

	1992	1993
Strongly agree	53	46
Slightly agree	40	43
Slightly disagree	4	6
Strongly disagree	1	1
No opinion	1	4

6. Your colleagues praise your work.

	1992	1993
Strongly agree	31	24
Slightly agree	47	53
Slightly disagree	13	12
Strongly disagree	3	2
No opinion	6	8

7. Your colleagues criticize your work.

	1992	1993
Strongly agree	21	16
Slightly agree	47	48
Slightly disagree	19	18
Strongly disagree	6	6
No opinion	6	13

8. You express yourself freely.

	1992	1993
Strongly agree		57
Slightly agree		34
Slightly disagree		5
Strongly disagree		1
No opinion		2

9. You are appreciated for the person you are.

	1992	1993
Strongly agree	64	57
Slightly agree	30	33
Slightly disagree	3	3
Strongly disagree	0	0
No opinion	3	6

10. You know what your superiors consider extraordinary performance in relation to your work.

	1992	1993
Strongly agree	18	18
Slightly agree	37	35
Slightly disagree	25	21
Strongly disagree	10	10
No opinion	10	18

11. Sbn Bank rewards extraordinary achievements.

	1992	1993
Strongly agree	9	8
Slightly agree	36	34
Slightly disagree	32	26
Strongly disagree	12	12
No opinion	11	21

12. Promotions are awarded on the basis of professional qualifications.

	1992	1993
Strongly agree	13	12
Slightly agree	40	36
Slightly disagree	27	24
Strongly disagree	7	8
No opinion	12	20

13. Promotions are awarded on the basis of human qualities.

	1992	1993
Strongly agree		8
Slightly agree		41
Slightly disagree		22
Strongly disagree		5
No opinion		23

Personal Development

14. Mistakes are used constructively as part of a learning process.

	1992	1993
Strongly agree	30	26
Slightly agree	49	48
Slightly disagree	14	14
Strongly disagree	2	2
No opinion	5	9

15. Sbn actively utilizes your strong points.

	1992	1993
Strongly agree	34	45
Slightly agree	46	41
Slightly disagree	16	8
Strongly disagree	2	2
No opinion	2	3

16. You have the opportunity to improve your strong points.

	1992	1993
Strongly agree	43	47
Slightly agree	43	41
Slightly disagree	10	6
Strongly disagree	1	1
No opinion	3	4

17. You can use your abilities to experiment with new ideas.

	1992	1993
Strongly agree	27	25
Slightly agree	43	40
Slightly disagree	20	17
Strongly disagree	3	4
No opinion	7	13

18. You have the opportunity for job rotation as part of your personal development.

	1992	1993
Strongly agree	34	35
Slightly agree	34	31
Slightly disagree	17	15
Strongly disagree	9	9
No opinion	6	10

19. Sbn Bank offers its employees training so they are attractive to other potential employers.

	1992	1993
Strongly agree	54	46
Slightly agree	30	31
Slightly disagree	9	8
Strongly disagree	3	4
No opinion	3	11

20. You are offered training courses outside your area of job expertise, but which contribute to your personal development.

	1992	1993
Strongly agree	55	46
Slightly agree	30	33
Slightly disagree	8	9
Strongly disagree	3	3
No opinion	3	8

Commitment/Teamwork

21. Your work is motivating and interesting.

	1992	1993
Strongly agree	67	66
Slightly agree	28	28
Slightly disagree	3	4
Strongly disagree	0	1
No opinion	1	1

22. Customers get friendly service.

	1992	1993
Strongly agree		73
Slightly agree		19
Slightly disagree		2
Strongly disagree		0
No opinion		7

23. You are proud to work at Sbn Bank.

	1992	1993
Strongly agree		60
Slightly agree		30
Slightly disagree		4
Strongly disagree		1
No opinion		5

24. The staff is divided into good teams.

	1992	1993
Strongly agree	23	23
Slightly agree	52	43
Slightly disagree	18	20
Strongly disagree	2	3
No opinion	6	11

23

Figure 5.2: *Sbn Employee Questionnaire (from Sbn's 1993 Ethical Accounting Statement)*

The dialogue circles, management's responses and the ethical budget essentially complete *the first* year's learning cycle: identification of the bank's stakeholders, identification of stakeholder values and associated test statements, questioning stakeholder representatives using the CATI-method, interpretation and publication of the results in the Ethical Accounting Statement, generation of more detailed and local 'internal' statements, and dialogue circles leading to proposals, ethical budgets and action as well as a modified design of the next year's questionnaire.

After the first year's cycle, it is seldom that new stakeholders are identified or that the list of stakeholder values is modified; these are considered to be very fundamental and stable. Nevertheless on a few occasions during the past six years some modifications have been made. Changes of the test statements have been regularly proposed at the dialogue circles in order to obtain greater precision, and a small number of improvements have been performed each year.

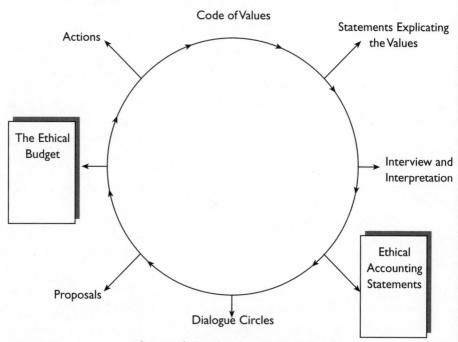

Figure 5.3: *The Accounting Cycle*

Sbn Bank has produced a detailed handbook which describes the whole process. In addition, the bank has developed a computer program which permits data collected via the CATI-method to be directly used in sorting, aggregating and printing the results, including the generation of tables and graphs, so that all that remains to complete the year's Ethical Accounting Statement is the interpretation and management's introductory report. To encourage other companies to generate their own Ethical Accounting Statements, the bank provides copies of the program at a minimal cost-price (roughly UK£1000). It can also be mentioned that extensive and detailed documentation of the bank's experience with Ethical Accounting is available in several Danish publications.[4]

BUT WHAT ABOUT AUDITING?

Surprisingly, this question has never been seriously raised in Sbn Bank – or in other applications of Ethical Accounting in Scandinavia. The attitude here has been that to even think of 'cheating' when presenting an Ethical Accounting Statement is an absurdity. Since it will be read with great interest by the stakeholders and will be actively debated _ for example – in connnection with the dialogue circles – attempts at presenting glorified depictions of stakeholder evaluations would be unveiled and therefore highly counter-productive. And why would a management want to run this risk of being attacked for transforming *ethics* into *cosmetics* – particularly when the whole underlying idea behind the process is dialogue, learning and accountability based upon shared values.

It is only via the recent co-operation with other European and American organizations working in the field of social and ethical accountability that we, in Denmark, have had to react to this query. I have met colleagues from the US and UK who have been amazed at the fact that neither management, the media nor the accounting profession has seriously challenged the existing methodology due its lack of formal external verification. In retrospect, I feel that this is probably due to the nature of our society, characterized by its smallness, homogeneity and a very high level of trust and transparency compared to most other parts of the world.

However, after having shared experiences with some of the other pathfinders in social and ethical accounting, I now feel that even though there has not been internal or external pressure pressures as to auditing here, this might in fact be valuable. This is not so much with respect to verification of procedures, data collection, processing and presentation, nor to giving the statement a stamp of approval from a respected outside agency (which most likely would cost quite a bit and place more demands on the whole process). Instead, it is due to the inspiration which could result from an outside party criticizing the process and suggesting where improvements could be made.

MANAGEMENT'S COMMITMENT

The following excerpts from the Sbn management report of the most recent Ethical Accounting Statements give an indication of the extent to which management is commited to the ethical learning process at Sbn Bank.

The Ethical Accounting Statement was something of an experiment when it was launched in 1990. It has now become part of our daily lives. Our departments pay just as much attention to our ethical performance as measured in the Ethical Accounting Statement as to purely financial matters.

> The results of Ethical Accounting show that it provides the organization with valuable information and that the concept still invites further development. Five years' experience in working with Ethical Accounting will now be used to further develop the approach. We will evaluate if the accounting statement can be made even more informative by supplementing it with other information on the bank's development and interplay with its stakeholders. The goal is to provide a holistic picture of the bank and its development.

The former CEO of the bank, who was very active in initiating the whole process and its implementation, recently stated:

> The Ethical Accounting Statement improves management options within the bank. The information collected provides us with the opportunity to see the results of each individual organizational unit. It allows us to initiate a dialogue and to act promptly should we become aware of developments which are contrary to the values shared by the stakeholders and Sbn Bank.... Without this supplement to the financial statement, we would lack an important indicator for managing our company. It would be like having a watch with only one hand.

It is my experience, having worked closely with the bank's top management for almost six years and having established close personal ties to several members of the management team, that the focus on organizational ethics, value-based leadership and Ethical Accounting has transformed not only the bank but its leaders as well. Their perspectives on leadership and on what the 'good life' is, both for the bank and for themselves, have undergone significant transformations over the years they have been involved in the process.

STAKEHOLDER REACTIONS

In such a short chapter, it is not possible to do justice to the wealth of information which is now available on stakeholder values, expectations and commitment. Instead, I have selected a few noteworthy examples, all based on recent Ethical Accounting Statements. The first is a list of several of the statements on *employee* values, which developed most positively from 1991 to 1992, and my comments to these developments.

> Management makes the bank's code of values visible by its actions *(an increase of 10 per cent to 59 per cent)*. This is noteworthy – management is living up to its value-based commitments, it practices what it preaches.
>   The bank's code of values can be used in connection with solving problems and conflicts *(an increase of 6 per cent to 66 per cent)*. This time it is not management which is said to live up to its commitments, but the employees themselves who say they can

use the code. It should be noted, however, that the employees' evaluation developed negatively in the period from 1992 to 1993, perhaps due to the fact that the wording was changed from the hypothetical: 'The bank's code of values can be used', to the factual 'is used'. This indicates how important it is to find the correct expression of the values via the statements.

You feel secure in your employment situation *(an increase of 7 per cent to 58 per cent): quite a positive development when seen against the background of extensive layoffs in the Danish bank sector.*

You involve yourself in shared goals *(an increase of 6 per cent to 73 per cent). Amazing. Ask a random employee in a random company if he or she even knows what the company's goals are. Here the employees indicate: they know what the goals are, and that they support them actively.*

Sbn Bank lives up to the maxim: It is easier to obtain forgiveness than permission *(an increase of 6 per cent to 68 per cent). What this tells me is that if an employee finds herself in a new situation, where rules and/or precidence are not available as guides to behavior, she knows that she should not turn her back on the situation or desperately seek permission from a boss, but should act according to her knowledge of the company's values.*

A dialogue is taking place throughout the organization *(an increase of 6 per cent to 58 per cent). This is a confirmation of the bank's improvement in the bank's dialogue culture – which is really paramount to what ethical accounting is about.*

A look at the other side of the coin is provided by a list of several of the statements on employee values which developed most negatively, this time from 1992 to 1993. The reason for this change in period is that in 1993 many statements were evaluated more negatively than in 1992 (in contrast to the more postive developments from 1991 to 1992).

As a general rule, you manage to do your daily work within normal working hours without suffering from stress *(a decrease of 18 per cent to 50 per cent). 1993 was a tough year for the bank. Management commented on this in the Ethical Accounting Statement for 1993: 'Recent hard times have perhaps caused us – briefly and unconciously – to tone down the basic values of the bank. It is therefore now that the concept of Value-Based Management must prove its worth.*

Sbn Bank offers its employees training so they are attractive to other potential employers *(a decrease of 8 per cent to 77 per cent). Although the level of agreement is still high, there is a strong indication here that management's commitment to the personal and professional development of its employees has slackened.*

You are given sufficient information on what goes on in the management of your department *(a decrease of 6 per cent to 72 per cent). The openness and communication which have charac-terized the bank is now being criticized – even though the level of agreement is reasonably high.*

All in all, during 1993 the staff gave Sbn Bank a high evaluation as a workplace – according to the 1994 statement: 'far in excess of 90 per cent of the employees consider their work to be meaningful, motivating and interesting as well as providing conditions so that they are happy in their work'.

As to *customers'* values, the following is a listing of those statements which received the most positive evaluations in 1994. You get friendly service (97 per cent). Sbn spends sufficient time on serving you (94 per cent). You are served by qualified personnel (92 per cent). You get fast service (92 per cent). And the following is a listing of those statements which received the least positive evaluations in 1994! Sbn advises against investments which, in its opinion, are too risky (38 per cent). Sbn acts on the basis of its customers' criticism and proposals (39 per cent). Sbn expresses its opinion on important local and societal matters (49 per cent). You know why Sbn contributes to activities in North Jutland (52 per cent). You are confident that the fees you pay are reasonable, considering the service you get (61 per cent).

Finally, the following presents some noteworthy *shareholder* evaluations from 1994, including my comments.

> You have confidence that Sbn Bank will continue to be an independent regional bank *(87 per cent). Clearly, this is a solid message of support for the bank policy – but represents a decrease of 5 per cent compared to 1993.*
>
> In the short term, it is more important to you that Sbn creates new activities and jobs in North Jutland than that you receive dividends on your shares *(73 per cent). Quite an amazing evaluation. This defies most presuppositions on the motives of shareholders and is an indication of the multiple roles of most of the bank's shareholders; they are not only shareholders but often are customers (62 per cent of the shareholders are customers) and dedicated members of the region of North Jutland as well. But the result also contains another message to management: it represents a decrease of 7 per cent compared to the results two years earlier, perhaps indicating that earnings are beginning to play a greater role in shareholder expectations.*
>
> The bank's vision: 'to be the power center for economic and human resource development in North Jutland' is important for you as a shareholder *(63 per cent) – down from 70 per cent the year before and perhaps another indication of an increased emphasis on more short-term economic results.*
>
> It would be a good idea for Sbn to close down unprofitable branches *(64 per cent). The fact that one third of the shareholders apparently defy what the textbooks define as economic rationality provides yet another indication of the ties that many shareholders have to the region, and that there are more motives to having shares in the bank than just earning money.*
>
> You are aware of Sbn's ideals and goals, ie Sbn's plans for future development *(57 per cent). This is not a very good score indeed and indicates the need for improved communication as to these important matters.*

In concluding this section on stakeholder reactions, it should be noted that the process also permits evaluating how different stakeholder groups react to the same general themes. Cross-sectional investigations were performed in 1994 on differences in replies from various subgroups within a stakeholder group – for example, female vs male employees and management vs non-managerial employees. The results turned out to be extremely provacative. Therefore, they were particularly highlighted in the 1994 statement and provided all parties involved with considerable food for thought – and action.

These, along with other such feedback, have provided management with a sensitivity they otherwise would have lacked. This is probably why the Ethical Accounting Statement for 1993, in connection with its presentation of customer evaluations states: 'One of the cardinal merits of the Ethical Accounting Statement is the fact that it can reveal tendencies in its stakeholder' reactions. It provides Sbn with an early warning system upon which it can base its plan of action.'

DOES IT PAY TO CARRY OUT ETHICAL ACCOUNTING AT SBN BANK?

This question pops up from time to time, particularly in the media and occasionally from shareholders at a general meeting of the bank. There is, however, no clear-cut answer to this question. No amount of statistics (and only six years' data are currently available) will permit a reasonable answer. And there is no simple cause-and-effect relationship between an organization's embracement of value-based leadership and its financial results. Furthermore, ethics and profitability each belong to their own domain: *presumably* the bank's motivation for carrying out Ethical Accounting is not an increased profitability but an increased awareness of its stakeholders' values and expectations and an increased competancy in meeting these expectations. As the bank's first statement pronounced: '[Ethical Accounting] demonstrates that there are other values to be promoted than power and money. The Ethical Accounting Statement measures the degree to which the company lives up to these shared values and thus supplements the financial statement's bottom line.' But, as was mentioned earlier, 'since values not only concern conduct, but also motives, they are neither visible nor precise measuring rods'. No one can say to what extent increased financial performance also was and is a motivating factor in implementing Ethical Accounting. Nor is this distinction crucial; what really matters is the way that the bank reflects upon its actions, evaluates them and relates to its stakeholders. Although it is not possible to give a clear answer to the question: 'does it pay?' there are certainly a number of costs to be considered. The following is a brief summary of some of the problems which the bank has met in its work with Ethical Accounting and value-based management.

Successfully implementing the process required considerable *time* and *patience*. It took several years before the employees were accustomed to communicating in terms of values and before *mutual trust*, which is a precondition for value-based dialogue, developed between the employees themselves in their working units and between the employees and management. This was a challenge to the organization in an epoch when everyone speaks of turbulence and uncertainty and when young MBAs consider the ability to make quick decisions as the sign of a leader. Perhaps this is why Jørgen Giversen, the former CEO of Sbn Bank, wrote:

We live in a society with large changes. Therefore, we must work with leadership modes which prepare the organization for co-existing with permanent instability. The bank has chosen to lead itself using values. In an enterprise like ours, which thrives on change and service, money and power are insufficient for steering the organization. Shared values and visions are necessary and these presuppose dialogue.

Experience showed that many leaders – particularly members of middle management – felt most secure keeping their cards close to their vests. Ethical Accounting at Sbn Bank clearly demonstrated that *openness* is a precondition for trust and for the whole ethical learning process. Therefore *all* results must be published, including those which are strongly critical. The whole process around Ethical Accounting also required *commitment* and *integrity*. Ethics is a big, value-laden word. Nothing can threaten the viability of the process more than top management's not 'walking its talk'.

And finally, the process required a considerable *expenditure of time, effort and resources*. The direct costs are by far the least of these; at Sbn Bank they amount to roughly UK£6000 yearly (covering data collection, printing and disseminating the statement, direct costs associated with dialogue circle meetings, etc). To this must be added the salary of the economist in charge of the process (he uses roughly 30 per cent of his time here, both as an internal process consultant and in leading the whole process and interpreting its visible results) and the time devoted by the employees and the management in participating in the process. But it may be unfair to categorize these expenditures as costs; after all, reflecting and communicating about corporate-existential questions, about values and expectations and about conflict are at the very core of what leadership at any level is all about.

PERSONAL OBSERVATIONS

I have observed the bank since it commenced its ethical learning process in 1989. During this period, the bank has undergone a slow but consistent metamorphosis. Ethical Accounting and shared values are no longer abstract terms which could bring blushes to modest Danish faces but are now part of the daily jargon of employees and management – and of many customers, shareholders and local citizens as well. They are elements in an expanded repertoire of concepts and perspectives which give meaning and identity to the organization. They have slowly but surely changed the behavior and the perspectives of management. Of course, it has helped considerably that the term 'Ethical Accounting' no longer is just a local matter but is now a theme which appears in many different parts of Danish society; there are courses, conferences and books on it, universities have research projects on it, it is regularly mentioned in the media – and a highly diversified group of companies and governmental organizations have implemented it.

I feel convinced that the methodology developed originally at Sbn Bank will be further developed in the years to come. Activities are already underway to introduce benchmarking into the accounts, hereby permitting *inter*organizational comparisons over and above the current procedure's *intra*organizational perspective. External auditing procedures can also contribute to the methodological development. Finally, the growing and highly diversified body of users are providing a wealth of empirical evidence which will contribute to the future development of Ethical Accounting.

ENDNOTES

1   Copies of Sbn Bank's Ethical Accounting Statements can be obtained by contacting the bank: Sbn Bank, PO Box 162, DK-9100 Aalborg, Denmark. Phone: +45 98 18 73 11. Fax: +45 98 18 91 03. It should be noted that aside from the statement for 1993, the statements are in Danish.

2   The Danish article was later published in modified form in English as 'Conflict and Consensus: Ethics as a Shared Value Horizon for Strategic Planning', *Human Systems Management* 9, 1990, pp135–151.

3   P Pruzan and O Thyssen, 'The *Ethical Accounting Statement* in a Nutshell', an English language version of the introduction to the 1991 Ethical Accounting Statement from Sbn Bank.

4   There is an extensive Scandinavian literature on the theory and practice of Ethical Accounting. In particular, reference can be made to the following books which provide extensive empirical documentation: C Bak (1996) *Ethical Accounting: Introduction, Experience and Practice* (Danish) Handelshøjskolens Forlag, Copenhagen; M Morsing (1991) *The Ethical Practice: An Introduction to Ethical Accounting* (Danish) Handelshøjskolens Forlag, Copenhagen; and *Ethical Accounting: A New Approach to User Influence and Quality in the Public Sector* (Danish) Frydelund, Copenhagen. See also P Pruzan (1994) 'Ethics, value-based leadership and the Ethical Accounting Statement' in S Hildebrandt and E Johnsen (eds) *Management Now – 10 Danish Professors on Modern Leadership* (Danish) Børsens Forlag, Copenhagen, pp97–154.

6

Accounting for Ethics: Traidcraft plc, UK

Richard Evans
(Director of Social Accounting, Traidcraft Exchange)

> *It is our intention that the process we have engaged in here will
> result in a methodology and approach that can be applied to any
> business to audit its social and ethical performance, and that such
> 'social audits' will become a significant indicator of success in the
> business world of the 21st Century.*
>
> (Zadek and Evans, Auditing the Market, 1993)

TRAIDCRAFT PLC

Traidcraft plc had its origins in a recognition that something was profoundly wrong and needed to be put right. In the late 1960s and early 1970s, the usual responses to the problem of endemic poverty in the 'Third World' were not aimed at radical change, but were predominantly intended to treat the symptoms of poverty, rather than tackle the causes. They were about relief and welfare, not about *fairness*.

Traidcraft was set up in 1979 to show that to eradicate the poverty of millions of people in the South, businesses and consumers in the North had to behave differently. The idea was simple enough. If small farmers and artisans in the non-market economies of Asia, Africa and Latin America were paid fair prices and were allowed to sell their products freely to the rich markets in the North, international trade could directly benefit their families and communities, instead of being a major cause of poverty.

Traidcraft is a public limited company based in the north-east of England. It has a turnover of around UK£7 million. The company imports and markets a wide range of food and handmade products from farming cooperatives and community businesses in Africa, Asia and Latin America. Traidcraft describes itself as 'a community of purpose', and the community is surprisingly large and geographically dispersed. At its 6000 square metre warehouse and office premises in the north-east of England it employs 150 people. Its share capital of just under UK£2,000,000 is owned, in small lots, by about 4,000 individual shareholders. At least 2,000 people all over the UK belong to Traidcraft's Voluntary Reps Scheme and sell its products in their homes, schools, churches, village halls, community centres and markets. Many reps have regular committed customers; there are probably around 40 to 50,000 of these supporters and customers. Most of the 400 or so small retailers who buy from the company are also strongly committed to justice and sustainability and identify themselves with Traidcraft's values and name. Around 200,000 people buy Traidcraft products from its own mail order catalogues and those of campaigning organizations such as Amnesty International, Greenpeace and The World Wide Fund for Nature (WWF).

This Traidcraft community of maybe 250,000 people in the UK has consciously committed itself to selling and regularly buying the products of more than 100 small businesses and farmers' co-operatives in 26 countries who are Traidcraft's trading partners in Asia, Africa and Latin America. Although the company is small, a recent Gallup survey found that 13 per cent of members of the public questioned recognized Traidcraft's name and logo and that three-quarters of these showed they understood its values by selecting one or the other of the following descriptions of our aim: 'helps Third World people by buying their products' or 'tackles the problem of poverty in the Third World by paying higher prices'.

TRAIDCRAFT'S FOUNDATION PRINCIPLES

Traidcraft's articles and mission statement contain a set of foundation principles which include 'promoting love and justice in international trade' and 'a commitment to practical service and partnership for change, which puts people before profit'. However, it is not a development charity. It is a business that will only survive if it trades profitably. It has to demonstrate that social goals and commercial viability are compatible.

It is in Traidcraft's foundation principles that the idea of creating 'an inclusive community of purpose' was first stated. This phrase is Traidcraft's shorthand for a definition of the company as an integral part of the society and the environment we share with everyone else. It sees the business as a community of people making different contributions, but equally valued and committed to a common objective.

TRADING FOR PROFIT OR PROFIT FOR TRADING

While Traidcraft is not at the cutting edge of twentieth-century technology, nor a model of free market enterprise, it is revolutionary. Its founders rejected the Keynesian law of the free market in favour of the law of love and justice for people found in the Judaeo-Christian tradition. It even rejected the classical definition of the purpose of the business – making its shareholders rich. This business's *raison d'être* was to improve the market deal for small producers in the 'Third World' while ensuring, somehow, that everyone involved in Traidcraft was fairly rewarded for the contribution they made to its growth and prosperity. For many years the company traded under the slogan: 'Putting People before Profit'.

Traidcraft recognizes that without profit it cannot invest in training its staff, in developing, together with its suppliers, new products and designs and in acquiring new technology to make it more efficient and effective. But profit does not define its purpose.

It is far too abstract a summary of the outcome of business processes. It does not tell the real life story of how the company treats people, whether they are valued or exploited. Neither does it show whether the company is achieving its mission of expanding the UK market for fairly traded products.

THE CONCEPT OF THE STAKEHOLDER IN BUSINESS

For most businesses, since the idea of the limited company was enshrined in law 200 years ago, the stakeholder to whom managers and directors are accountable has been the shareholder. Traidcraft's first share issue in 1984 sought to revive the original idea of equity as a share in the mission or purpose of the company and the accompanying risks. But it also broke the tradition that the shareholders' interests preceded all others. At the time, James Erlichman wrote in *The Guardian*:

> *Traidcraft urgently needs a £300,000 cash injection from new shareholders – but it is offering them in return only 'love, justice and equity'. And equity to Traidcraft means putting a higher value on sharing the world's resources fairly than on its own share certificates. Investors must prefer goodness to greed and should never expect 'personal gain or profit' the prospectus warns.*

However, progress in defining a wider range of stakeholders in the business and finding a way of recognizing their rights and the expectations of the company did not arise until some years later.

The subordination of shareholders' interests to those of the partner enterprises in the developing countries was already well established. But how were the partners' interests, and those of employees, customers and the community, to be represented when policy was being formed ? This is where the concept of the stakeholder became important and the quest for ways to represent their interests began. Traidcraft plc defines its *stakeholders* as those key groups of people who can influence the business or are directly affected by its activities, and also the natural environment. The core stakeholders were identified, by the managers of the business, as suppliers, employees, voluntary representatives, retailers, customers, the local community, the environment and, of course, the shareholders. The company's commitment to creating 'an inclusive community of purpose' meant that not only are different stakeholders' needs and views to be recognized, but divergent aspirations and priorities must ultimately serve the 'common purpose' set out in the foundation principles.

THE IDEA OF A SOCIAL ACCOUNT OF THE BUSINESS

The trustees of the Traidcraft Foundation, who hold the voting shares in the company, asked the directors to develop a process of accounting for the company's social impact and to carry out an annual audit of its performance against non-financial criteria. Early in 1992 the board agreed to publish its first externally audited account, with its annual statutory accounts the following year.

The terms 'social audit' and 'social accounts' appeared to be there right at the beginning of the discussion and undoubtedly owed their place in the business ethics vocabulary to the work of Charles Medawar and Social Audit Ltd in the 1970s. We also learned a lot about corporate social reporting from Traidcraft's first managing director, Richard Adams, who left Traidcraft in 1989 to set up New Consumer, a UK-based public interest research organization dealing with corporate ethics.

Traidcraft's approach differed from what we knew of the existing practice of external audits and corporate social reporting in a number of ways:

* The social account would be based on a system of voluntary reporting produced by the company itself. Many would instinctively regard such a report as potentially damaging to the company's reputation and competitive position. Traidcraft believed accountability was a duty, but also, by exposing the company's activities more systematically to the view of its stakeholders and the UK public, it would learn and grow stronger.
* The accounts needed to record stakeholders' qualitative perceptions of the company's behaviour. We rejected earlier approaches to social accounting which attempted to reduce social impacts to a list of financial credits and debits. As a result, Traidcraft's social accounts would never provide a simple balance sheet with a numerical bottomline score for the company's ethical performance. As well as reporting against quantitative indicators of social or ethical performance, it would need to tell the stakeholders' stories.
* It recognized that each stakeholder group would have a different perspective. Somehow the report had to capture the differences so that each stakeholder group at least knew what the others saw as priorities. It was hoped that publishing these 'perspectives' would highlight points of agreement and lead to understanding and dialogue about points of disagreement.
* All aspects of the business were up for scrutiny, not just the safe areas selected by the management or directors. This aim was to be underwritten by inviting stakeholders to identify what aspects of performance were important to them and how they should be measured.
* In the same spirit of rigour, the report was to be produced annually. The principles of regularity and timeliness in financial accounting seemed just as relevant in social accounting. So the company adopted the practice of publishing social accounts at the same time as the statutory financial accounts.
* Like the financial accounts, we believed the company's social accounts report should be externally audited.

TRAIDCRAFT

Towards a Social Audit 1992

Traidcraft's mission is to work towards changes in the international trading system which will deliver justice and economic development to the poor. Traidcraft is valued because our aims extend beyond creating profitable and sustainable business opportunities for suppliers in the 'third world', to helping them achieve the skills and market knowledge to become effective exporters.

We aim to develop positive relationships with our employees and customers, to be environmentally sensitive and to express the Christian beliefs and spiritual values enshrined in our foundation documents.

Up to now we have had no systematic method for reporting how we perform against these objectives. In 1993 and in subsequent years, as well as the Financial Statements, the Directors intend publishing a separate report to evaluate the Company's activities against non-financial criteria. When established, this report or Social Audit will be subject to scrutiny by external assessors appointed by the Company in General Meetings in the same way that the Financial Statements are subjected to independent audit.

This review of 1991-92 is not an independent audit, but is published by the Directors to indicate the scope of future social audits. During the next two years we will develop detailed performance criteria and methods for reporting and auditing. We would especially welcome your comments.

On behalf of the Directors

Richard Evans
External Affairs Director

Box 6.1: *Towards a Social Audit*

DEVELOPING A METHODOLOGY

In July 1992 the company sent an eight page colour document entitled *Towards a Social Audit* with the annual Financial Statement to all its shareholders, employees, reps and suppliers. Soon after the publication of the document a happy coincidence occurred. Traidcraft Exchange, the charitable development agency set up by Traidcraft's trustees, invited a development consultant, Simon Zadek, to undertake an evaluation of the Exchange's Overseas Business Development Service programme in Tanzania. It was suggested that I join the team to see what might be learned, which could be relevant to social accounting.

Simon had decided to approach the evaluation from the perspective of the 'beneficiaries' of the Traidcraft Exchange programme. It would include elements of conventional economic and cost-benefit analysis, but would also be the story told by project holders and the clients of the Exchange's advisory service. It was, of course, essential that the partner organizations in Tanzania understood that they were being asked to make the evaluation. To a considerable extent they were to determine how success and good performance were to be defined. The Exchange also wanted to understand the impact of its own behaviour, rather than assess the partners' performance or use of inputs provided by the Exchange. Indeed, a thorough, frank and, where warranted, critical appraisal would be welcomed. The evaluator became the audience, or auditor, in the primary meaning of *one who listens*.

Creating a method that allowed clients to liberate themselves from a dependent recipient role promised and delivered a significant breakthrough in the quality and nature of the feedback. The method recognized that the Exchange's clients were stakeholders in the Overseas Business Development Service. We decided that we should elaborate the evaluation approach into a new methodology for organizational social accounting. The result was a 64-page booklet written by Simon Zadek and the author and published by Traidcraft Exchange and the New Economics Foundation, with the title, *Auditing the Market – a Practical Approach to Social Auditing*. The booklet came out in April 1993, just before we started on the process of compiling Traidcraft plc's first set of social accounts, for the year April 1992 to March 1993. In its preface it said:

> *What follows is an interim result. We are very conscious of the growing activity in this field, ranging from the development of indicators for assessing the value of community enterprise to the debate on corporate social responsibility. Traidcraft and NEF wish to participate in that debate and to learn from it. We are therefore very interested to receive your comments on this paper.*
>
> *It is our intention that the process we have engaged in here will result in a methodology and approach that can be applied to any business to audit its social and ethical performance, and that such 'social audits' will become a significant indicator of success in the business world of the 21st Century.*
>
> *Traidcraft plc's 1993 social audit, based on the methodology set out in this paper, will be published in July 1993.*

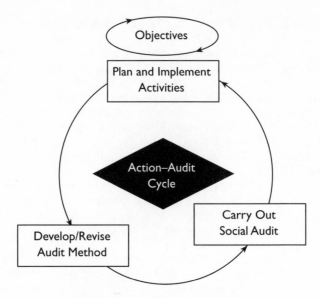

Figure 6.1: *Action–Audit Cycle*

The methodology booklet initiated a learning cycle, which we illustrated as the 'Action-Audit Cycle'.

The key elements of the methodology are:

- *Establishing the value base:* What are the social objectives and the ethical values against which the business's activities are to be assessed?
- *Defining the stakeholders:* Who are the key groups of people who can influence or are significantly affected by the activities of the business?
- *Establishing social performance indicators:* The principle of stakeholder evaluation requires stakeholder participation in determining the appropriate indicators for measuring performance. The scope of the indicators is limited by the objectives of the organization. However, stakeholders have their own objectives and represent wider social constituencies. The performance indicators agreed on and used inevitably recognize that these wider objectives exist and should be incorporated where there is a direct causal link with the company's activities.
- *Collecting the data:* As far as possible the data on which the 'accounts' are to be based should preserve the original and authentic 'voice' of the stakeholder.
- *Writing the accounts:* Internal production of accounts is the normal practice envisaged in the methodology and is analogous to the practice in business financial accounting. This involvement of the organization's own staff in data collection and preparing accounts reflects the methodology's basis in dialogue between the organization and its stakeholders, and its commitment to learn.
- *Auditing the accounts:* Social accounting carries with it the requirement that the organization submit its accounts to an independent audit.

*   *Publication:* The Accounting Statement approved by the auditor, together with the Auditor's Report, are published and distributed to all key stakeholders before the company's annual general meeting of shareholders.

SOCIAL ACCOUNTING IN PRACTICE: INDICATORS AND TARGETS

Most of the performance indicators we have used were developed in consultation with representatives of the relevant stakeholder groups in the first full social account in 1993. In practice it has been somewhat easier to agree on what should be measured – the indicators – than to agree appropriate targets. This has less to do with any significant divergence of views about what level of ethical performance and what social objectives are implied by the company's Foundation Principles than with issues of time scale where long-term objectives can be practically realized.

Some of the targets – for instance, in employment policies such as equality of opportunity and health and safety – are in line with, or intended to better, widely accepted mandatory or normative standards in the UK. Some, such as targets for realizing 'fair trade' objectives, will require extensive consultation with suppliers over a succession of annual social accounting cycles. In the meantime the management have set targets based on what they believe can and should be achieved given their current strategies and the performance of the business. These are not, however, arbitrary or intended to shelter the company from criticism, since the indicators, targets and performance reports are disclosed, open to debate among all stakeholders and open to revision.

A major consideration in developing indicators and targets has been whether actual performance against the indicator can be measured with reasonable accuracy and at a cost that is in proportion to business objectives, turnover and other expenditure.

The cost burden of the annual social accounting process has been limited by adopting a cycle of reporting in some critical areas that will be spread over a number of years. This is particularly the case with the account of overseas suppliers' perspectives on the company's performance. Collection of data and visits to all suppliers annually would be prohibitive in cost and time required. The suppliers' audit is therefore restricted to partners in one region: in 1993, the Philippines; in 1994, Kenya, Tanzania and Zimbabwe; in 1995, Bangladesh; and in 1996, India.

The complete picture will only emerge after a number of years, during which strategies and the company's performance are likely to continually change. However, all supplier partners are encouraged to compare their perceptions with the partial picture that emerges each year in the report and to advise the Annual General Meeting, the trustees, the directors, or the auditors if the findings are at odds with their experience.

The following excerpts from the schedule for the 1994/95 accounts illustrate the sort of indicators used for two of the stakeholder groups.

The payment of fair prices has been identified as the most important ethical aim of Traidcraft by all stakeholders. However, determining what is a 'fair price' is difficult. In the case of a few commodities, for example green

Table 6.1: *Indicators and Targets for Suppliers*

Area		Indicators/targets
Fair price	• external benchmark prices	Arabica coffee = US$1.20/lb Tea = average price at auction + fair trade premium
	• comparison with normal trade prices	Illustrated by examples
	• Proportion of price accruing to primary producers	Illustrated by price structure analysis of specific examples
	• comparison of value added (profit)	(this has potential for computer analysis through the social bookkeeping system, but the costing data is not currently available on a single database)

coffee, *external benchmark* prices have been set by international agreement between the so-called fair trade organizations. However, these are generally rejected as unrealistically high by commercial traders, who account for most of the world trade.

In practice, there are no such simple benchmarks available. Instead, we take the dual approach of asking the supplier's own view about the prices paid by Traidcraft and then make a series of comparisons and analyses of our prices and those of other buyers.

The fair trade principles set out in the constitutions of international organizations, the European Fair Trade Association and the International Federation for Alternative Trade include not only stipulations about prices paid to suppliers, but also require prompt payments, advances to be made to producers, where needed, to purchase raw materials, a safe and reasonable working environment, protection of employees' interests and rights, support and investment in suppliers' product development, and protection of the natural environment, and the development of long-term partnership relationships.

After several years of social accounting assessments of Traidcraft by its suppliers in different countries, it has become clear that producers' and suppliers' greatest concern is the uncertainty of the commercial market and the continuity of orders and long-term commitment promised by *fair trade* organizations.

Continuous growth in the value of purchases from its 'Third World' suppliers has been a critical indicator of achievement since Traidcraft started. The current retail recession in the UK and changing market conditions are likely to result in reductions in the immediate future. A test of the validity of social accounting for our 'Third World' suppliers will be whether suppliers, managers and the other stakeholders are able to subordinate immediate needs and priorities to achieve long-term goals, and how the company reacts.

Table 6.2: *Indicators and Targets for Suppliers (continued)*

Area	Indicators/targets
Continuity • Traidcraft's commitment to 'Third World' producers	(i) Total value of purchases (compared to previous years) Target: 25% real growth 91–95 (ii) Value of purchases by country (compared to previous years)
• continuity of purchasing	(i) Number of active trading partners (ii) Number of entries and exits (with commentary) (iii) Significant increases/ decreases in order volume/value (with commentary)
• demand forecasting	(i) Monitor quality and timeliness of information communicated to producers where demand increases or decreases by more than 20%

SOCIAL BOOKKEEPING

Traidcraft is conscious of the tension that exists between its desire for transparency and quality feedback, from those the company interacts with, and the cost of collecting and analyzing the required social impact data. In discussion with other more conventional, and profit-focused businesses, they have often made the point that social accounting is important for 'ethical businesses' such as Traidcraft but too expensive for them.

We are addressing the cost issue by developing a system of *social bookkeeping*. As the term implies, social bookkeeping captures data relevant to the social accounts on a continuous basis through the existing company management accounting systems or by developing a new *social management accounting system*.

In the autumn of 1994 Traidcraft plc arranged with Dundee University's Department of Accounting to place a doctoral researcher in the company's accounts department to investigate the scope for setting up such a system. The aims were to develop a software system that would:

- access data in the management accounting system and structure it for the purpose of reporting against social accounting indicators and targets;
- extend the range of indicators that could be monitored systematically through a computer database and reporting system;

Table 6.3: *Employees' Accounts Performance Indicators and Comparisons*

Pay & conditions	• pay	(i) Target: Earnings to rise in line with national average (ii) Target: Earnings for staff grades 1–5 at least national average (iii) Target: 3:1 differential
	• staff turnover • sickness and absence	Compared to national norms Compared with industry norms
	• changes in benefits	
Equality of opportunity	• gender distribution by grade	(i) Target: Increase to 33% proportion of women in Grades 7–10 by 1997.('93 approx 25%) (ii) Target: Increase proportion of women on board to 33% by 1998. ('93 less than 20%)
	• employment of registered disabled • ethnic minorities	Target: Department of Employment 'quota' and meeting criteria for the Disability Employer Award Quota and Equal Opportunities Policy by June 1994
Staff development	• skill development	(i) Total number of training days (compared to previous years); Target: Average N training days per employee. (ii) Percentage turnover spent on training
	• education	Target: M hours of educational input per employee
	• 'Third World' exposure visits	Target: x % staff over 2 yrs' service who have 'Third World' exposure
	• release for community service	Develop policy and targets by April 1995
	• staff representation	(i) Target: 2 staff directors (ii) Training and support for staff association (report staff assessment)

- allow managers to monitor social performance on a regular basis through desk-based report generation;
- simplify year-end accounting proceedures to simple standardized reporting routines, eg generating graphs, comparing annual performance against established indicators;
- facilitate the external auditing of social accounts.

Where data exists in the current management accounting system, the following areas have been identified and incorporated into a first attempt at a report-generating software system.

Producer-Related Indicators

- Proportion of total sales originating from 'Third World' suppliers;
- total value of purchases from 'Third World';
- comparisons of purchase value from different countries/ regions and suppliers;
- an exception report for deviations from payment period targets.
- value and period of advances to producers.

Employee-Related Indicators

- Total remuneration to employees compared to retail price index (RPI) and national and local pay indicators;
- salary grade distribution by gender;
- ratio of highest and lowest salaries;
- staff turnover;
- days lost due to illness;
- staff training statistics compared to targets.

The system is capable of extensive analysis of, for example, customer life cycles, purchase level and product choice profiles, choice of purchase channel, and geographical and demographic distribution – much of which overlaps with more general market research requirements. However, the data is valuable for social accounting when used in conjunction with qualitative responses from customers, and voluntary representatives or retailers, about ethical issues and their perceptions of the company's performance.

The use of the database system allows reports to be produced instantly with year-on-year comparisons, graphical presentation of trends, and performance against target ratios. It also has the potential to correlate performance against any of the indicators or other data in the management accounting database. The system is now available on a network of PCs throughout the company so that managers can monitor performance in areas relevant to their responsibilities and generate their own reports.

Key Performance Indicators

Sales of "third world" goods[1]
TARGET 1991-1995 Business Plan set a target of 25% volume increase during the plan.
OUTCOME 23% (5.7% IN 1994/95)

% of total sales from "third world" goods
TARGET minimum 66%
OUTCOME 67% (93/94-68%, 92/93-67%)

Income to "third world" partners[2]
TARGET Continuous growth - no quantitative target.
OUTCOME 10% IN 94/95 £2.2 million
[93/94 £2.0 million]
[92/93 £1.6 million]

Fig 1. Sales Sourced from "Third World"

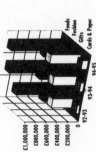

Fig 2. "Third World" Purchases 93-95

Figure 2 shows significant growth in Gifts (13% in 1993/94 and 31% in 1994/95). Crafts and fashion have the highest added value for Traidcraft's producers.

PRODUCERS' PERSPECTIVES

Objectives

Traidcraft's Foundation Principles state the mission of the organisation.

To establish a just trading system which expresses the principles of love and justice fundamental to the Christian faith.

Traidcraft plc is a business based on the common goals and shared action of its stakeholders. Its primary business objective is to increase the volume, value and quality of fair trade with primary producers in the "third world".

Scope of the Producer Accounts and Consultation Process

Each year Traidcraft has undertaken an intensive consultation with producer partners in one country or region - 1993 The Philippines, 1994 Kenya, Tanzania and Zimbabwe, and in 1995 Bangladesh. The selection has been made by Traidcraft with the aim of building a balanced and inclusive view over time of the company's relations with its "third world" suppliers.

Richard Evans, Traidcraft's Director of Social Accounting visited Bangladesh in March. The producers' organisation ECOTA helped organise visits to producers and suppliers. Structured interviews based on a list of topics identified by producers as key determinants of fair trade during the consultation process for previous Social Accounts were recorded by Traidcraft and checked, amended and endorsed by the senior manager present for the discussions in each of the organisations visited.

In addition, there is an overall analysis of Traidcraft's performance in 1994/95 in relation to the issues its producers have identified, and short reports on the producer group selection reviews referred to in the Directors' Response to last years' report on page 22.

The report has the following sections:
Key performance indicators
Producer perspectives - Bangladesh
Review of craft sourcing
A new food sourcing policy

Key Performance Indicators

We have used the same indicators for growth as in previous years to measure performance against the key objective of expanding fair trade for our "third world" partners.

We have continued to monitor payments in advance to suppliers and the amount of contact time with producers spent by Traidcraft's product development and design staff. This year we have introduced an overall review of the company's performance in terms of the continuity of orders. Producers have emphasised the importance they attach to continuity as a differentiating characteristic of fair trade.

Commentary on continuity of orders

Traidcraft emphasises continuity of relationship in its Purchasing Policies, but has not systematically monitored changes in order values at the year end. The new social bookkeeping system (see p22) will facilitate monitoring of year on year order variations for individual partners, as well as country and regional changes. Year on year comparisons will not take account of distortions arising from changes in ordering or delivery patterns. Changes in value may reflect changes in currency values as well as changes in order volumes.

- 21 of the 26 "third world" countries supplying Traidcraft had increases in the value of goods shipped to Traidcraft in 1994/95.

- Africa (60% increase) and Latin America (100% increase) benefited mostly from direct sourcing of teas and coffees. The African result also includes a £92,000 (90%) increase in shipments of T-shirts, cards and papers from Dezign Inc in Zimbabwe received during the year.

- 5 countries had falls in the value of goods supplied: Indonesia down 44% (a reduction of £63,000), Zambian Cashew Company delivered one sixth of previous year's value (a reduction of £16,000); Bangladesh deliveries were down 5% (a reduction of £8,000); Nepal down 39% (a reduction of £2,000) and there was no order to the Nicaraguan instant coffee processor Encafe.

Figure 6.2: Extract from Traidcraft Social Accounts 1994-5

HOW NOT TO LIE WITH STATISTICS

A key characteristic of the Traidcraft approach is allowing stakeholders to make their own observations about the organization's performance and to record these in the accounts and in the published report. This approach not only limits the scope for misleading statistics and biased accounting, but also enriches the report with a wealth of detailed statistical data and with the real human experience of Traidcraft.

THE IMPACT OF TRAIDCRAFT'S SOCIAL ACCOUNTS

None of this information would have much power to change the company unless it were published. Surprisingly, the directors not only agreed that this was a logical outcome of the methodology, but that publication, even of the first 'experimental' reports, would speed the process of refining the method by encouraging feedback. While recognizing that stakeholders would criticize as well as praise the company's performance, this too was accepted as a necessary contribution to improving performance.

AUDITING

In Traidcraft's first social audit, the data collection and production of the written accounts was managed by an 'external accountant' in the person of Simon Zadek of the New Economics Foundation. In the second year, as we began to feel more confident about the process, the accounts were prepared by Traidcraft itself.

While the practice of using 'in-house' accountants raises questions about whether stakeholders will express their views frankly and honestly to another company employee or a manager, it is essential if social accountability is to be embedded in the company's relationships with internal and external stakeholders. By exposing managers directly to the issues, priorities and shortcomings stakeholders see, the social accounts become part of the company's learning experience. Also, in a transparent process, stakeholders have many opportunities to correct incomplete or biased reporting of their views and to appeal to management, the trustees and other stakeholders – should their honesty result in discrimination against them. A further safeguard against dishonest or incomplete accounting is the audit. How does it work ?

Financial auditing depends on the development over several hundred years of codes of standard practice in accounting and auditing. These allow the auditor to verify that the accounts have been prepared in accordance with the Accounting Practice codes and give a 'true and fair view' of the company's affairs at the time. Shareholders, for whom the accounts are made, should know what the standard accounting practices are and consequently the scope of the auditor's statement – what it does and what it does not say. There are no such recognised codes of practice for social auditing, and therefore the basis on which the auditor declares that the accounts give a 'true and fair view' is unclear. Social accounts are also less susceptible to statistical checks and other verification techniques.

In the absence of a code of practice, Traidcraft and the New Economic Foundation (NEF) have found it useful, up to the completion of the 1994–95 accounts, to base the auditor's report on the advice given by a group of independent experts and practitioners in fields that are related to our business activity – in addition to the auditor's own supervision of the accounting process. The members of this audit review group are given the draft report the directors intend publishing as the annual social account, and have access to relevant parts or all of the detailed accounts and records on which it is based. They meet with the auditors and the company's 'internal accountant' and discuss the accounting statement. The auditor also monitors and advises on how the accounts should be carried out and makes his own checks on the draft report. On the basis of his own judgement and the advice of the review group, an Auditor's Report is written and included in the published report. The following example (Box 6.2) is taken from the 1994/95 Social Accounts.

Traidcraft is among a group of organizations and researchers in social and ethical accounting who have recently launched the Institute for Social and Ethical AccountAbility, described elsewhere in this book (Chapter 4). Among its aims is the development of international codes and standards for SEAAR.

THE IMPACT ON TRAIDCRAFT

Traidcraft was not interested in compliance but in learning. Rather than seeing social accounting as a threat, the board, the shareholders, the staff, the customers and our suppliers have welcomed it as a unique forum where different stakeholders, many of whom will never meet, communicate with one another about how the company affects their lives.

Social bookkeeping, developed to reduce the cost of the annual social accounting and auditing process, allows us to build more of the 'ethical and social' performance measures into the routine management accounting systems of the company. The idea is that managers can see how we are doing regularly and make business decisions that take account of the social impact as well as the effect on bottomline profits. It would be satisfying to claim that greater accountability and greater attention to the new measures of performance resulted in booming sales and better profit performance. At the time of writing, this is not the case and Traidcraft is currently undertaking a radical review of business processes and structures aimed at increasing efficiency and overall profitability.

Directors and managers have recognized that the company will not achieve its strategic aims of widening the customer base and doubling sales of fairly traded products by the end of the decade with the current organiza- tion. Already departmental structures are being replaced by process managing teams driven by a new priority to win and retain new customers who support the company's 'justice in trade' mission.

As these new ways of working emerge, so are new methods of measuring performance against the combined business and social goals. The company's commitment to social and ethical accountability requires that all changes pass the test of whether they meet stakeholders' aspirations in the long term. The next stage of the social bookkeeping development will involve building these tests and indicators into the social and management accounting

BOX 6.2: AUDITOR'S REPORT

We have studied the Social Accounts of Traidcraft plc for the period April 1994 to March 1995. We have monitored each stage of the accounting process and provided related advice and support. We have obtained views on the Social Accounts by an Audit Advisory Group comprising people with relevant expertise and experience in relation to the interests of each stakeholder group, and business ethics more generally. Finally, we have considered the accounts in the light of the Auditor's recommendations contained within Traidcraft plc's 1993/94 Social Audit Report.

Traidcraft plc is to be commended for its decision to produce a third set of Social Accounts. The company has complied wherever possible with the key principles of social accounting, thereby opening itself to public scrutiny well beyond current statutory requirements. Many of the Auditor's recommendations from last year have been taken into account this year.

We are satisfied that Traidcraft plc's Social Accounts for 1993/94 provide a fair and reasonable basis for understanding key aspects of the company's social impact and ethical behaviour in relation to its aims and those of the stakeholders for the period in question.

We appreciate that Traidcraft plc wished to further advance the quality of its own social accounts, as well as contribute to the growing body of practical experience from which other organizations can learn and benefit. The Audit Advisory Group, furthermore, has identified aspects of the accounts that could benefit from further development. We would like, therefore, to recommend that future social accounting by Traidcraft plc reflect improvements in the following areas: strengthening external verification of producer consultation; developing consultation with the company's local community; clarification of environmental concerns of key stakeholders and reporting performance against those concerns; further investigation of stakeholders' perceptions of each others' expectations and associated trade-offs; and the further strengthening of the company's social bookkeeping systems to enable both more systematic accounting and in-depth auditing. Finally, we would suggest that Traidcraft plc might wish to report on the effects of social accounting to date on its activities and social impact.

The New Economics Foundation

system. However, we believe that being honest with our customers about shortcomings in our fair trade performance has increased their trust and kept sales growing in a very depressed economic environment.

SOCIAL ACCOUNTS IMPACT ON FOOD SOURCING

A good example of this 'warts and all' approach is that in the 1993–94 social accounts, Traidcraft reported the results of a review of its Food Product

Sourcing Policy and Practice. Traidcraft's Purchasing Policy sets out the ethical criteria to which the company aspires in the selection of all suppliers and products, including foods and beverages. However, because many foodstuff are traded as commodities, there is not always the same close link between the company and the primary producer as there is with our craft product suppliers. So, purchasing conditions were modified to include indirect buying of foods from national export agencies where the country had effective land reform and economic support policies for peasant farmers. Traidcraft reported, in the 1993–94 accounts:

> It had been aware of the weakness of this approach, and as we now have access to a number of Third World suppliers through our fair trade partners in Europe, we will aim to phase out indirect sourcing and replace it with sourcing directly or through a fair trade partner.

On the basis of an initial review, the 1993–94 accounts reported:

> ...about three-quarters of the products come from apparently acceptabe sources, where the producer receives a fair price, though it should be noted that evidence may be indirect;
> at present Traidcraft has information about the environmental aspects of production of only a few of its food and beverage products. In about one fifth of all products the company has some evidence that growers and producers are using organic methods; with about a fifth of the products in the present range, some of which include a mixture of the 'Third World' and UK/European context, apart from ensuring that we buy from reputable suppliers, we have not applied specific fair trade criteria.

By the following year, using a revised and stricter food purchasing policy, 64 per cent of the products matched the new criteria, accounting for 67 per cent of the sales revenue for foods and beverages in 94/95; 36 per cent of the products did not conform to the new policy.

Customers asked questions at the company's annual general meeting and some of the sales reps wrote expressing their concern that they had been selling goods as fair trade products which did not meet the company's published criteria. However, they said the new sourcing policy and review 'were a perfectly adequate response to a difficult situation' and 'Traidcraft is at least honest about the shortcomings and the criteria are good.' Another wrote:

> I understand the problems involved in breaking into the commodities market and I am satisfied that Traidcraft is working towards the perfect solution. I do not expect perfection overnight. As long as Traidcraft is not motivated by the protectionism and greed of the big boys I am happy to trust your judgement on behalf of the suppliers and those of us who sell the goods.

Throughout the period since the first 'bad report', sales of Traidcraft's food and beverages have continued to grow in spite of the stagnant retail market and static or falling sales in other areas of its business. Honesty, if it has had an effect, has been beneficial.

It has also exposed Traidcraft's management to continuing scrutiny by its customers and shareholders and has undoubtedly forced the pace of research into more appropriate sources for food products. The analysis of the food range in 1995/96 shows around 90 per cent of the sales revenue coming from products that meet the revised criteria.

THE IMPACT OUTSIDE TRAIDCRAFT

Traidcraft plc was the first business in the UK to develop voluntary social accounts and to publish independently audited reports. That, too, has drawn much more attention to the company's mission and activities. Traidcraft recognizes that its contribution to fair trade will have only a tiny and localized effect on the problem of poverty. So it is vital that we win the hearts and minds of the public to chose justice instead of indifference when they go shopping, and to see sacrifice as a virtue rather than the self-indulgence encouraged by advertizing and the media. This means providing information and being honest and open. Social audit reports, therefore, have a real public relations function to fulfil – not in interpreting the company's activities in the most favourable way, or deliberately misleading the public, but in providing detailed accounts for people to make their own judgements.

For the last two years we have sent copies of our social audit reports to the chief executives of the top 100 companies in the UK. Sadly, only a minority bother to respond at all, but among those who do there is a growing interest in our activities and recognition that people do come before profit; the onus is on individual businesses to prove that they deserve public support. We have also had excellent coverage in the business sections of internationally known British papers such as *The Financial Times*, *The Guardian*, *The Independent* and *The Observer.*

Other companies in the United Kingdom have followed Traidcraft's lead, and we are now increasingly involved in work with other companies and organizations which are interested in introducing social and ethical accounting in their own businesses.

The use and testing of the accounting methodology, social bookkeeping and the development of auditing practices in different organizational environments are seen by Traidcraft as an essential part of the evolution of social accounting into an effective, and recognized, system of assessing for an organization's impact on all its stakeholders. Traidcraft Exchange has set up an organization funded by trust and donated income and consultancy fees to pursue this objective of developing the method through application. At the same time, Traidcraft's links with the New Economics Foundation, the Centre for Social and Environmental Accounting Research and the organizations involved in setting up the Institute for Social and Ethical AccountAbility ensure that we maintain an objective and critical approach to the development of the method and its application.

7

Integrated Ethical Auditing: The Body Shop International, UK

Maria Sillanpää
(Team Leader, Ethical Audit)
and David Wheeler
(Head of Stakeholder Policy)

The Body Shop International first committed itself to an active programme of integrated ethical auditing at the beginning of 1994.[1] This followed successful experience in implementing audit programmes for environmental protection and health and safety at work, and supplier screening programmes for animal protection.

This paper describes The Body Shop's business activities, together with the company's ethical policies and how these are audited. The company's environmental and animal-protection related auditing activities are discussed briefly to provide some context for what is meant by 'ethical auditing'. The methodology adopted for social auditing is described in more detail. Emphasis is given to the importance of auditing and disclosure of performance as the key to establishing legitimacy for active engagement in the wider socio-political arena.

BUSINESS AND SUSTAINABLE DEVELOPMENT

Throughout the 1990s there has been increasing emphasis on the need for transparency and especially public disclosure of environmental impacts by industry.[2] In addition, the relevance of environmental management and auditing systems to wider issues of socially responsible business behaviour is now becoming understood. Thus, in 1992, the key document emerging from the United Nations Conference on Environment and Development, Local Agenda 21, emphasized the importance of environmental management, auditing and public disclosure of environmental impacts in pursuing the broader goal of sustainable development.[3] In preparation for the UNCED conference, Schmidheiny and others produced a radical prescription for altering business behaviour to take into full account the need to balance environmental conservation and economic development.[4] This analysis has stimulated work in the Business Council for Sustainable Development and elsewhere on issues such as eco-efficiency and ecological tax reform.[5] It has produced resonance in progressive business circles and in more forward-thinking national and international agencies.[6, 7, 8]

However, it is only recently that the management implications of the wider business agenda have become apparent. Thus, heads of corporations and business leaders still talk about sustainable development when they really mean environmental protection and the conservation of natural resources.[9, 10] Companies whose activities could hardly be less sustainable act as leading players in international fora promoting environmental management initiatives which are claimed to be compatible with unrestricted free trade and patently unsustainable consumption.[11] Even terms like eco-efficiency, life-cycle assessment and eco-management are promoted as technical devices devoid of the wider issues of global social responsibility and intergenerational equity.[12]

For businesses to be able to effectively progress towards the goal of sustainablity, it must develop pioneering management systems which are based on a wider perspective of how environmental protection and conservation relate to business obligations. If we are to avoid the kind of crisis foreseen by some and move towards a more genuinely ecocentric approach to business, new techniques are needed.[13] These techniques may borrow from existing management theory and practice, including techniques used in environmental, health and safety, or total quality management and auditing. In the case of environmental audits, The Body Shop elected in 1991 to follow the European Union Eco-Management and Audit Regulation (EMAS)[14] as the most rigorous, comprehensive and rational framework available.[15] The company published three independently verified environmental statements in 1992, 1993 and 1994.[16, 17]

But business will need a broader and more holistic set of values, together with systems for implementing those values if it is to make a genuine commitment to sustainable development. A paradigm shift is needed, complete with methodological underpinning.[18, 19] Integrated ethical auditing which takes into account social, animal and environmental protection issues is one technique which may help.[20, 21]

THE BODY SHOP APPROACH TO SOCIAL RESPONSIBILITY

At a general level, The Body Shop has defined its approach to socially responsible business as operating on the following three levels:

1 *Compliance:* The first step is to take into account the responsibilities of business not to abuse people, the environment or animals wherever the company operates. This means accepting and behaving in accordance with defined regulations, norms and standards of human rights, social welfare, environmental protection and, where relevant, animal protection.

2   *Disclosure*: Only through public disclosure can a real process of dialogue and discussion with stakeholders be achieved and the right direction charted for the future. The second step is, therefore, for companies to go beyond compliance with standards and be open about their performance record. This transparency develops relationships of trust and sets an example.

3   *Active Engagement*: For The Body Shop, a committed socially responsible business takes a third step after compliance and disclosure. This is to play an active part in campaigning for positive change in the way the business world works, with the ultimate aim of making a positive impact on the world at large. This step requires an acceptance that business does not exist in a political vacuum. This does not mean party politics but it does require the conviction of stakeholders to come together on a common platform to affect social change.[22]

THE BODY SHOP'S FIRST VALUES REPORT

In January 1996, The Body Shop published an integrated statement of its ethical performance which is called *The Values Report 1995*. Each component of the report has an element of independent verification in line with established best practice where this exists. The report also included a guide to The Body Shop's approach to ethical auditing.[23]

The three main components of the report were:

1   *Environmental Statement*: The Environmental Statement covered issues at the company's principal operating sites in Watersmead (Littlehampton, UK), Wick (Littlehampton, UK) and Wake Forest (North Carolina, US). In all cases, The Body Shop's environmental management systems and data were subject to external verification in line with the provisions of EMAS.[24]

2   *Animal Protection Statement*: The Animal Protection Statement covers systems and procedures at Watersmead where the majority of product and ingredient purchasing decisions were made during the audit year. Procedures for checking the animal protection credentials of the company's suppliers are partially decentralized to purchasing departments on subsidiary sites and to two franchise operations (Canada and Australia). However, these activities are overseen by systems which operate at the Head Office level. Thus, independent verification of activities in 1994/95 concentrates on the Watersmead audit and management systems.

The Animal Protection Statement of the Report included an independently verified assessment of the company's Against Animal Testing procedures to International Standards Organization quality systems standard ISO 9002.[25] This standard is aimed particularly at assessing conformance to specified requirements by a company's suppliers.

A summary of
The Body Shop Values Report 1995

MEASURING UP

February 1996

The Body Shop publishes its first Values Report this January. This Report comprises three statements covering the Company's track record on the environmental, animal protection and the human relationships within our business.

The Road Ahead

The Body Shop is a large, multi-local business. It is not a one-woman show, but a global operation with franchisees running their own businesses and thousands of people working towards common goals. It is a curious, committed and passionate work in progress.

We want it to be obvious for anyone to see why we do what we do - and how we do it. This applies to every level of our business, from the manufacture and marketing of skin and hair care products to our activities as a socially responsible company. But we've had to make our own roadmap - there are few signposts along the way. Our Values Report is an ambitious document which defines our future challenges. There is much in the Report that delights us but more than a little that we are very disappointed by.

There is clearly a lot to take in at once. So, we've summarised it to give a sample of the highlights and low points. The title says it all. This is our - and your - yardstick to assess The Body Shop performance. It is only the first of many.

" I would love it if every shareholder of every company wrote a letter every time they received a company's annual report and accounts. I would like them to say something like: Okay, that's fine, very good. But where are the details of your environmental audit? Where are the details of your accounting to the community? Where is your social audit? **"**

Anita Roddick, BODY AND SOUL, 1991

Why?

In January 1996 The Body Shop releases more details on its ethical activities than ever before.

It has done this because:

■ The Company believes that business has a moral responsibility to tell the truth about itself and face up to things that need to change;

■ The Body Shop is a high profile advocate of social and environmental causes. Sometimes this kind of advocacy upsets people, so if a company wants the licence to campaign on public issues it must demonstrate its own commitment to reflection and self-improvement on issues like environmental protection, animal protection and human rights;

■ For The Body Shop to continue to mix business with politics, cosmetics with campaigns, it has to take its supporters and stakeholders (including customers, employees and suppliers) along with it.

What?

The instrument used to release details of our ethical performance is called the Values Report 1995. Each component of the Report has an element of independent verification in line with established best practice where this exists. There are three components:

SOCIAL AUDIT
A social audit requires measurement of performance against policies, internal management systems, programmes and targets, stakeholder expectations and external benchmarks. During 1994/5 The Body Shop worked with the New Economics Foundation (NEF) on a consultation process with our stakeholders. The results, verified by NEF, are published in the Social Statement.

ENVIRONMENTAL AUDIT
The Environmental Statement section of our Report covers issues at our principal operating sites in Watersmead (Littlehampton, UK), Wick (Littlehampton, UK) and Wake Forest (North Carolina, USA).

In all three cases our environmental management systems and data have been subject to external verification (audit) in line with the provisions of the EU Eco-Management and Audit Scheme (EMAS). The Environmental Statement also includes information from international markets around the world.

ANIMAL PROTECTION AUDIT
The Animal Protection Statement section of our Report includes an independently verified assessment of our Against Animal Testing procedures and purchasing criteria according to International Standards Organisation standard ISO 9002. This standard is aimed particularly at assessing conformance to specified requirements by a company's suppliers.

How?

If the word 'audit' conjures up for you the drier areas of high finance, you should know that in recent years many new types of audit - environmental, medical, and ethical - have emerged which have little to do with money, and everything to do with responsible management. The Body Shop approach to ethical business operates on three levels:

COMPLIANCE
The first step is to take into account the responsibilities of business not to abuse people, the environment or animals wherever the Company operates. This means opening up to defined standards of human rights, social welfare and worker safety, environmental protection and, where relevant, wider ethical issues like animal protection.

DISCLOSURE
The second step is for companies to go beyond compliance with standards and be open about their records on social, environmental and animal protection. This transparency develops relationships of trust and sets an example.

Only through public disclosure can a real process of dialogue and discussion with stakeholders be achieved and the right direction charted for the future. The Values Report 1995 also includes a report on our approach to Ethical Auditing.

CAMPAIGNING
The really committed socially responsible business takes the third step after compliance and disclosure. This is to play an active part in agitating and campaigning for positive change in the way the business world works, with the ultimate aim of making a positive impact on the world at large.

It requires a political outlook to campaign. This does not mean party politics but it does require the conviction of stakeholders to come together on a common platform to fight for a fairer world (*listed on the back page are some areas we have campaigned on*).

THE BODY SHOP

Figure 7.1: *The Body Shop International's Values Report 1995*

Table 7.1: Scope of Audit and Verification Activities for Main Sites and Activities of The Body Shop International Social Audit 1995

	Watersmead Site (UK)	Wick Site (UK)	Wake Forest Site (US)	Easterhouse Site (Scotland)	UK Company Stores	US Company Stores	International Franchisees	UK Franchisees	US Franchisees
Staff employed at 28 February 1995	863	367	240	150	669	989	5500*	3200*	1595*
Environmental management & audit procedures	XXX	XXX	XXX	XX	XX	—	X(X)	XX	--
Animal protection & audit procedures	XXX	XX	XX	XX	N/A	N/A	XX	N/A	N/A
Social audit procedures	XXX	XXX	X	XXX	XXX	—	XXX	XXX	XXX

Key

XXX   Information presented, internally audited and externally verified
XX   Information presented, internally audited
X(X)   Information presented, internally analysed
X   Information presented
—   No information presented
N/A   Not applicable or relevant
*   Estimated number of staff based on average number of staff employed in Company stores

This chart includes all areas of the Company employing more than 100 employees

3   *Social Statement*: A social audit requires measurement of performance against policies, internal management systems, programmes and targets, stakeholder expectations and external benchmarks. The Body Shop's first Social Statement focused on the company's impacts on stakeholders directly affected by its UK operations. During 1994/95 The Body Shop worked with the New Economics Foundation (NEF) on a consultation process with the company's stakeholders.[26] The results, verified by NEF, are published in the Social Statement.

The principal subject of the *Values Report 1995* was the company's wholly owned business in the UK. Most of the information relates directly to its Watersmead (UK) site, home to The Body Shop's manufacturing, production and warehousing and its international head office.

In arranging the *Values Report 1995* in this way, The Body Shop believes it has systematically covered most relevant issues as far as environmental protection, animal protection and social issues are concerned. Naturally, the scope of each report needs to be fully understood. For example, as noted above, in the first cycle The Body Shop was unable to include quantitative information from staff employed directly by the subsidiary company in the US in its Social Statement, although it has initiated the process which will allow the company to do that in future years. Similarly, because it is a relatively small facility, the soap factory's environmental management programme has not yet been included in independent verification, although it is covered by the company's internal ethical audit systems. Below is a framework to help the reader understand the scope of the *Values Report 1995* and the extent to which information in each statement has been subject to internal audit and external verification.

From Table 7.1 it is clear that the main areas of The Body Shop International are being addressed for all three areas of ethical concern in the UK. Further progress needs to be made in the US – especially with respect to environmental information gathering and auditing in the company stores. In addition, appropriate social audit procedures need to be developed and put in place for the US operations. Nevertheless, 1996 did not see tangible progress in both areas. Programmes for international franchisees necessarily take more time to develop, but the company has been very pleased with the environmental auditing and information gathering activities of franchisees since 1992. This will be further consolidated during 1997 and appropriate social audit programmes introduced as soon as practicable.

Financial auditing and reporting is currently carried out separately to the above areas of ethical auditing. However, financial information is utilized especially in the Social and Environmental Statements, and it is envisaged that the use of financial performance indicators will increase in the future, possibly offering opportunities for further integration between financial and ethical auditing.

THE BODY SHOP

Mission Statement

OUR REASON FOR BEING

To dedicate our business to the pursuit of social and environmental change

To creatively balance the financial and human needs of our stakeholders: employees, customers, franchisees, suppliers and shareholders.

To courageously ensure that our business is ecologically sustainable: meeting the needs of the present without compromising the future.

To meaningfully contribute to local, national and international communities in which we trade, by adopting a code of conduct which ensures care, honesty, fairness and respect.

To passionately campaign for the protection of the environment, human and civil rights, and against animal testing within the cosmetics and toiletries industry.

To tirelessly work to narrow the gap between principle and practice, whilst making fun, passion and care part of our daily lives.

Figure 7.2: *The Body Shop Mission Statement*

THE BODY SHOP

OUR TRADING CHARTER

The way we trade creates profits with principles

We aim to achieve commercial success by meeting our customers' needs through the provision of high-quality, good value products with exceptional service and relevant information which enables customers to make informed and responsible choices.

Our trading relationships of every kind – with customers, franchisees and suppliers – will be commercially viable, mutually beneficial and based on trust and respect.

Our trading principles reflect our core values

We aim to ensure that human and civil rights, as set out in the Universal Declaration of Human Rights, are respected throughout our business activities. We will establish a framework based on this declaration to include criteria for workers' rights embracing a safe, healthy working environment, fair wages, no discrimination on the basis of race, creed, gender or sexual orientation, or physical coercion of any kind.

We will support long-term, sustainable relationships with communities in need. We will pay special attention to those minority groups, women and disadvantaged peoples who are socially and economically marginalized.

We will use environmentally sustainable resources wherever technically and economically viable. Our purchasing will be based on a system of screening and investigation of the ecological credentials of our finished products, ingredients, packaging and suppliers.

We will promote animal protection throughout our business activities. We are against animal testing in the cosmetics and toiletries industry. We will not test ingredients or products on animals, nor will we commission others to do so on our behalf. We will use our purchasing power to stop suppliers animal testing.

We will institute appropriate monitoring, auditing and disclosure mechanisms to ensure our accountability and demonstrate our compliance with these principles.

Figure 7.3: *The Body Shop Trading Charter*

THE BODY SHOP APPROACH TO ETHICAL AUDITING

Policies and organizational structure

The company's current Mission Statement was adopted in mid 1994. It dedicates the company to the pursuit of social and environmental change. It is a holistic document, embracing human and civil rights, ecological sustainability and animal protection. The Mission Statement also makes clear that the company should work 'to narrow the gap between principle and practice'. Underpinning the Mission Statement is a Trading Charter which addresses the three principal ethical concerns of The Body Shop while committing the company to 'appropriate monitoring, auditing and disclosure mechanisms to ensure our accountability and demonstrate our compliance' with the company's trading principles.

Together with The Body Shop Memorandum of Association, which also affirms the values-led nature of the business, the Mission Statement and Trading Charter provide the central thrust for the company's ethical policies and its desire to demonstrate accountability on ethical issues. At the present time, The Body Shop maintains a number of formal policy, guideline and procedure manuals which underpin the ideals expressed in the Mission Statement. Some are still under development and await formal release. However, the current picture is depicted in Figure 7.4.

In early 1994, in order to promote compliance with its ethical policies, The Body Shop set up an integrated Ethical Audit department. This both brought together already existing auditing functions (eg environmental, health and safety) and helped to establish certain functions formally within the company (eg social and information audit). The 14-staff department aims to provide support for the company's ethical stance in the following areas:

* policy development and maintenance;
* auditing and reporting;
* advice and training.

The Ethical Audit department has six areas of professional expertise:

* animal protection;
* environmental protection;
* social issues;
* health and safety at work;
* information management;
* training.

The department is organized along stakeholder lines, with each of the main professional groupings taking special responsibility for the needs of particular stakeholders (see Figure 7.5). This integrated matrix-style approach to ethical auditing has proven effective in streamlining communications and avoiding head office departments and stakeholders being confused by differing values-related audit demands. Each grouping also works through relevant departments: for instance, through purchasing groups for supplier issues and through human resources for employee issues.

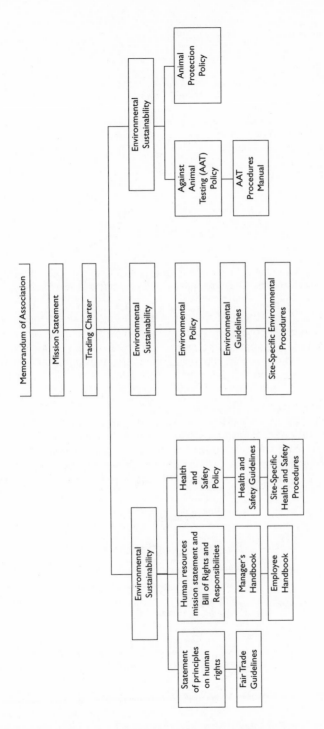

Figure 7.4: *Guide to The Body Shop International Key Policies on Ethical Issues*

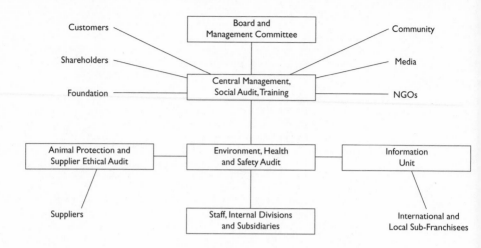

Figure 7.5: *Structure of Ethical Audit Department: How Professional Groups Take Responsibility for Ethical Issues of Relevance to Principal Stakeholders*

The position of the Ethical Audit department with respect to the rest of the company is shown in Figure 7.6. It may be noted that as part of the Values and Vision Centre the department reports directly to Founder and Chief Executive Anita Roddick and is represented on the management committee in the CEO's absence.

The Ethical Audit department is not usually responsible for day-to-day operational management of ethical issues. Where it is necessary to develop a management system for quality control centrally, the Ethical Audit department may take provisional responsibility for it. But this is always with the intention of floating the system off into the relevant business entity at the earliest appropriate opportunity. For example, the supply division maintains its own health, safety and environmental management group, the purchasing

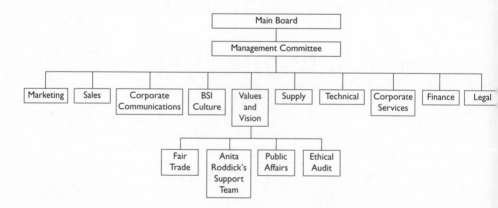

Figure 7.6: *Structure of The Body Shop International Principal Divisions: Details of Values and Vision Centre*

group has its own systems for supporting suppliers in moving forwards on ethical issues, and the technical division maintains its own systems and records on the ethical profile of product ingredients. This split, which may be likened to the difference between quality *control* and quality *assurance*, avoids potential conflicts of interest and ensures maximum integration of ethical programmes within the business.

ENVIRONMENTAL PROTECTION

Environmental reviews and audits have come a long way since the early 1980s. Pioneered in the United States, early audits tended to equate environmental risks with health and safety ones. This was a natural development for industries such as energy and petrochemicals which already had long track records of health and safety auditing. The experiences of the Soviet authorities in Chernobyl, Union Carbide in Bhopal and Icmesa in Seveso certainly served to emphasize the relationship between occupational and environmental risks.

However, growing environmental awareness among the general public prompted a growth in environmental auditing in companies which had lower levels of exposure to risks of industrial accidents. Thus, new techniques reflect wider public concerns and often go beyond the limitation of risks or compliance with legal responsibilities for health and safety or pollution control. Audits now examine how to save money on waste treatment and disposal and how to reduce energy consumption; both are especially relevant for organizations which want to justify spending money on improved environmental performance. Audits can also cover: procurement policy (including suppliers); global environmental responsibilities (eg the reduction of CO_2 emissions); education and awareness raising; and a company's whole approach to environmental strategy. Because these issues often strike at the very heart of an organization's culture and can affect profits – either positively or negatively – it is not surprising that methodologies available for environmental auditing have been examined in some detail in recent years.

Happily, despite the growing diversity of organizations involved in auditing, standards and approaches have been converging in recent years. Auditing is now seen as a tool to be employed within a formal environmental management system (EMS). An EMS establishes effective ways of detecting and responding to environmental problems.

In late 1991, The Body Shop adopted the (then) draft European Community Eco-Audit Regulation as the principal framework for the company's environmental management, auditing, and public reporting. The first Environmental Statement was published in May 1992, focusing particularly on the environmental performance of the main headquarters and manufacturing site at Watersmead, UK.

During 1992 and 1993, the draft Eco-Audit Regulation underwent further negotiation and development, eventually emerging as the European Union Eco-Management and Audit Scheme (EMAS). The scheme retained its voluntary nature, a point of some concern to The Body Shop. But several essential components, most notably continuous improvement of performance, a commitment to best practice and independently verified public disclosure, ensured that the measure retained credibility.

The Body Shop's experience of EMAS has been very positive. Despite the parallel emergence of British (BS 7750) and international (ISO 14001) standards on environmental management systems, we believe that EMAS represents by far the most exacting framework for ensuring best environmental practice in industry.[27]

ANIMAL PROTECTION

Organizations which conduct animal experiments are usually subject to some degree of external surveillance and control. In most countries, licensing arrangements are handled by governmental bodies who seek to ensure the minimization of animal suffering during and after experimentation. In the UK, licensing is handled by the Home Office. In addition, scientists are often subject to professional or institutional codes of practice which also seek to ensure the humane treatment of test animals. Depending on the type of licence, the nature of the experiments and the purpose of the research, surveillance might involve site visits by regulatory agencies.

For organizations which choose not to undertake or commission animal tests there is clearly no compulsion to obtain licences or become subject to external or internal professional audit of practices. However, in the cosmetics and toiletries industry, where the avoidance of animal cruelty embraces not just the company's own behaviour, but that of suppliers, some type of assessment is necessary. Companies which market cosmetics are now well aware of the interest of consumers in avoiding cruelty to laboratory animals. Historically there have been four levels of company response to this consumer concern:

- Some companies prefer to continue to test or commission tests either to provide arguments against liability claims (should product safety ever be challenged) or to satisfy third-party requests for such testing.
- Some companies have found it possible to terminate the testing of finished products but reserve the right to continue to test, or ask suppliers to test individual ingredients.
- Some companies do not test or commission tests on animals either for finished goods or ingredients; however, they may tolerate using suppliers who do test raw materials used for their products, eg for regulatory or marketing reasons.
- Some companies do not test or commission tests and use some kind of standard or purchasing rule against which to judge their suppliers and avoid encouraging the perpetuation of testing in the supply chain.

Over the years, animal welfare and animal rights groups have recognized these different approaches by placing companies on approved or disapproved lists. These lists are almost universally based on information supplied by the companies themselves; thus, although the information is made public in order to help advize consumers, there is no guarantee that a company is actually doing what it says it is doing on the animal testing question. This uncertainty has led to some confusion and public debate – particularly where animal welfare groups exercise different criteria for judging company behaviour.

Recognizing this source of uncertainty, in 1994 The Body Shop started talking to animal welfare societies about how its own procedures and purchasing criteria could be subject to some type of external independent assessment leading to public disclosure of the company's performance in this area. The idea was, if The Body Shop's supplier screening systems (established in 1986) could be verified, then so could other companies' too. These discussions led to a decision to engage a quality systems assessor to check The Body Shop procedures against the ISO 9002 quality standard. This standard is aimed particularly at assessing conformance to specified requirements by a company's suppliers; the logic is that companies can provide a better service or product quality to their customers if their suppliers are also performing adequately.

ISO 9002 is versatile enough such that any company with a non-animal testing stance which is actively seeking to check the performance of its suppliers could be assessed according to this new dimension of quality. The particular purchasing rule or standard is thus somewhat less important than the management systems and procedures which are in place to back it up. This finally overcomes the fairly futile debate over differing purchasing rules and should allow animal welfare groups to unite by classifying companies using a common, independently verified standard.[28]

SOCIAL ISSUES

The publication of the Social Statement 1995 marks the first attempt by The Body Shop to systematically audit, verify and disclose the company's performance on social issues. The company sees this as the starting point for more *effective* dialogue and communication with all its stakeholders. The entire process behind the first statement took approximately three years, including researching, planning and implementing.

In developing the social audit methodology, the company took as its philosophical starting point the belief that all stakeholders should have an effective voice in commenting upon and shaping a company's behaviour. The Body Shop does not believe that a company is only in business to serve the interests of a limited number of stakeholders.

Our methodology has drawn heavily on our own research into the history of private and public sector social accounting, auditing and assessment. The Body Shop has, in particular, learned a great deal from the recent experiences of organizations like the Sbn Bank in Denmark, Traidcraft plc in the UK and Ben & Jerry's Homemade, Inc in the US. All three have a good track record in public disclosure, and although they all have adopted different methods appropriate to their organizations, they have each been successful.

In 1994, The Body Shop started to work with the New Economics Foundation, who had been advising Traidcraft, to tailor a social audit methodology that would be appropriate to an organization as large and structurally complex as The Body Shop. By drawing on these various experiences, we have endeavoured to synthesize and develop an approach which makes sense not just for The Body Shop, but, we hope, for other large organizations too.[29]

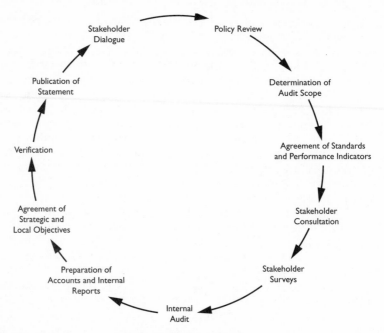

Figure 7.7: *Framework for Social Auditing and Disclosure at The Body Shop International*

Although work is under way, there are, as yet, no universally agreed standards or frameworks for social auditing, there is no accepted terminology, and there are very few sources of expertise to call on. The framework presented below is therefore tentative. It is the framework which is currently in use by The Body Shop. It endeavours to synthesize some aspects of environmental management and auditing systems with recent experience of leading practitioners in social auditing and disclosure.

COMMITMENT

The Body Shop committed itself to a formal social audit process in 1992.[30] This followed the publication of Anita Roddick's autobiography in 1991 in which she wrote: 'I would love it if every shareholder of every company wrote a letter every time they received a company's annual report and accounts. I would like them to say something like, "OK, that's fine, very good. But where are the details of our environmental audit? Where are the details of your accounting to the community? Where is your social audit?"'[31]

There is no doubt that had it not been for the commitment of the founders of the company and the development of an 'accountability ethos' within The Body Shop in the early 1990s, the company would not now be in a position to publish a statement of its social performance. As with environmental management and auditing, clear leadership is probably the most important single factor in driving a process of social auditing and disclosure to a successful conclusion.

POLICY REVIEW

For any audit process to be meaningful, it is essential to understand which policy statements are relevant and which need to be developed in order that the organization's performance can be measured against a set of strategic goals. For The Body Shop's first social audit, the main policies against which performance might be judged were the company's Mission Statement and Trading Charter. More specific policies and guidelines existed for health and safety at work, human resources (managers' and employee handbooks) and community trade (fair trade guidelines). These were also used as the basis for assessing the ability of management systems to deliver on policy commitments.

DETERMINATION OF AUDIT SCOPE

Because parallel systems already existed at The Body Shop for auditing and reporting on ethical performance with respect to animal protection and the environment, the subject area of the social audit focused on people: human stakeholders who may affect or be affected by The Body Shop. The number of individual stakeholder groups could theoretically be quite large, and a decision had to be taken as to which groups should be included in the first and subsequent audit cycles. The Body Shop took the view that in the first cycle, the net should be cast as wide and as deep as possible. But inevitably some groups and subgroups could not be reached for practical reasons.

Another important factor in the scoping of a social audit is geography. Where a company has wholly or majority-owned operations in different countries, a decision has to be taken as to whether one or all countries are to be covered in each cycle. For The Body Shop this meant choosing not to include US stakeholders in any great depth in the first year but to concentrate mostly on UK-based groups. So although some US information was gathered with respect to franchisees and customers, this was a less-comprehensive effort than that devoted to the UK process.

The last factor to be taken into account in scoping a social audit is the level to which indirect stakeholders may be embraced. For The Body Shop this required a decision about whether, for example, staff of franchisees or non-governmental organizations in franchised markets should be consulted. It was decided that it would be more appropriate for such stakeholders to be directly consulted by franchisees at such a time when they were able to conduct their own audit processes.

Table 7.2 sets out the scope of those stakeholder groups consulted during the first audit cycle. Consultation was done by using a mix of focus groups, open meetings and market-research type surveys as described later.

As far as reporting of quantitative information goes, it is the company's intention to publish this on a regular basis, whatever the mix of tools used in consultation in the first audit cycle of 1994/95.

The general picture, for stakeholders, was outlined as follows:

* Year 1: mostly UK-based but with some US input;
* Year 2: deepening dialogue with UK-based stakeholders not fully covered

Table 7.2: *Scope of Stakeholders in First Social Audit*[32]

Stakeholder	Size of the Stakeholder Group
UK Staff	
(directly employed by The Body Shop International)	2199
International Head Franchisees	40
UK Franchisees and Partnerships	104
US Sub-Franchisees	82
UK Customers	34 million
	(customer transactions)
US Customers	10 million
	(customer transactions)
Suppliers	1,309
Community Trade Partners	12
Shareholders	6809
Local Community	23,301
	(Littlehampton population)
UK Non-Governmental Organizations	352
	(mailing list entries)
Foundation Applicants	
• Successful applicants 1994/95	72
• Unsuccessful applicants 1994/95	7500

in Year 1 plus full roll-out to the US;
• Year 3: introduction of parallel processes in certain international franchised markets; return to full portfolio of Year 1 consultation in the UK.

As part of the scoping exercise for the first audit, predictions for the following year were also made regarding the inclusion of new groups who were not consulted as part of the first audit. The Social Statement commits to consulting such groups as the media, ethical investment community and regulators. The Statement also invited stakeholder groups who felt they had been missed in the first cycle to identify themselves as groups who should be consulted.

As the above illustrates, determining the scope and boundaries of social auditing is potentially a more complex exercise compared to environmental auditing, where the boundaries can mostly be determined based on geographical locations. Therefore, time and thoughtfulness should not be spared, especially in determining the first audit scope.

AGREEMENT OF STANDARDS AND PERFORMANCE INDICATORS

A crucial step in the development of the audit methodology was the establishment of a clear framework for what standards and associated performance indicators should be used in assessing the company's performance. Partly based on the previous work done by other companies, the following three groups were defined and used as generic categories of measurements.

Performance Against *Standards* (Benchmarks)

These should reflect nationally and internationally available information or recommendations on best practices for activities and policies that relate to any organization's social performance. Indicators may be both quantitative and qualitative and proposed, for instance, by government agencies, professional bodies and special interest groups representing certain stakeholder interests.

Standards for The Body Shop's first social audit were agreed in memoranda of understanding with relevant departments, which then had the responsibility for collecting and providing relevant information to the internal audit team. In a similar way as with environmental auditing, the accuracy of the data is validated by the audit process.

Table 7.3: *Examples of Performance Standards Used in the 1995 Social Statement*

Human Resources	• Staff turnover and stability rates
	• Salary differentials
	• Equal Opportunities related statistics
Health and Safety at Work	• Sickness/absence rates
	• Incidents/accident rates
Customers	• Complaints and Inquiries
Fair Trade (Community Trade)	• Fair Trade spend of total purchasing
	• Pricing structures
Shareholders	• Dividends
	• Share price performance
Community Involvement	• Staff community volunteering statistics
	• Foundation donations

Stakeholder Perception of Performance Against *Core Values*

These core values are essentially defined by the organization itself. Each stakeholder group is consulted to establish their perception of how closely the organization's performance matches its stated values. In The Body Shop's case, these core values are defined in its Mission Statement and Trading Charter.

Stakeholder Perception of Performance Against Specific *Needs of Stakeholders*

These needs are particular to individual stakeholder groups. They are identified as salient through dialogue with stakeholders in focus groups and measured in market-research style surveys as discussed below.

STAKEHOLDER CONSULTATION

If social auditing is about giving a voice to stakeholders, one of the most important and sensitive processes is the engagement of stakeholder representatives in dialogue. It is especially important to identify salient issues for each group in face-to-face conversation before conducting wide-scale surveys. The Body Shop used focus groups in order to allow stakeholder views and concerns to be expressed. For example, before conducting an employee survey, 10 per cent of the UK-based employees were involved in focus groups facilitated by the Ethical Audit department. Focus groups excluded managers from The Body Shop who were responsible for those stakeholders participating in the discussion, in order to avoid inhibiting the free expression of views. In the case of one stakeholder group, it was felt appropriate for the independent audit verifier to facilitate a focus group. And in all cases the verifier was invited to attend as an observer. In this way the verifier could be assured of fair play and open dialogue in the discussions.

STAKEHOLDER SURVEYS

Following the focus groups, when specific issues had been identified as salient or of particular interest to stakeholders, questionnaires were designed to measure more wide-scale opinion. These questionnaires were intended to capture perceptions of the company's performance against both stakeholder-specific needs and core values articulated by the company. Questionnaires were designed with professional assistance to avoid inadvertent introduction of bias. Space was also allowed on the questionnaires themselves for open-ended commentary on the company's performance.

Surveys were done using the largest manageable sample size; respondents completed the questionnaires anonymously and returned them to an independent survey organization for confidential analysis. Only statistical summary information and lists of comments were submitted to The Body Shop for inclusion in the audit process. The open-ended comments on the company given by respondents were analyzed by both the independent survey organization and the external verifier, who selected a representative sample of comments for inclusion in the Statement.

In some cases the resulting response rates were high (eg for staff who were given one hour off work to complete them) and in others quite low (eg for non-governmental organizations who received the questionnaires by post). In most cases the resulting sample size was large enough to draw quite clear conclusions. In some cases the sample size was relatively small and care was needed in analyzing the results.

Table 7.4: *Response Rates of Stakeholder Surveys*

Stakeholder	Size of Sample	Return Rate
UK Staff	2199	72%
International Head Franchisees	40	57.5%
UK Sub-Franchisees and Partnerships	104	52%
		55%
US Sub-Franchisees	82	51%
UK Customers	1000 (omnibus)	N/A
Suppliers	285	38%
Shareholders	1473	25%
UK Non-Governmental Organizations	137	32%
Foundation Applicants		
• Successful applicants 1994/95	50	48%
• Unsuccessful applicants 1994/95	50	16%

THE INTERNAL MANAGEMENT SYSTEMS AUDIT

There were three main sources of information for The Body Shop's first social audit process:

* the results of the focus groups and surveys described above;
* the documentary information provided by departments which had agreed quantitative and qualitative performance standards; and
* the output from confidential audit interviews with staff and managers.

This latter source of information was based on the kind of 'management systems' structured interviews used in environmental and health and safety auditing. Checklists were developed specifically for the purpose of the interviews and results used to build up a dynamic picture of departmental and divisional handling, and knowledge of social issues and company policies relevant to social performance.

The checklists evolved through examination of best practice in relevant policy areas, through consideration of existing recommendations (eg in the field of equal opportunities), and through consultation of internal and external experts on different policy areas. The checklists have been designed so that they facilitate year-on-year comparisons and thus help track progress.

These checklists are currently being up-dated and the scope of the internal audit programme expanded to include policy areas such as customer services. In future years it is intended to integrate management-systems interviews from all The Body Shop's 'ethical audit' procedures: health and safety at work, social audit, environmental protection, animal protection and information audit.

PREPARATION OF ACCOUNTS (THE SOCIAL STATEMENT) AND INTERNAL REPORTS

To avoid a Social Statement becoming too densely packed with statistics or too discursive and 'woolly', a balance has to be struck. Information from surveys has to be presented in a concise, user-friendly way and linking text has to avoid bias without becoming turgid. Statistics and performance indicators have to be balanced with quotes and views of stakeholders to bring the document alive. Finally, a sense of dialogue has to be created in which the company is seen to respond to stakeholder views, set out a direction and commit to future progress on stakeholder relations. So the preparation of a social statement requires great care, but is not in any sense a mechanical process.

The format chosen for The Body Shop's first Social Statement was based on a stakeholder model, with each group given its own section within the report. An introductory section gave a general explanation about the scope of the audit and how the information had been compiled and what assumptions were used. The company founders also gave their overview in a foreword, thereby setting a tone and direction for the document.

Each stakeholder section then followed a common format:

- the basis for the company's *approach and aims* for each group (with reference to relevant policies, etc);
- the *methodology used* for each consultation process (ie what combination of focus groups, surveys and discussions were used to capture stakeholder perceptions);
- the *results of stakeholder consultation* with perception surveys described in as even-handed and neutral a way as possible so as to avoid premature interpretation, together with direct quotations from stakeholders selected in an independent fashion;
- quantitative and qualitative *standards of performance* where these exist; and
- a *company response* in the form of a statement from a main board member or senior manager setting out their reaction to the stakeholder views and noting where progress is already being made, and/or where improvements are clearly required.

The reasoning behind setting out the accounts in this way was to promote further dialogue after the publication of the Social Statement and to allow stakeholders to take a view on the adequacy or otherwise of the company response to the results. In order to make the follow-on dialogue process efficient, stakeholders receiving the social statement were encouraged to complete a response card and attend a discussion with representatives of the company.

The final components of The Body Shop Social Statement were a verification statement from the New Economics Foundation, a summary chapter including commitments to consult stakeholders who could not be included in the cycle, and a list of strategic targets. The external verification process should have an influence on the tone, format and style of the Social Statement. The extent of this influence is guided by the verifier, as discussed later.

In addition to the published Social Statement, the social audit team prepares internal reports that are mostly based on the results of confidential management-systems interviews. Reports based on these audits are submitted to the company's senior management who then have the responsibility to implement recommendations. This follows the practice of environmental auditing. In future years, it is intended to integrate internal reporting from all The Body Shop's 'ethical audit' procedures.

AGREEMENT OF STRATEGIC AND LOCAL OBJECTIVES

As with environmental auditing and reporting, a very important part of the process is to set strategic objectives for the business which can help clarify the future priorities of the company and unite all stakeholders behind a common purpose. Setting strategic objectives and placing these in the public domain requires a significant amount of internal discussion, management commitment and senior 'sign-off'. It is not a process which can be rushed. Strategic objectives must also be underpinned by subsidiary or localized objectives which apply more specifically to individual stakeholder groups or parts of the company. The latter are in some ways simpler to negotiate because they involve fewer decision-makers at the corporate level. However, the endorsement and support of the company main board and central management committee are essential if more localized objectives are to be executed speedily and efficiently and kept in line with wider business goals.

As mentioned earlier, the individual stakeholder sections in The Body Shop's first Social Statement all included a response from a senior manager most directly responsible for a particular stakeholder group. In the majority of cases, these 'next steps' included local objectives set by departments or divisions as a response to the audit results, but it was also possible to include a programme of strategic targets to the year 2000. Based on the experience gained from four years of environmental auditing, it is envisaged that the programme of strategic social targets will become more extensive and detailed in future years as the audit process becomes more established within the company.

VERIFICATION

Unlike verification of an environmental audit process and statement, where verification can safely be left towards the end of the cycle, social audit verification requires engagement throughout. The main reason for this is that when verifying a process aimed at an audit of human relations, it is not enough to examine documentation, conduct interviews with representative staff and test the accuracy of data. The very process of collecting views from stakeholders has to be witnessed as fair and open. To ensure fair play throughout the consultation process, the external verifier was therefore able to observe, and in some cases, facilitate stakeholder focus groups of its choice. In addition to direct participation in the consultation process, the verifier involvement in finalizing stakeholder questionnaires is needed to ensure that the forms reflect the stakeholder's specific needs and issues raised in the focus groups.

A social audit verifier has to engage and participate at every part of the cycle. This could result in the verifier becoming compromized, ie too involved to be objective. So they engage, in turn, a formal advisory panel which meets to assess both the process and the output of the audit. The Body Shop's first social audit was verified by the New Economics Foundation; NEF appointed 13 people with expertise in a wide range of policy areas relevant to the company's audit. The panel of experts met on two occasions and contributed significantly to the framing of the Social Statement. NEF also produced a Verification Statement which summarized their view of the process and which included areas to be addressed in future audit cycles.

PUBLICATION OF STATEMENT

The Social Statement needs to be a true and fair picture of the social impacts of the organization, in so far as the defined scope of the audit allows. It needs to be comprehensive and systematic, but above all be understood. Because of the complex nature of a social audit and because of the variety of stakeholder needs for information, a multitier approach has been adopted for the publication of The Body Shop's first Social Statement. The full Statement was published based on the approved, verified accounts as part of The Body Shop *Values Report 1995*. In addition, more detailed information was provided to staff on specific results relevant to them and their part of the company. A summary document of all the ethical statements (including the Social Statement) was produced for wider scale distribution alongside even briefer material appropriate for customers and other large audiences. The entire *Values Report 1995* was also made available through an Internet web-site. In each case readers were made aware of how they could obtain more detailed information.

DIALOGUE

Following publication of the results of the social audit, it is vital to obtain feedback from stakeholders and engage them in dialogue about how they react to the findings presented in the Social Statement. This process of dialogue helps shape future audit cycles, enables indicators and data presentation to be fine-tuned for future cycles and helps set priorities for future action by the company. Ideally, dialogue should be driven by those departments and divisions which have direct responsibility for stakeholder groups, but facilitated and attended by the audit team to ensure continuing openness of communication.

CONCLUSION

In recent years, business leaders have been forced to take seriously the demands of stakeholders for safer and more environmentally responsible

BOX 7.1: SEVEN DO'S AND DON'TS OF SOCIAL AUDITING AND DISCLOSURE

Do start with environmental auditing and disclosure if these are relevant to your organization. Environmental audits are simpler to organise and conduct than social audits.

Do consider joining the Institute for Social and Ethical AccountAbility – an important source of independent advice and experience.

Do involve departments, managers and staff at every level, especially in deciding the scope for the audit. Key departments are those that have most to do with stakeholder groups, eg. human resources, communications/PR, investor relations, etc.

Do set up an internal audit system or department and have them report to a main board director.

Do exercise real care in selecting an independent verifier; they will have access to the very soul of the organization and their integrity is paramount. Always network to find verifiers with experience who are recommended by others.

Do allow plenty of time for drafting and finalizing the social statement. Audited departments will be very keen to be involved in putting results in context and proposing priorities for improvement.

Do report: formally and informally, publicly and internally. Stakeholder understanding is crucial to progress,as are targets and objectives for the future.

Don't launch into a social audit without talking to someone who has done one. It is a long-term commitment, so plan ahead at least two audit cycles.

Don't forget the importance of training for social auditing: for managers and auditors. In its current form it is a new science and the principles and pitfalls need to be understood.

Don't forget to focus on the benefits and business case for social performance measurement and disclosure for all stakeholders. Good social auditing should make an organization more responsive and efficient.

Don't omit to publicize the role of the audit team and its purpose; people may feel more threatened by a social performance audit than by an environmental audit.

Don't forget that you may also need other sources of expert advice, eg survey design and analysis.

Don't allow one stakeholder voice to outweigh others. Take into account minority views but don't let them take over; a good external verifier will act as wise counsel on the right balance to be struck.

Don't be afraid of including both good and bad aspects of social performance; better that you draw attention to your faults than your critics do.

operations. This has been manifested in the adoption of diverse technical solutions and an increase in environmental accountability on the part of larger corporations which have elected to publish accounts of their environmental performance.

These developments, though welcome, cannot deliver sustainability for business and industry while philosophical and economic barriers persist. New paradigms are needed, together with complementary management theories and practices. New economic models and new measures of performance are required in order to promote more sustainable behaviour by business and industry. Finally, there must be an integration of ecological and social agendas and a willingness on the part of business to be held accountable for its performance across the spectrum of ethical concerns of stakeholders: economic, ecological and social.

> *The Body Shop sets itself very tough standards and has an exceptionally ambitious mission – to dedicate its business to the pursuit of social and environmental change. Measuring how well the company matches up to its ideals has been an extraordinary challenge. Doubtless our auditing and reporting practices can be improved and we look forward to the continued networking with leading thinkers and practitioners in this field. In the long run I hope ethical audits and reports will be seen not just as exercises in accountability and openness but vital components of running inclusive, efficient, and sustainable companies in the twenty-first century.*
>
> *Anita Roddick*
> *Founder and CEO of The Body Shop International*

FURTHER INFORMATION

The Body Shop Values Report 1995 consists of the following separate statements:

* Environmental Statement;
* Animal Protection Statement;
* Social Statement;
* The Body Shop Approach to Ethical Auditing.

The *Values Report* is available on the Internet – http://www.think-act-change.com

Other publications:

* *Measuring Up* (Summary of the Values Report 1995);
* *Our Agenda* (How The Body Shop values are integral to its business, 1995).

Hard copies of all the above publications can be obtained from:

The Body Shop International
Mailorder
Watersmead
Littlehampton
West Sussex BN17 6LS

ENDNOTES

1 The Body Shop International (1994) *The Body Shop Annual Report and Accounts* The Body Shop International, Littlehampton.
2 DTTI, Sustainability and IISD (1993) *Coming Clean: Corporate Environmental Reporting* DTTI, London.
3 United Nations (1992) *Agenda 21* UN, Geneva.
4 S Schmidheiny with the Business Council for Sustainable Development (1992) *Changing Course: A Global Perspective on Development and the Environment* MIT, Cambridge, Mass.
5 Business Council for Sustainable Development (1993) *Getting Eco-efficient: First Antwerp Eco-efficiency Workshop* Antwerp, November 1993, Geneva.
6 Hawken, P (1993) *The Ecology of Commerce: A Declaration of Sustainability* Harper Collins, New York.
7 B Taylor, C Hutchinson, S Pollack and R Tapper (1994) *Environmental Management Handbook* Pitman, London.
8 International Institute for Sustainable Development (1992) *Business Strategy for Sustainable Development* IISD, Winnipeg.
9 O Williams (1994) 'Business Response to the Earth Summit' *ICC World Business and Trade Review* pp123–124, ICC, Paris.
10 R Gray and J Bebbington (1994) *Sustainable Development and Accounting: Incentives and Disincentives for the Adoption of Sustainability by Transnational Corporations* University of Dundee, Dundee.
11 A C DeCrane (1994) 'Energy and Sustainable Growth' *ICC World Business and Trade Review* pp127–128 ICC, Paris.
12 D Wheeler (1993) 'The Future for Product Life Cycle Assessment' *Integrated Environmental Management* (20) pp15–19.
13 P Shrivastava (1994) 'Ecocentric Management for a Crisis Society' in *Proceedings of The Second Nordic Network Conference on Business and Environment* Norwegian School of Management, Oslo.
14 Council for the European Communities (1992) Proposal for a Council Regulation (EEC) allowing voluntary participation by companies in the industrial sector in a Community Eco-audit scheme Com (91) 459 *Official Journal of the European Communities* C76, pp1–13.
15 D Wheeler (1992) 'Memorandum by The Body Shop International' in *A Community Eco-audit Scheme 12th Report of the Select Committee on the European Communities House of Lords Paper 42* HMSO, London, pp58–59.
16 The Body Shop International (1992, 1993 & 1994) *The Green Book* 1, 2, 3 The Body Shop International, Littlehampton.

17 D Wheeler (1995) 'Auditing for Sustainability: Philosophy and Practice of The Body Shop International' in Harrison, L L (ed) *The McGraw-Hill Environmental Auditing Handbook: A Guide to Corporate and Environmental Risk Management* McGraw-Hill, New York.

18 E Callenbach, F Capra, L Goldman, R Lutz & S Marbur (1993) *Ecomanagement: The Elmwood Guide to Ecological Auditing and Sustainable Business* Bernett - Koekler, San Francisco.

19 J Carlopio (1994) 'Holism: A Philosophy of Organisational Leadership for the Future' *Leadership Quarterly* 5(3/4), pp297–307.

20 E Mayo (1994) 'Social Auditing' *New Ground*, Winter (41).

21 S Zadek (1994) 'Making Business More Socially Accountable' *Co-operative News*, January 24, 1994.

22 The Body Shop International plc (1996) *Measuring Up – A Summary of The Body Shop Values Report 1995* The Body Shop International, Littlehampton.

23 The Body Shop International plc (1996) *Values Report 1995.*

24 Verification of the Environmental Statement 1995 was carried out by Environmental Resources Management.

25 Verified assessment of the animal protection management procedures was carried out by SGS Yardsley.

26 The New Economics Foundation is a leading UK think-tank focusing on the social and environmental dimensions of economics and business With over a decade's experience of working in the UK and internationally, NEF has challenged conventional wisdom in promoting economic alternatives that support key principles of social justice and environmental sustainability NEF has been at the forefront of developing social auditing for the 1990s in conjunction with socially responsible businesses.

27 For a detailed description of The Body Shop's environmental management and auditing practices, see: The Body Shop International plc (1996) *The Body Shop Approach to Ethical Auditing* The Body Shop International, Littlehampton.

28 For a detailed description of The Body Shop's animal protection screening procedures and related auditing practices, see The Body Shop International (1996) *The Body Shop Approach to Ethical Auditing* The Body Shop International, Littlehampton.

29 M Sillanpää & D Wheeler (1994) *Social Auditing at The Body Shop - A Conceptual and Methodological Framework* The Body Shop International, Littlehampton.

30 The Body Shop International (1993) *The Body Shop Annual Report and Accounts* The Body Shop International, Littlehampton.

31 A Roddick (1991) *Body and Soul* London, Ebury Press.

32 For more detailed information, see The Body Shop International (1996) *Social Statement 1995.*

8

The Expert View: Ben & Jerry's Homemade, Inc, US

Alan Parker
(Corporate and Investor Affairs, Ben & Jerry's Homemade Inc)

Since 1988, Ben & Jerry's Homemade, Inc. has performed a Social Performance Assessment yearly and published it in the Company's Annual Report to shareholders. As far as we know, no other company has been at this task as long. Certainly, no publicly traded company in the US has done so.

There is a compelling case to be made for an honest, independent review of the 'social performance' of any organization, whether it is a business, a non-profit agency, or a governmental organization. The case becomes more compelling when an organization is closely identified by its stakeholders, as Ben & Jerry's is, with the principles of corporate social responsibility. While our social initiatives are not conceived for marketing purposes, it is certain that we have enjoyed tremendous goodwill in large part because of our public commitment – as conceived by our founders and consistently ratified by our board of directors – to the cause of social responsibility in commerce. This fact of our history is nothing more than a demonstration of the principle of 'doing well by doing good.'

Given this reservoir of goodwill, an impartial assessment of the impact and effectiveness of our social initiatives has two purposes. First, it results in a critical internal document which allows us to see what works, what does not work, and why. Second, given Ben & Jerry's position as a company committed to social responsibility, the standards by which people judge our performance is higher than those applied to companies that make no specific commitment to greater involvement in social issues. Consistent, forthright self-criticism, as expressed in our social reports, allows us to discuss an ideal of commerce's role in the social fabric without being sanctimonious in the light of our own shortcomings.

A BRIEF CORPORATE HISTORY

A bit of history. Ben Cohen and Jerry Greenfield were, as much as anyone can be, children of the 1960s. They met in junior high school. Coming of age as they did during the era of civil rights marches, Vietnam war protests, and the cultural experimentation of that time, they never saw themselves as being hard-driving businesspeople. After living both apart and together around the US in their early twenties, they decided to open a small business together – one that would be fun for them to operate and fun for their customers. After reviewing their options, they settled on the idea of an ice-cream shop. In 1978, they realized their goal and Ben & Jerry's was born. One of their criteria for a home for their business was that it be a college town. They felt at home with the cultural and political orientation – and the love for ice-cream – of college students. Ben & Jerry's first home was a renovated gasoline station in the downtown business district of Burlington, a city of 40,000 people and home to the University of Vermont.

Ben and Jerry undertook a social mission as soon as the company opened its doors. Highly informal at first, their community involvement centered on such things as showing free movies projected on the outside wall of their small ice-cream shop, festivals and ice-cream giveaways of all sorts, and, as Ben once said, a commitment to 'reducing the price of lemonade whenever the price of lemons went down.' The founders' public commitment – that business must assume a larger share of responsibility for addressing social and environmental problems – grew out of this simple community spirit and became a cornerstone of the company's relationship to its customers.

This history is important if you want to understand how Ben & Jerry's undertook social accounting as part of its business practice. As the business grew (the ice-cream they made was incredibly delicious and very popular), the founders came face to face with the realities of running a real enterprise. It was no longer a hobby, no longer a diversion. They were managing significant amounts of money. They had employees who counted on them. Distribution was a problem they had never even thought of. Their customers, though appreciative of their products and the fun atmosphere in their shop, demanded quality, consistency, innovation, and a continuing commitment on the part of the founders to the light-hearted, community-minded atmosphere that they had come to expect. In the counter-culture of the time, business was, if not the root of all social disruption, at least a place for gentle-spirited political radicals to avoid. Confronted with the realization that they had become real business-people, in 1983 Ben and Jerry came very close to selling their business.

Rather than sell the company, however, they began to form a vision of how they might run their business differently by focusing as much on their positive role in their community as on making a profit. This focus led to the formal adoption by the Board, in 1987, of a three-part mission statement which outlined the company's mission as being equally committed to product quality, financial success, and social innovation.

The mission statement is as follows:

> *Ben & Jerry's is dedicated to the creation and demonstration of a new corporate concept of linked prosperity. Our mission consists of three interrelated parts:*

Figure 8.1: *Ben and Jerry's Homemade, Inc, Mission Statement*

- **Product Mission:** *To make, distribute and sell the finest quality all-natural ice cream and related products in a wide variety of innovative flavours made from vermont dairy products.*
- **Social Mission:** *To operate the company in a way that actively recognizes the central role that business plays in the structure of society by initiating innovative ways to improve*

> the quality of life of a broad community: local, national and international.
> • **Economic Mission:** *To operate the company on a sound financial basis of profitable growth, increasing value for our shareholders and creating career opportunities and financial rewards for our employees.*
>
> Underlying the mission of Ben & Jerry's is the determination to seek new and creative ways of addressing all three parts, while holding a deep respect for individuals, inside and outside the company, and for the communities of which they are a part.

Once this mission statement was in place, we quickly realized the necessity of finding a way to measure our performance against the social mission component of this statement. We already had measurements of performance – albeit imperfect ones – against the product and financial missions.

LOOKING FOR MEASUREMENT MODELS

What we lacked was a model on how to proceed with measuring of our social performance. We had seen some research done by universities that attempted to create equations of a sort to quantify the financial or social impact of socially driven decisions. These models seemed hopelessly complex and, finally, arbitrary. The board and management of the company felt that the social mission was fundamentally about innovation and experimentation, while part of the social mission was to create a safe, dignified, environmentally responsible, and appropriately rewarding workplace. The mission further challenged us to find ways to do business differently, to reach into the community and find brand new ways of creating partnerships with stakeholders – suppliers, community members, franchisees, distributors, shareholders, and customers who, in a more traditional business structure, would either be transactional partners or would have no relationship with Ben & Jerry's at all. If this type of initiative was the real challenge of the social mission – beyond fair wages, safe workplace, environmental responsibility, etc – then measuring social performance should account for experiments that might not succeed. Such accounts should appropriately 'celebrate failure' – not in and of itself, but for its suggestion of a willingness to challenge the limits of what business might do to 'improve the quality of life in a broad community'. For example, we once tried to find a source of peaches grown by African-American farmers.

In the winter of 1989, we did our first social performance report. Like all subsequent reports, it took roughly three months from the beginning of information-gathering to the final edited report. At that time, several organizations were emerging in the US that sought out and encouraged socially responsible investing and purchasing opportunities. Among the more widely known organizations of this type was the Council on Economic Priorities (CEP). CEP had published a booklet called *Shopping for a Better World*, which rated hundreds of companies for their practices in such areas as healthfulness of products, environmental compliance, animal testing, opportunities for women and minorities, defense contracting, and willingness to be evaluated.

We retained John Tepper Marlin of CEP to be our first social performance auditor, or assessor. (Our financial auditors objected to the use of the term 'auditor' for this new undertaking. Their concern was that the term 'auditor' implies the application of a standardized process, broadly understood and accepted in the business community, to the matter of reviewing and passing judgement on the quality of records. Their concern was based on their dedication to such a process in financial accounting and their correct belief that no such process exists – at least not yet – in social accounting.)

Our first report took what has come to be known as 'the stakeholder approach,' in which we evaluated our performance in terms of the effect of our actions on five stakeholder groups: communities, employees, customers, suppliers, and investors. Marlin interviewed people who represented these groups, and took volumes of notes. His interview subjects included employees, state regulatory officials, customers at scoop shops, dairy farmers who supply milk and cream, and franchisees. From his notes, and from discussions with him about the interviews he performed, the report was written by our own staff and submitted to Marlin for comment and editing. The report was printed in our Annual Report, accompanied by a letter from Marlin in the style of an auditor's opinion. His letter described his role in the process and attested only to the accuracy of the report's contents. As such, the judgements in the report, both positive and negative, were expressed as the judgements of the company, not of the reviewer.

This report focused on outcomes – on the impact of our actions – which, while not entirely inappropriate, did not serve to measure our performance against goals. This was essentially our responsibility, because we had not at the time developed specific goals for our social mission. Nonetheless, because we wrote the report using Mr Marlin's notes and conclusions, we were critiquing ourselves based not on internal goals, but on the reviewer's assessment of what was appropriate to expect from the company in the way of social performance.

For example, one of the most substantive criticisms aired in the report was that there were virtually no minorities employed by Ben & Jerry's at the time. Marlin saw this as an area of critical importance, one that, by a review of outcome, we had not adequately addressed. While we would agree that creating employment opportunities for minorities is an important responsibility of business, our situation at the time was that of an employer in a state with a very small (the smallest in the nation) minority population. We had not made any significant effort to recruit either managers or production and support staff outside our region. To quote the report, 'We are looking at ways to expand the pool of applicants to include more minorities, but we see our primary task as being to meet the employment needs of the region where we live and work.' It was natural that Marlin, accustomed to viewing corporate hiring practices on a national scale, would observe that minority hiring was an area where most companies needed to do better. Our key priority at the time, however, was simply to staff our company in response to our rapid growth. This was a hugely difficult task, even without making the admittedly desirable long-term commitment to recruiting minorities and attracting them to move to Vermont.

In our second year of social reporting, we wrote the report internally and retained an outside party to review the document and conduct interviews to verify the substance of our report. The outside party's role in the process was far less active than in our first year. This was the choice of the reviewer, William Norris, the founder and chairman emeritus of Control Data Corporation. Information-gathering was done by a volunteer committee of employees, rather than the reviewer. Employees interviewed customers, suppliers and regulatory officials and provided to the reviewer the names of those interviewed for follow-up and verification.

While the structure of the report remained similar to the first year's, it began to move toward an issue-based review of social performance. This approach seemed a natural outgrowth of the process, driven by staff rather than by an independent party. The report began to reflect the company's performance against what employees saw as the goals and the key initiatives of the company in the social mission arena. More data appeared in the report, including measurements of the percentage of waste material recycled and the percentage of supplier purchases made from what we deemed to be progressively oriented suppliers. With staff involved in the process of preparing the report, it became clear that, for the document to be of value as a springboard for improvement, we needed better record keeping in areas such as energy consumption and workplace safety.

In some ways, the employee-led fact-finding was more critical of performance than had been the reviewer-driven analysis of the previous year. For example, in planning the task of preparing the report, several employees pointed out that they felt Ben & Jerry's was too hard on its suppliers – that we did not make our expectations clear, that we changed our minds about what we needed and when, and that we demanded unreasonably short lead times. In posing questions on this subject to suppliers, as the report stated, 'we did not uncover such sentiment'. The report then added, 'To the extent that we see a shortcoming on our part in this area, we have an obligation to address it.' The committee felt that asking suppliers questions in this vein was no guarantee that they would answer honestly. It is relatively rare that a company invites its suppliers to point out its shortcomings, and suppliers may have felt uncomfortable offering such criticism. It may be that having company employees do interviews with suppliers on this sensitive subject was not the best way to elicit frank responses to such questions. Or it may be that our performance in this area was not so far out of the norm that our suppliers saw our requirements of them as unusual.

The inherent tension to be found in the role of an independent assessor began to emerge in the 1989 report. Since the report was employee-driven, it reflected internal priorities more than our first report did. At the same time, however, we felt that the assessor's role was too passive to be of great value. It is not an uncommon trait for people both to want and not want advice. This is the essence of the tension that an independent reviewer must balance. In designing and preparing the report, our staff people felt and expressed great pride in some of our accomplishments during the year, such as the development of an innovative supplier relationship with a source of sustainably harvested Brazil nuts from the Amazon rainforest; our early opposition to a controversial growth hormone being tested for use on dairy cows; and our growing ability to make financial contributions to charitable organizations. We felt it appropriate to celebrate these accomplishments in our report.

At the same time, as with the question about our relationships with suppliers, we felt that there was something not quite right about the way we managed these relationships. We couldn't put our finger on the problem, and we wanted some guidance from an impartial observer about what the norms are and what the world expects in such dealings. This uncertainty points up a larger question about the social responsibilities of business. Are these responsibilities defined by a consensus that exists in the wide world? Or, if no consensus exists, is it the task of a business to create its own definition of social responsibility and measure its performance on its own terms? Intellectually, one can say that the answer lies somewhere in the middle. Finding that point where internal and external expectations meet, however, is a difficult task.

In 1990, the independent review of our social performance report re-established an activist role for the outside reviewer. James E Heard, President of Institutional Shareholder Services, Inc., was given the task of independent reviewer. He assumed a vital role in the design of the information-gathering process and the report's structure. His commentary at the close of the report gave voice to his concerns about issues on which the company did not measure up. As Heard stated:

> There are... however, areas in which Ben & Jerry's performance falls short of what is expected of a leadership company. Nutritional labelling, parental leave policy, employment of minorities, energy consumption, and franchise relations are five such areas. Ben & Jerry's has yet to print nutritional information on the packaging of its original superpremium ice-cream; it has no paid parental leave policy; it has only one minority in a senior management position. Due to inadequate recordkeeping, the company is unable to report on energy conservation actions. Relations with franchisees have improved; even so, the company's communications with franchisees about the social mission have been uneven.

The report for 1990 was the most comprehensive review of our social performance we had undertaken. It established six key areas for assessment:

- *Products and marketing* – including nutrition and healthfulness and the integration of product development and marketing resources with social concerns;
- *Internal policies and operations* – including employee benefits; opportunity for women, minorities, gays and lesbians; workplace safety; and the company's first-ever comprehensive survey of employee attitudes;
- *Resource management* – including recycling, wastewater treatment, and energy consumption;
- *Relationships with suppliers and franchises*;
- *Philanthropy*;
- *Taking a stand* – including the company's active presence in debate

about social and political issues such as nuclear power, opposition to the Gulf War, legislation guaranteeing workplace rights for people who are HIV-positive, and other issues.

The central challenge issued by the 1990 social performance report was for the company, as Heard stated, 'to establish company-wide and departmental social performance goals.... The absence of goals has ... made it more difficult to measure and evaluate social performance.'

This was a difficult challenge for the company. It was also a challenge that needed to be met in areas of operation beyond the scope of the social mission. There was something almost whimsical about the very nature of the company and its products, and spontaneity had always been something close to a core value for Ben & Jerry's. This may be the essence of entrepreneurship – the feeling that, if a good idea comes to the surface it should happen regardless of the obstacles, that process and planning are subordinate to pouncing on great ideas as they come up. It would be hard to deny the power of this notion in any enterprise. Ben & Jerry's was a case in point, having succeeded beyond its founders' wildest dreams (and its critics' most dire predictions). The trick would be to foster this can-do, spontaneous spirit while committing the company to writing down its short- and long-term goals and sticking to them, even if doing so meant that some great new ideas might not find room to grow, or at least might have to wait their turn.

Milton Moskowitz, a noted author and commentator on business and workplace issues, took the task of social reporter in 1991. For the first time, Ben & Jerry's gave the job of writing the report to the reviewer himself. Moskowitz's information-gathering strategy was essentially the same as had been used in previous years. He interviewed employees, community members, shareholders, suppliers, state regulatory officials and senior managers and directors of the company. His report was wide-ranging, conversational and subjective. For example, he wrote, with regard to nutrition and health: 'Ben & Jerry's has not exactly covered itself in glory. It procrastinated for years about putting nutritional information on ice cream packs. It wasn't required to do so, so it didn't. [Such] labels are finally going on the pints in ...1992, just in time to conform with new food and drug administration regulations.' Further on, he noted that, 'One of the year's unmitigated flops was the "Save Family Farms" campaign.... The campaign was like a drive for motherhood; everyone's for it but what do you do about it?'

Moskowitz also noted, however, a visit made by seven Ben & Jerry's employees to northern Quebec to visit the native people whose culture and homeland is threatened by a huge hydroelectric development project. These employees came back from a week of living with the Cree Indians of the region, convinced that the hydro project is environmentally and socially inappropriate. They drafted a statement to that effect and the statement was placed as a full-page ad in Vermont's largest newspaper, thus adding their voice, on behalf of Ben & Jerry's, to a debate in Vermont about whether the state should enter into a power purchase contract with the project.

The report for 1991 noted that the company had added senior staff in the role of director of social mission development, regarding this as a positive step in moving the company toward strengthening the focus and priorities of the social mission. This staff addition was, it could be said, in part a response to previous criticisms that the company's social mission lacked goals. Still, as Moskowitz noted, 'The consensus on the 1991 social and political activity was that the company's efforts were too scattered.' In the area of environmental protection, he made note of progress and innovation and of the company's signing of the Valdez Principles as put forth by the Coalition for Environmentally Responsible Economies, but pointed out that the company had still 'not set rigorous reporting standards [for environmental programmes] and has therefore failed to generate the numbers needed to measure results.'

In 1992, we chose Paul Hawken to act as our independent social assessor. Hawken was retained in this role for the following two years as well, marking the first time we had used the same assessor in consecutive years. As in the previous year, the company gave responsibility to the assessor both for gathering information and actually writing the report. Hawken was a co-founder of Smith & Hawken, a company that marketed specialty gardening tools and an early leader in the growing corporate social responsibility movement. He has written several books on business and on corporate social responsibility. His assessor's report focused on five areas: employees, ecology, the customer, the community, and openness of the system.

Under Hawken's direction our social assessment moved toward some numerical quantification of performance in key issue areas, such as pay equity for men and women, workplace injuries and the percentage of stock owned by employees, which was found to be very low. His report also took a more aggressive approach to environmental assessment than had been taken previously. Citing the energy intensiveness of our manufacturing and distribution systems, the report challenged the company's decision to build a new plant in Vermont, given that ever-larger percentages of our products are being sold to distant markets. Hawken also expressed concern about construction of a manufacturing plant in the environmentally strained and sensitive area of the St Albans Bay on Lake Champlain. This was an issue that Ben & Jerry's board had debated on the basis of the company's longstanding commitment to using Vermont dairy products as our sole source. The report acknowledged the validity of this commitment, saying that: 'This commitment to local [dairy] production is at the heart of the company's concept of linked prosperity and social responsibility.' The report also pointed out measures the company had taken to improve energy efficiency and minimize waste in the new plant. The report concluded, however, that 'the scale and siting of the new...plant virtually ensures that for many years to come, the company will have a high embedded energy component to every pint of ice cream.'

In the 1993 and 1994 social performance assessments, still managed and written by Paul Hawken, increasing attention was paid to internal management issues as being the core of the social mission, as opposed to the political stances, alliances with non-profits, or innovative supplier relationships that have always been the most visible expression of Ben & Jerry's commitment to social responsibility. The areas most extensively critiqued in these most recent social performance reports were environmental performance, workplace safety, and employee morale. Hawken's perspective in these reports was that, while Ben & Jerry's has been tremendously innovative in making social activism part of its normal course of business, it has not been in the forefront in some areas more close to home – the nuts and bolts, if you will, of making an enterprise safe, rewarding to its staff, and one which addresses the environmental impacts of its normal course of business.

On balance, criticisms of the company's performance in these areas were relatively mild. What Hawken, and previous assessors as well, most often pointed out was that, while the company made many good-hearted efforts to improve performance in these areas over the years, and while the company was generally in compliance with laws and regulations, the management of the company had not demonstrated a commitment to leadership in these areas. Especially because Ben & Jerry's had always been perceived as a leader in corporate social responsibility (and in some important areas was so), its lack of leadership in these areas seemed particularly glaring.

The report for 1993 noted that the company had retained a firm to do a comprehensive environmental audit. This area of performance had been noted as needing attention in several previous social assessments, and the report in 1993 stated that: 'The company is to be complimented... for its commitment to a broad and thorough examination of the complex issues involving large-scale manufacturing and distribution of foodstuffs.' The audit was not completed in time for a summary of its results to be in the 1993 social performance report, but the scope of these audits was described and the baseline information about energy consumption, waste generation, and materials usage began to emerge as a yardstick by which to measure future improvements.

Workplace safety was highlighted as needing attention in both the 1992 and 1993 reports. The report for 1994 noted that: 'The company turned this situation around with impressive results. Statistics for 1994 show a dramatic improvement in key safety indicators..' In the seven years of social reporting at Ben & Jerry's, this is likely the best example of the report actively pointing out the company's need for improvement in a particular area and then acting on it. The issue of employee morale was perhaps the most difficult subject Ben & Jerry's has ever treated in its social performance report. It is an issue that points out clearly how social missions and business mission are ultimately inseparable. Morale problems are usually about uncertain leadership. This was certainly the case at Ben & Jerry's. We had grown fast and very successfully until 1993, when the heat of growth cooled for the first time. The growth of consumption of superpremium ice-cream slowed dramatically. The weak links in the company's organizational and operational structure became evident. The company did not see its future as clearly as it perhaps once had. Staff people at many levels of the company, who had signed on to the wild, exciting ride of Ben & Jerry's, felt themselves misdirected, undirected, and generally unsuccessful in their work. The company's long-term ability to meet all parts of its mission was truly challenged, in a way it never had been before.

The growing awareness and treatment of this issue was closely related to the social reporting process. While the leadership issues raised would surely have, in some part, been resolved without benefit of the report, the formal discussion of the issue – for public view in the Annual Report – was quite extraordinary. It indicated more clearly than anything previously covered in the report how serious the company is about self-examination and criticism. While not a solution in itself, the acknowledgement of how critical sound leadership is to the company's social mission was essential to protecting that mission's integrity.

The report for 1994 also discussed Ben & Jerry's marketing of Rainforest Crunch ice-cream, and the connection of this product with fair trade issues. In essence, the report's discussion was about 'whether representations made on Ben & Jerry's Rainforest Crunch ice-cream package give an accurate impression to the customer' about how the nuts in the product were harvested. The larger question about the impact of this and similar sourcing arrangements on the people and ecology of the Amazon rainforest led to a recommendation in the social performance report that 'the company should employ a consultant from the Fairtrade Foundation to review purchasing and labeling practices to bring its procurement policies into alignment with broader agreements that exist worldwide on how properly to interact with indigenous organizations.'

This issue continues to be debated in the media, and Ben & Jerry's has been criticized for being involved in the kind of sourcing relationship about which this debate exists. We stand by our achievement of our original goal for the project, which was simply to be part of an effort to increase demand for sustainably harvested rainforest products. There is, admittedly, a lot that businesses, including ours, must learn about how to develop successful, equitable trading relationships with native peoples.

Each social performance report that Ben & Jerry's has performed has shone a light on both successes and failures. The purpose here is not to describe the fullness of each report, only to demonstrate the kind of issues that have surfaced in our attempts to assess ourselves. We cannot say at this point that we have a defined process for undertaking such a report, nor have we in all reports assessed performance on a standardized, comprehensive list of subjects. But over the course of all the years we have done this report, we have addressed most of the issues that a consensus on the social issues of commerce would dictate need to be discussed. The process has been ragged at times and sometimes quite uncomfortable, like cleaning out a messy garage. But it has addressed, at one point or another, every issue from basic employee benefits, workplace safety, and environmental performance to experiments in sourcing and franchising designed to address social needs in the context of commerce.

Reactions to our efforts at social reporting have been varied. Those who view the efforts of businesses such as Ben & Jerry's to redefine the social role of business as being nothing more than elaborate marketing ploys tend to see our social report in the same light. The *New Republic*, in its 11 September 1995 issue, says, 'Like Ben & Jerry's, many of the socially responsible businesses publish their own social audits, in which they publicly flagellate themselves over minor failings.' Whether or not a full airing of the issues around rainforest sourcing or leadership and morale problems within the company is a discussion of a 'minor failing' is open to debate. On the other hand, in a recent phone conversation with us, David Olive of the Toronto *Globe & Mail* cited our social performance reports as being extraordinary in their openness and unparalleled in anything he had ever seen from a business about its social performance. The United States Trust Corporation, a socially responsive investment firm, stated in the August 1995 edition of its newsletter *Values*: 'Ben & Jerry's, which publishes unedited conclusions of its independent social auditor, remains the "gold standard" in open, self-critical evaluation'.

On balance, addressing such issues in a public way has served us well. It is far better to acknowledge a shortcoming than to try to explain it away after being discovered trying to hide it. This is a lesson most of our parents taught us young children and it makes sense that the same counsel would be wise for a business. More important than the protection of our reputation, however, is that the process requires us to sit down and ask ourselves what works and what doesn't. In the arenas of finance and product quality, such processes are regarded as essential to success. Social reporting is as legitimate a reality check on our social vision as a financial statement is a check on our financial goals.

The test of the value of social reporting is whether it affects an organization's social performance. By this measure, we call our experience successful. It is likely that no reporting system – financial or social – could claim to be the only source of decision-making and change, but it is also true that there is no substitute for stating an issue or a problem in clear, black-and-white language to focus one's attention on it. Once one has shone a light on a problem, there is a better sense of its dimensions. And if we train a light on such problems in public, then we make an implicit contract with all who see them to work toward their resolution.

Critical issues that have arisen in our social reports over the years have generally been addressed, though not always with complete success. These include workplace issues such as job safety, formal parental leave policy, leadership and internal organizational problems, and employee ownership. While no one at Ben & Jerry's would argue that we have entirely solved all of these problems, the full discussion of them in our social reports has brought attention to them and helped to put them on the agenda. Our efforts at alternative, or fair trade, sourcing have received greater, more analytical attention in light of their shortcomings being noted in our social report. We are measuring our critical environmental indicators far better than we first did, and we are setting improvement goals with the knowledge that we can assess whether we have met them.

The social performance report we publish is only a part of the process by which we examine our successes and failures, but because we commit to doing it and disclosing its results, we – and all who know us – are reminded not just of what still needs work, but also that our social mission is not, as some allege, about marketing; it is about trying to figure out what is right. And this is not easy. What society expects from our commerce varies from one person or institution to the next. Most thoughtful people can agree that safety and fair treatment of workers are requisites of socially responsible business. Most will also agree that businesses should clean up after themselves. It seems likely that, as social accounting grows, we will discover standard ways of reporting on the performance of businesses in these areas. The CERES Principles, as the Valdez Principles have come to be known, offer a serviceable early model of how to measure environmental performance. Many large corporations have now signed onto these principles and by doing so have committed to opening their environmental performance to measurement by a widely acknowledged standard. Compliance with labor, safety and environmental laws is relatively easy to measure. Philanthropic giving can be counted.

Still, questions abound. For example, what does fair treatment of workers really mean? Are layoffs fair? And if they are not fair, can anyone really expect such fairness? Is there a difference between, on the one hand, two large, profitable banks merging and eliminating thousands of jobs and, on the other hand, a manufacturing business laying off workers in response to slow sales? Debate about commerce now often focuses on environmental and economic sustainability. There are easy examples of unsustainable economic activity, but few widely agreed-upon models of sustainable activity and what it requires of both producers and consumers. If a company sources a product that adversely affects people or the environment, will its customers support a more expensive way of sourcing? If they won't, should the company stop making the product?

These are the kinds of questions Ben & Jerry's and other companies have just begun to face, but they give a hint as to the range of issues which businesses will face in any honest effort to assess social performance. The array of such questions is dizzying. They come from within and from outside any company that undertakes social reporting. As such, the process of social accounting is confronted with questions for which there is no agreement on the answers. At Ben & Jerry's, these puzzling questions have coloured our efforts to develop a standard method of social reporting. Part of the reason we have yet to develop a protocol for doing so is that we have used different reviewers, or assessors, and given them leave to design the reports as they deem appropriate. We have sought new advice and perspectives by engaging different people to manage the task. As we gave over the actual task of writing the report in the past four years, the final product has become longer and more narrative in style. In some ways, this has made the report more difficult to digest, and less standard from one year to the next, but it has also resulted in treating complex issues in a more complete way.

At the time of writing, beginning our eighth social report, we have contracted the New Economics Foundation to serve as our social auditor. A body of work in social auditing, led largely by NEF's efforts, has grown around making social reporting more standardized, disciplined and thus verifiable. We do need to bring more of these qualities to our social reporting. We cannot measure trends without looking regularly at the same indicators of our performance. We cannot draw conclusions about the quality of our relationships with various stakeholders without asking them, in a careful and comprehensive manner, for their own conclusions. The company is understandably less eager to make changes based on stories and impressions than on consistently measured benchmarks. And we cannot build the credibility of our own reporting system, much less advance the idea of social reporting to the wider world, unless we can demonstrate how we obtained our information. If people inside or outside the company are to trust our social reports' conclusions, they must be able to pick up the thread of our own investigations of issues and arrive at essentially the same conclusions that our reports set forth.

In past reports, we have asked someone to come into our company and essentially judge our performance. We have been fortunate to have wise, thoughtful people do this task, and we have gained insight into the wide range of issues that constitute corporate social responsibility. The cumulative effect of our work in this area, as well as the work of other businesses and interested people, is that we have a better sense than we had eight years ago of what needs to be measured. Now, rather than hire a judge of our social performance, we have hired a guardian of a process – a process that is designed to gather information and present it in a more or less standardized fashion. The conclusions that we and others draw from this information may still differ, for there is as yet no consensus on what the social responsibilities of commerce really are. But that's okay. In social accounting, just as with financial accounting, the first task is to develop a common language. We then have reason to hope that a common understanding will follow.

This process is ultimately about discussing the moral issues of commerce. That sounds lofty, but it is just the natural growth of a discussion that has been going on for a long time. Many companies are now asking hard questions on the subject from within the mainstream of business. Perhaps an ancillary benefit of our efforts at social reporting, beyond what we have said and learned about our own enterprise, is that we have been part of making it more common to ask the questions and, by doing so, helping to redefine what the community expects commerce to contribute to the well-being of society.

No one will find the answers without asking the questions. As to the matter of which are the right questions, one of our senior managers, when asked about how to do this job – where to start – offered the advice given to her once by a strawberry farmer when asked where to start picking: 'Just put your bucket down and start where you are.' We took that advice in social accounting. We are still picking, and we are in the good company of others doing the same.

9

Co-ordinating Expectations: Municipality of Aarhus, Denmark

Carl-Johan Skovsgaard
(Sector Manager, Municipality of Aarhus)
and
Tom Christensen
(Chief Consultant, EKL Consult)

Providing care and assistance to senior citizens is very much a municipal responsibility in Denmark, but several municipalities have started asking private companies to submit tenders for service tasks. At present, increased social attention is directed to the quality of services offered by the public sector in return for the payment of taxes. Thus, many Danish municipalities are beginning to focus on the requirements of users and on their evaluation of the level of service they receive.

Since 1993 Ethical Accounting has been used to improve the quality of services received by senior citizens in the municipality of Aarhus, the municipality with the second-largest number of inhabitants in Denmark. Using the Ethical Accounting method has involved new thinking. Instead of making decisions and acting on other people's behalf based on experts' professional knowledge and ideas, a dialogue culture develops where stakeholders ask themselves what is important to them in their interactions with the service provider, whether their expectations are fulfilled, and how they think things can be improved. When Ethical Accounting is used in senior citizen service, the relationship between users, services and staff is in focus. Therefore, the method can be used, no matter if the service provider is public or private.

In the municipality of Aarhus, Ethical Accounting was first used at two decentralized local centres servicing senior citizens. Experience from these two centres is now being used to develop the method, so that it can be applied with optimum results in other parts of the senior citizen sector where there is growing interest in using Ethical Accounting for quality development.

THE SENIOR CITIZEN SECTOR IN THE MUNICIPALITY OF AARHUS

The municipality of Aarhus has 275,000 inhabitants and 32,000 of these receive services from the Senior Citizen Department. In Denmark, services to senior citizens are organized within a legal framework established by parliament. The state pays old age pensions to all persons above the age of 67. The counties take care of hospital services, special institutions for handicapped persons and public health insurance payments. The municipalities take care of nursing, help and technical aids for senior citizens in their private homes, the provision of nursing homes, sheltered homes and pensioners' flats, as well as health services and care, social activities and meals-on-wheels.

In the municipality of Aarhus the Social and Health Services Department is divided into the Children and Young People Department, the Department of Family and Labour Market Affairs and the Senior Citizen Department. The clients of the Senior Citizen Department are defined as all inhabitants in the municipality above 67 years of age, and the total number of employees in the department is 5200, including a central staff organization and local centres.

In the municipality there are 37 local centres servicing senior citizens; therefore, all senior citizens have a centre near their homes. The local centre serves partly as an open recreational centre to the senior citizens in the local area. On the premises of all local centres there are activity rooms and meeting facilities which the users can administer themselves. The local centres also offer a number of housing options for those local-area citizens who cannot cope in their own homes. In addition, the centres provide a variety of on-site services: the nursing and home-help staff of the area work at the local centre; activity staff and therapists offer help for a healthy body and mind; and other staff offer advice and guidance on issues such as pensions, housing benefits, meals-on-wheels and aids to daily living.

Finally, the local centre is the place where users can have direct influence on local-area policies for senior citizens. This is possible through the user councils that are elected at all local centres every second year. Any person who lives in the local area and receives old-age or anticipatory pension, or voluntary early retirement pay, may stand for election and has the right to vote. The user council can take initiatives on any matter it considers to be of importance for senior citizens. At the local centre the council participates in the operational planning, is responsible for some of the centre activities and has a say in the recruitment of staff. The management of the local centre is responsible for all local staff, ie nursing, home help, activity and guidance staff, for their activities and service delivery, and for the economy of the centre.

The Senior Citizen Department has a central staff organization employing less than 100 people, which is the link between the city council, the Social and Health Services Department and the local centres. The central staff organization is responsible for planning, development and the overall economy of the Senior Citizen Department.

USING ETHICAL ACCOUNTING IN THE SENIOR CITIZEN SECTOR

In 1993, the Senior Citizen Department in the municipality of Aarhus decided to launch a major quality development project. Initially, two local centres were selected as test centres for the Ethical Learning Process as part of the larger project. Ethical Accounting Statements would be made for each of the centres and the results would be followed up in dialogue circles in order to prepare an Ethical Budget. After evaluating the process, it would be decided whether the Ethical Learning Process would be used at other local centres.

The Ethical Learning Process was chosen as a method for quality development in the senior citizen area in the municipality of Aarhus because the management felt that the traditional quality development methods did not sufficiently focus on users. In the social service area, quality depends heavily on the interaction between users and employees instead of on tangible product characteristics. Therefore, the fulfilment of underlying values and expectations as to the service and the people involved in providing it become more relevant than firm quality targets. The sector manager had already worked with the Ethical Learning Process in a former job as a consultant, and he knew that this method can clarify values and expectations and measure their fulfilment.

When using the Ethical Learning Process for quality development in the municipality of Aarhus, *quality is understood as living up to values/standards formulated in a dialogue between users and staff, taking into account the consumption of resources.* The Ethical Learning Process is based on interactions between the groups of people who influence and who are influenced by the quality of services. The aim is to create a better accord between services offered and the expectations of the users of those services.

The Senior Citizen Department decided to involve Tom Christensen, leading consultant at EKL Consult in Aalborg. Tom Christensen has extensive experience in using Ethical Accounting as the basis for Learning Processes in Danish private and public enterprises. Concurrently with his work for the Senior Citizen Department, the external consultant is training two project consultants employed by the municipality of Aarhus. After three years, they should be able to implement the Ethical Learning Process on their own.

CLARIFYING EXPECTATIONS AND VALUES

It is necessary to know the opinion of various stakeholder groups when focusing on the quality of a local centre which services senior citizens. Relevant groups may be users, potential users, relatives of users, staff members, hospitals, tax payers and the central organization of the Senior Citizen Department.

For this pilot study, two important groups affecting, and affected by, the quality at the local centres were chosen as the most important stakeholders: users of personal services and staff. Carrying through the pilot study with two stakeholder groups was a clear and easy task with regard to time consumption and costs. In later Ethical Learning Processes, the number of stakeholder groups may be extended.

Several meetings at the two local centres were held to provide information about the quality development project and the method to be used. User councils, liaison committees and management at the two local centres were given an especially thorough introduction to the method before they agreed to join the project.

In February/March 1994 randomly picked users and staff members were invited as representatives of the stakeholder groups to so-called 'value group meetings' at each of the two participating centres. These meetings clarified the expectations of the representatives. They were asked to express what was necessary to make them feel satisfied and to define what good quality meant in relation to each local centre. These value-based expectations created a basis for formulating relevant questions about quality that were later posed to all users and staff members at each centre.

Participation by physically and/or psychologically weak users in the value group meetings presented a problem, however. Some had difficulties, due to illness or age, in expressing what they expected from a good local centre. It may, therefore, prove better to clarify the expectations of weak users by means of personal interviews in their own homes, where relatives might be present.

All people have their own ideas about what constitutes good quality. Thus, one senior citizen's expectations of services provided in the senior-citizen service area range from the importance of a friendly reception by staff to the quality of the food brought out to his home. Another elderly person might emphasize the importance of involving users in tasks at the centre, while a third person might stress the importance of getting the required home help. Many expectations of good quality were introduced at the value group meetings. Expectations in the same area were then grouped under a so-called value by the meeting facilitator.

Users' values at the two local centres are:

- friendliness and warmth;
- peace of mind;
- dignity;
- good communication;
- good quality of services;
- good organization and planning of work;
- good physical surroundings.

Staff values are:

- job satisfaction and well-being;
- good cooperation;
- good communication/information and dialogue;
- good quality of services;
- good organization and planning of work;
- personal and professional development;
- good work norms;
- good physical surroundings.

FROM EXPECTATIONS TO QUESTIONNAIRE

When the facilitator had listed the values, he rephrased the matching expectations – grouped under each value – into a series of statements. A questionnaire was then developed for each stakeholder group at each centre. Representatives of the various stakeholders received the questions for review and criticism. This was done to ensure that everything raised in the value groups conveyed the meaning intended. At the same time, the representatives could add more expectations, if they thought of something not covered by the questionnaire.

Since the issue was: what should we expect from a good local centre, the questions were phrased as positive statements to which the respondents would indicate their degree of agreement.

Examples of Statements Illustrating a Value: Friendliness and Warmth

Users at the Næshøj local centre noted:

- The staff members are always friendly.
- We experienced friendliness and warmth the first time we were in contact with the staff at Næshøj.
- When we came to the centre, we received a cordial welcome.
- The staff members are almost always happy.
- The staff meets us with a co-operative attitude.

Good Work Organization and Planning

Users at the Næshøj local centre observed:

- The staff members plan their work well.
- The telephone service at Næshøj is good.
- The staff always keep appointments.
- The staff are good at involving volunteers.
- The staff are open to new ideas.
- The management of the local centre is appropriately visible.

Good Communication/Information and Dialogue

Staff at the Næshøj local centre stated:

- You get the information required in your work situation.
- You know the users' expectations.
- You get good information about what is happening at Næshøj so that you can see the centre as a whole.
- Your immediate leader is good at keeping you informed.

- Your immediate leader is open and attentive to your ideas.
- There is a good dialogue with the management.
- Your colleagues are good at keeping up-to-date on the work situation.

An additional value group meeting was held with each group in which the participants discussed the values and expectations from the first meeting. This caused problems. There was disagreement about the definition of values made by the facilitator. In some cases, the representatives had difficulty in recognizing their own statements from the questionnaires. One of the reasons for this was the positive formulation of the questions. Furthermore the consultant had added some questions taken from the corresponding group at the other local centre in order to be able to compare the investigations. This was rejected by the participants.

The result was that each group got its own questionnaire, formulated on the basis of its own expectations. Service provider organizations are different, and so are humans. However, a certain comparability was achieved by identical phrasing of questions dealing with the same expectation. Furthermore, the values were identical in both groups of users and both groups of staff members.

In the future the values will be phrased at the value group meetings and all participants will be encouraged to participate in the conversion of expectations into questions at the meeting itself. It is also important to stress that Ethical Accounting is context-dependent and should reflect the service provider in question, even though this may limit the possibility of making comparisons between providers.

GATHERING INFORMATION

All 194 users and the 47 staff members at the Næshøj local centre received the questionnaires developed by the stakeholder representatives together with the facilitator. Similarly, questionnaires developed by the stakeholder representatives at the Vestervang local centre were sent to all the 515 users of Vestervang and the 96 staff.

The questionnaires were distributed in April 1994. Background information about the respondents was also obtained from the questionnaires. In the case of the users, this information included such matters as sex, age and use of the various services. The information was collected in order to target quality improvements for the subgroup(s) which might turn out to be dissatisfied with the fulfillment of their expectations. At the same time, there was also space on the questionnaire for the respondents to supply extra comments.

Users were offered the assistance of an independent person not connected with the local centre if they wanted assistance in answering the questionnaire. This gave weak users a better chance of participating.

Some users and staff did not approve of the positive wording of the statements and thought that they were manipulative. In the future, questions may be presented in a more neutral way.

RESULTS AND INTERPRETATION

In order to encourage users and staff to answer the questionnaire, the poll was talked about regularly at the centre. Staff also mentioned the poll in connection with home nursing visits and home help. Finally, reminders were sent out to everyone who had received a questionnaire.

The questionnaires were sent from, and returned to, the central Senior Citizen Department. This was done so that respondents would not refrain from answering due to the fear of being identified. At Næshøj, there was a 72 per cent response from users and 81 percent from staff. At Vestervang 52 per cent of users and 70 per cent of staff completed the questionnaire.

Even though the poll gives some clear indications about what is working well and what can be improved at the two local centres, a 52 percentage response is low. It was therefore necessary to be careful when interpreting the results. Also, the interpretation was hindered by a high degree of 'no knowledge' answers to many of the questions asked. The large number of 'no knowledge' answers is probably due to the fact that the users are a hetero-genous group; some of them are fit and well and only attend activities at the centre. These users could not judge the quality of home help. Others, for example, receive home nursing visits and do not attend the centre. They could therefore not answer questions about the centre.

It is our experience that one must look at the relevant subgroups in relation to expectations when assessing whether or not an expectation has been met satisfactorily or unsatisfactorily. Another alternative might be to divide the stakeholder groups into larger subgroups, hold separate value group meetings with the subgroups and use a questionnaire adjusted to suit the individual group. More general questions about service and performance could still be included, in order to provide an overall view.

REPORTING BACK

When reporting back on the investigation, the results were presented in the Ethical Accounting Statement as a number of signals concerning what worked well at the local centres and what could be improved upon in terms of quality. The drawing of firm conclusions about what was good and what was bad was avoided. Similarly, no comments were made on the possible reasons for positive or negative results.

In order to ensure impartiality, the consultant was given the task of analyzing the statistical material and reporting back. The results were made public, since the assessment of quality, its causes and possible solutions to apparent problem areas was to occur in interactions between stakeholder groups taking part in the investigation and the leadership of the local centres via so-called 'dialogue circles'. Using the Ethical Accounting Method, interpre-tations and solutions are matters for the parties involved.

It took time to collate the statistical material into interpretations without making them appear as definitive truths. Later, however, doubt was expressed about the interpretations. It is questionable, therefore, to what extent statistical material ought to be collated. In general, though, a certain degree of collation is necessary, since some readers find it difficult to relate to tables, diagrams and the like. To ensure the greatest possible degree of objectivity, the interpretation must be carried out by someone outside the service provider in question.

Table 9.1: *Ethical Accounting at the Naeshøj Local Centre – user satisfaction*

Value	Agree on fulfillment	Disagree on fulfillment	No knowledge
Friendliness and warmth	73 %	10 %	17 %
Peace of mind	58 %	8 %	34 %
Dignity	57 %	12 %	31 %
Good communication	54 %	16 %	30 %
Good quality of services	71 %	19 %	10 %
Good organization and planning of work	39 %	14 %	48 %
Good physical surroundings	39 %	10 %	52 %

Table 9.2: *User satisfaction with the value 'Friendliness and warmth' – Naeshøj Local Centre*

Expectation	Agree	Disagree	No knowledge
Staff members are always friendly.	75 %	11 %	14 %
We experienced friendliness and warmth the first time we were in contact with the staff at Næshøj.	74 %	14 %	12 %
When we come to the centre, we receive a cordial welcome.	72 %	7 %	21 %
Staff members are almost always happy.	71 %	9 %	21 %
The staff meet you with a co-operative attitude.	75 %	9 %	17 %

DIALOGUE CIRCLES – ON THE WAY TO AN ETHICAL BUDGET

When the Ethical Accounting Statements for the two local centres had been drawn up, work on the Ethical Learning Process was increasingly delegated to the local centres themselves so that they could control the further work through dialogue circles and Ethical Budgets. Each of the centres set up its own steering group, including representatives of the User Council.

In the autumn of 1994, dialogue circles were set up at the centres to prepare proposals for improvements. The work topics for the dialogue circles were determined at a meeting with the users of each centre. Together with the staff and management, 70 users at Næshøj and 80 users at Vestervang decided on the topics for their own local centre. The topics to be considered in the dialogue circles were chosen after discussing the results of the centre's Ethical Accounting Statement – in particular, those values and expectations where it was felt that the level of satisfaction should be higher.

At Næshøj, the result of the meeting was the establishment of a dialogue circle for the topics: regard for the weak users, communication and information; peace of mind and friendliness and warmth. Dialogue circles were also established at Vestervang to work on the topics 'weak users' and 'co-operation between users and staff'. To keep the process going, the local centres may take up other topics and work on them, even though they were not at first chosen as topics for the dialogue circles.

EXAMPLES OF PROPOSALS FROM THE DIALOGUE CIRCLE AT NÆSHØJ

Information and communication

* Develop a monthly newsletter for users of the centre and users of home help.
* Improved signposting – including suggestions as to where and how.
* Telephone calls must always be answered at the centre.
* Users and staff should attend a proposed course where they learn to listen openly and honestly.

Each dialogue circle at the centres consisted of representatives of users and of staff. This was meant to ensure agreement on proposals for improvements, which of course affect both groups. It is our experience that the management should assist in the choice of users and staff, so that they are equally represented in the dialogue circles. Moreover, the dialogue circles are a good tool for attuning the expectations of different stakeholder groups to each other and in this way preventing conflicts. When problem areas are identified and solutions are found in common, the stakeholder representatives reach an insight into the conditions and views of the other stakeholder groups.

Whether the management should participate in the dialogue circles must be considered: the quality of services is very much determined by the interaction between users and staff. At Vestervang, the centre manager decided to participate when she judged there was a need for it. Experience dictates that whether the manager should participate depends on the topic. But the manager should, perhaps, be called in by the dialogue circle according to need.

The future may call for the greater use of consultant support to determine how dialogue circles should operate. This is partly because the consultant is impartial and partly because, at times, it is difficult for local centres to operate dialogue circles independently whilst looking after the day-to-day tasks. The impartiality of the consultant is also an advantage if the dialogue circle has problems in reaching agreement or if some of the members try to dominate.

ETHICAL BUDGETS

The work of the dialogue circles was completed at the turn of the year 1994/95. Proposals were presented and discussed in the user council and at a meeting between the user council and the staff liaison committee. Finally, in order to prepare the Ethical Budgets, the managements of the local centres started to assess and prioritize proposals from the dialogue circles with due consideration to finances and to overall viewpoints, which may be considered important at the local center level. The Ethical Budget describes the values which the individual centre will promote in the coming year, and how and when this will happen.

The Ethical Budget at the Næshøj local centre presented most of the proposals for information and communication from the dialogue circle. The newsletter, for example, was published for the first time in February 1995 and in the autumn the centre arranged a day of talks on how to become better at listening to others. The major part of the suggestions from the dialogue circles to which Næshøj local centre committed itself did not imply extra costs but could be kept inside existing financial limits. It was relatively inexpensive to implement the suggestions; the money had already been earmarked for changes in the areas concerned – all the local centre needed were good suggestions for solutions.

Examples of suggestions from the dialogue circles which were not included in the Ethical Budget were those concerning 'regard for the weak users'. The dialogue circle wanted time to be found for excursions for the weak users, escorted by staff members. Another suggestion was that each weak user should have an extra hour each week, together with a member of staff, to do things which it would otherwise be difficult to find time to do, such as buying new clothes for the user. The dialogue circle also suggested that the staff should create more time for these activities by leaving other tasks undone or by giving them lower priority. The management at the Næshøj local centre rejected the suggestions for more activities, together with the staff, because the staff have to follow a list of priorities decided by the municipality of Aarhus. This list states that, first of all, the staff must carry out nursing and welfare tasks for the weakest users; available time, if any, is to be distributed among the users with the greatest need.

In this area. therefore, there was a conflict between user expectations and the rules that were made to allocate staff resources in the best way. Nevertheless, a solution to the problem was found because the dialogue circle had also suggested that the strong users should, to a greater extent, help arranging excursions for the weak users. This suggestion was extended to make the strong users help the weak users in other areas. After that, an investigation was made of the need for help and the way the help was to be organized. There were also some proposals from the dialogue circles at Næshøj which the local centre management was unable to act upon, since the proposals required changes in regulations and legislation. But the central organization of the Senior Citizen Department can still follow up on these proposals.

At the end of 1995, almost a year after the Ethical Budgets were presented and first initiatives were taken to promote specific values at the local centre level, the local centre manager at Næshøj summed up the results of the Ethical Learning Process. Although the process had not led to drastic changes at the centre, it had proved valuable in increasing mutual understanding and agreement between users and staff. For example, the stronger users gained a better understanding of what the staff already does to help the weaker users at the centre. And through the work in the dialogue circles, the users and staff realized that as many people as possible should feel satisfied with the services instead of only thinking of one's own wishes.

4. DET MENER BRUGERNE

Venlighed og varme

68% af brugerne på lokalcentret Vestervang oplever i gennemsnit venlighed og varme. Tilfredsheden er næsten lige stor på alle spørgsmål. 27% har besvaret spørgsmålene med intet kendskab.

Brugerne oplever et venligt personale, samt venlighed første gang de kom på Vestervang

Mest enige er brugerne i, at de ved første kontakt med personalet på Vestervang oplevede venlighed og varme. Tillige synes de, at personalet er venligt overfor brugerne.

Mindst enige er brugerne i, at brugerne er venlige over for hinanden.

De brugere, der ikke får hjemmehjælp eller hjemmesygepleje, er dog mere tilfredse end de, der modtager disse ydelser. Ligeledes er man mere tilfreds, jo hyppigere man kommer på lokalcentret.

Spørgsmål om varme og venlighed	enig %	uenig %	intet kend-skab %
Personalet er altid venligt over for dig	78	3	19
Du oplevede venlighed og varme første gang, du havde kontakt med personalet fra Vestervang	74	6	20
De øvrige brugere er venlige over for dig	60	2	39
Brugerne på centret bliver venligt modtaget af personalet	61	4	35
Personalet er næsten altid i godt humør	66	6	29
Der bliver altid vist imødekommenhed over for dig	69	6	25
Gennemsnit for spørgsmålene om varme og venlighed	68	5	27

Tryghed

51% af brugerne på lokalcentret Vestervang føler sig trygge. Tilfredsheden er lidt svingende fra spørgsmål til spørgsmål. 41% har besvaret spørgsmålene med intet kendskab.

Brugerne oplever et godt samarbejde med personalet, men de mener ikke, at der bliver taget nok hensyn til de svage brugere

Brugerne oplever, at de har et godt samarbejde med personalet, som de tør sige deres mening til.

Mindst tilfredse er brugerne med det hensyn, der bliver taget til de svage brugere.

Af baggrundsoplysningerne fremgår det, at jo ældre brugerne er, jo mere tilfredse er de med behandlingen af de svage brugere.

Figure 9.1: *The Municipality of Aarhus' Ethical Budgets*

REACTIONS TO THE ETHICAL LEARNING PROCESS

Management and staff at the two local centres wish they had known from the beginning how extensive and time-consuming work with the Ethical Learning Process would be. They wish they were better prepared to face the problems raised and how to tackle them. However, uncertainty is one of the conditions of undertaking pioneer work and the local centres were test sites for work with the Ethical Learning Process in the municipality of Aarhus. In the future, other local centres and institutions will have some experience to draw on, if they also choose to apply the Ethical Learning Process.

The experiment has, however, taken too long. It is important that progress be made continuously without too much time passing between the various tasks, so that management and others involved can see change in context, and so that interest does not fade. It is also important that the Ethical Learning Process should be allowed to stand on its own two feet and not disappear into other development tasks or projects.

As mentioned, the pilot study started in autumn 1993 by defining expectations and values in the stakeholder groups, and the first round in the Ethical Learning Process ended at the beginning of 1995 with the publication of Ethical Budgets for the two local centres. It is difficult to sum up exactly how many human and financial resources the process has required. At the beginning of the pilot study the external consultant estimated that the consultancy assistance would amount to 260 hours. To this must be added the time some staff members from the central staff organization in the Senior Citizen Department, and some staff members from the local centres, have spent on project group meetings, meetings in dialogue circles and practical tasks in connection with the implementation. Meetings in connection with the Ethical Learning Process are, however, constructive and point forward to the development of the organization. They may, therefore, reduce the need for meetings focusing on problems in the organization, whose fault the problems are, etc. In addition to consultancy assistance and meeting activity, there have been costs for information meetings for users and staff, for collection and processing of the data material and for printing of the Ethical Accounting Statements.

It is important to realize that commitment by the external stakeholder groups implies no major costs. When the organization shows an interest in the opinion of the stakeholders, and when the organization takes their opinions and suggestions seriously, many customers or users of a service are willing to make a considerable voluntary effort. After the pilot study, for instance, the 35 other local centres in the municipality of Aarhus expressed considerable interest in the Ethical Learning Process. In the course of 1995, the method was developed and implemented within the senior citizen area as an important component of the overall quality development programme. Just when the other local centres will begin to develop their own Ethical Accounting Statements and their own learning processes will be decided at the local level.

It is also important that both the local centres and other organizations and companies, who are interested in development through the Ethical Learning Process, take their own organization and their own stakeholder groups as a starting point. Values and expectations cannot be borrowed from others – it is necessary to find out exactly what they are in relation to the special stakeholder groups who characterize one´s own organization. Therefore, no general ethical rules can de deduced from the process at the two local centres, but, then, this was not the intention. However, the results may give food for thought and inspiration to others servicing senior citizens.

In time, some general experience may appear, however, when the Ethical Learning Process is spread to several organizations within a certain field of work. Such experience may well lead to ethical principles, rules or priorities which all the organizations can adopt as their own.

In addition to the development of Ethical Accounting Statements at the two local centres, the Senior Citizen Department has also organized a two-day seminar where an Ethical Accounting Statement was prepared. The central management and staff of the Senior Citizen Department and the leaders of the local centres, participated as stakeholder groups. The Ethical Learning Process has also been started at two other local centres. Here, the expectations and values of senile clients, other residents, relatives of senile clients, and staff of the centres are being examined. This project has required developing a method to understand the values and expectations of the senile clients, since value group meetings and questionnaires cannot be used in the ordinary way.

ETHICAL ACCOUNTING AND TOTAL QUALITY MANAGEMENT

It is clear that Ethical Accounting is relevant and suitable for improving the quality of services, whether the service provider is public or private. The Ethical Learning Process contributes to making otherwise intangible expectations and values measurable. These measurements provide a starting point for a dialogue between the people who influence the quality of service and those who have to live with it. It should, however, be noted that the process contributes to an ongoing dialogue which has no natural conclusion. People develop, and as this happens the life demands which they make also change. Their self-awareness and the ongoing dialogue contribute to the development of identity and responsibility – and also to new demands and expectations.

If Ethical Accounting and the Ethical Learning Process are taken as a starting point, the result will be new thinking in quality development. This new thinking considers what is important to different people. Values and expectations are discussed before the concrete contents, thereby putting quality development in a different perspective. If a discussion commences based on tangibles, the client may well get what has been decided for him – but his own values and expectations may not even come near to fulfillment.

When a company is working with Ethical Accounting, the management will try to run the company by values rather than by rules and power. The stakeholders know the value foundation because they have all influenced it. This also gives the stakeholders a better understanding of the management decisions in the Ethical Budget: what are the values and expectations the company should focus on.

When the value foundation has been established in relation to the different stakeholders, a definition is formed of measurable quality targets that are more concrete than the values and expectations. One expectation of service in the senior citizen sector could be that home helps arrive on time. In co-operation with the user, the relevant quality target can be defined in such a way that 'arrive on time' means arrival half an hour before or after the agreed time, since something unexpected can always happen at the homes of other users.

Ethical Accounting, therefore means measuring how well the service supplier lives up to the values and expectations of the stakeholders; *Ethical Budgets*, on the other hand, mean prioritizing which values and expectations the service supplier will live up to in the year to come. This entails establishing quality targets, quality measurements, quality reportin and adjusted action.

The Connection Between the Ethical Learning Process and Quality Management

Total quality management (TQM) is a management philosophy which can be described by the following elements:

- management involvement (leadership);
- focus on customers and staff;
- current improvements;
- focus on facts;
- total participation.

The TQM method can contain a lot of the elements of Ethical Accounting. But in some of the existing TQM versions the main contents are detailed control and development tools. The ethical aspect, however, is more related to philosophical company issues where the stakeholders contribute to developing the company through a dialogue. Therefore, it is worth considering the use of Ethical Accounting and the accompanying dialogue as the first step before the organization starts working with TQM and establishes the actual quality targets. Nevertheless, the dialogue and the Ethical Learning Process can be used concurrently and should not just be an introduction to quality development. Quality development is improved by the use of dialogue, since dialogue can be used both to find out what to improve and how to do it, as well as to find out how well the improvements succeed. Finally, dialogue can be used to do it even better next time.

FURTHER INFORMATION

Copies of the Aarhus Ethical Accounting Statements – only available in Danish – can be obtained from the municipality of Aarhus at:

Aarhus Kommune,
Aeldresektoren,
Telefontorvet 4,
DK–8000 Aarhus C,
Denmark.

10

Building Dialogue Culture:
Wøyen Mølle, Norway

Lise Nørgaard
(Consultant in Leadership and Organizational Development)

THE NECESSITY OF DIALOGUE

Many of today's challenges rise as huge as mountains. Our society seems to become more and more unpredictable and complex. No one has *the* answer to what is right and what is wrong. Morals have become a private matter. At the same time voices are heard from many directions, searching for 'closeness', 'core values', 'ethics' and 'solidarity'. It seems, therefore, necessary to pause for a moment to consider what is important and valuable to us. What are our needs and what expectations do we have of the organizations and communities of which we are part?

If we are to nurture what is valuable to us, we must find a decent way to talk about it. It seems more and more necessary to develop a dialogue culture with those who are, or will be, involved in our activities, decisions and behavior. It is very likely that there will be disagreement and maybe conflict, but the point is that we have to find ways and places to talk about such matters. And in the worst case: how can we live with disagreement in a decent way? The development of a *dialogue-culture* may be one way of responding to and challenging the disintegration of society today.

WHAT IS AN ETHICAL ACCOUNTING PROCESS AND AN ETHICAL ACCOUNTING STATEMENT?

In a Norwegian setting the Ethical Accounting Process has turned out to be a very constructive approach to developing and maintaining an ongoing conversation between an organization and its stakeholders. The main questions underlying this dialogue-culture are: 'What values do an organization's stakeholders want to see embodied in the organization, and how should these values be translated into practice?' and 'What activities and behavior should be promoted so that organizational practice is in reasonable harmony with stakeholder values?'

The Ethical Accounting Statement provides a temporary answer to the question: 'to what extent does the organization live up to its stakeholders value-based expectations?' In Latin 'accounting statement' means: 'to settle one's doings'. The Ethical Accounting Statement, therefore, provides a richer and broader picture of organizational activity than the economical picture permits. While an operating statement provides a perspective on organizational succes and failure based on the narrow vocabulary of money, an Ethical Accounting Statement provides a multifaceted depiction based on the values the organization shares with its stakeholders. 'Ethics' in this connection is to be understood as 'the obligations the organization faces if it is to live up to the shared values it has agreed to promote.'

WØYEN MØLLE – AND THE DIALOGUE ON SHARED VALUES

In August 1994 Wøyen Mølle published its first Ethical Accounting Statement, and so became the first organization in Norway to present such a statement. Our experience indicates that it is not the Statement itself that is important, but the *process* leading up to its publication and the ensuing dialogues.

Wøyen Mølle was established in 1975 and is beautifully situated 20 km west of Oslo, on the banks of a picturesque waterfall. The building is an old mill ('*mølle*') – therefore the name 'Wøyen Mølle'.

In the early 1970s the number of youths with alcohol, drug and social problems increased, and the municipal politicians in the county of Bærum decided to establish a job-training centre to meet at least *some* of the needs of these young people. Today, 20 years after it began its activities, Wøyen Mølle is developing into a competence-centre for those having special problems in finding and maintaining employment. Most of the participants who are connected to the programmes have had social problems for a long time; they have low self-esteem and many of them have not even completed their primary education.

Wøyen Mølle does not operate commercially. It is organized as part of the Social Services in the county of Bærum, with economic support from the Norwegian Department of Labour. The total budget of roughly US$3 million a year comes from public means. As of summer 1995, 24 people were employed at Wøyen Mølle, working on three different programmes with a total of roughly 150 participants.

The philosophy at Wøyen Mølle is that every person has qualities, competancies and possibilities which could be utilized in a more productive and satisfying manner. It is our duty to make the participants aware of their potential and to help them put it into practice. We believe that having a job in an ordinary workplace is important for developing a positive identity, pride, self-satisfaction and responsibility.

The programmes include:

- On-the-job training, which means that roughly 50 young people are employed by a firm or organization in the region for one year. Each participant in the on-the-job training programme also has an advisor from Wøyen Mølle whose most important task is to make him or her

concious about which choices and steps should be taken in order to best develop the way of living he or she realistically aspires to.
*   Faith, Hope and Charity, a kind of network-group for single women with children. These women not only receive support to help them success-fully tackle a part-time job. The network group also provides them with the possibility of sharing experiences and problems with other members of the network – eg the difficulties of single parenthood, how to tackle loneliness and alienation, discussing dreams.
*   Project Nygård: a programme for 15 long-term unemployed people who are presently restoring an old farm. When the renovation work is completed, the farm will be a place to visit for kindergartens and schools as well as the centre of many other cultural activities. All the future activities will also be led and carried out by long-term unemployed under the supervision of Wøyen Mølle. The participants in the programme receive support in improving both their professional and social qualifications.

Wøyen Mølle could not have offered these programmes if it had not been for the practical support provided by many private companies and public organiza-tions in the region. The management of these enterprises is seriously concerned with the negative consequences of the high rate of unemployment. These programmes give people a chance to show their concern and live up to their feelings of social responsibility by offering a job to a participant for one year.

At Wøyen Mølle we like to refer to ourselves as 'marriage-brokers of problems'. We have known people who want to get a job, but for years they have been standing at the rear of the unemployment line. We have the money, but we do not have the jobs our participants need. The employers have work to be done, but not the money to pay for the salaries. (Norway, like other Scandinavian welfare-countries, has a very high minimum wage, providing many social benefits and long vacations compared to many other western European countries.)

For 20 years now employers in the region have co-operated with Wøyen Mølle in order to give young, long-time unemployed people a chance to show that they have the guts and the capabilities which are needed on the labour market.

Since Wøyen Mølle was established in 1975, the organization has been concerned with developing and implementing educational and supportive methods which can provide the participants with the best possibilities for developing a better way of life. In this process we have often asked ourselves to what extent our conduct, methods and activities live up to the ethical standards we have adopted. Do we really do what we say we do?

During recent years Wøyen Mølle has conducted several 'inner talks with itself' – all employees have discussed which values and norms should constitute the identity of the organization. We have promoted an atmosphere conducive to both individual reflection and discussion in smaller groups and we have held seminars where all employees participated.

These inner talks resulted in the identification of five core values which should serve as guiding principles for every employee at Wøyen Mølle. These shared core values were presented in a small booklet with artistic metaphoric illustrations.

By 1994 the time had come to find out to what extent the organization's sayings and doings actually corresponded to the needs of its stakeholders. The Ethical Accounting Statement provided us with an intellectual framework and an operational approach to finding some of the answers to the existential question: is there harmony between words and deeds? At the same time there had been growing frustration, both at Wøyen Mølle and in other parts of the Social Services, because politicians and the regional administration only evaluated us according to our budgets and showed just a minimum of interest in how we managed to take care of the many fundamental needs of our stakeholders.

We wanted to be able to reflect upon and to evaluate ourselves according to a wider range of standards of success. Most of all, we wanted to find out if there were certain core values and norms that could be accepted by both the organization and its most important stakeholders. We asked ourselves the following question:

'What values in the interaction between the organization and its stakeholders are so important that we can hardly co-operate without them? What concrete practices and activities do the stakeholders expect in their interaction with us?' This also brought up some tensions within the organization:

- Would we be able to meet all the expectations we imagined would come from the stakeholders?
- Would the values of the stakeholders be in harmony with the core values of the organization? And what if they were not?
- Did we need a political acceptance of the whole project and, if we sought acceptance, could there be interference and delays we did not want?

The last question was solved by a meeting with the administrative leader of the county. He gave us his support and did not suggest that it was necessary to open a political discussion. Rather than starting a discussion regarding such touchy matters as citizen participation in the political administrative process, his advice was: 'Get started, keep me informed and save the possible political debate until later.' This support really eliminated some of the tension we felt in the begining.

As to the two first questions, this is what the Ethical Accounting Process is about. We must be able to see and to communicate that Wøyen Mølle is more than the sum of its parts – that the organization is nothing *in itself* alone, but is created and recreated in its ongoing dialogue and interaction with its stakeholders. In this connection we often used the following anecdote to emphasize that every one of us has a bigger purpose than just doing our job:

> One day a wanderer came up to a quarry where three quarrymen were working. It was obvious that they put very different effort into their work – and the wanderer became curious.

He went up to the least enthusiastic quarryman and asked him what he was working on. 'Well, I am just getting some stones out of this quarry', he said, and went on working without any enthusiasm. The wanderer moved on to question the second quarryman who seemed to put more energy into his work. 'Oh, I am just cutting a cornerstone,' he said. But the third and most enthusiastic quarryman straightened up, smiled and said proudly, 'I am building a cathedral.'

THE ETHICAL ACCOUNTING STATEMENT – FROM DENMARK TO NORWAY

My connection with Wøyen Mølle has really been from the inside. I have worked with the youth of our region from 1979 to 1993 – and I was co-manager at Wøyen Mølle from 1986 to 1990 and manager from 1990 to 1993. In September 1993 I received a two-year scholarship from the Ministry of Administration for a project on 'The importance of ethics and shared values in developing the culture of an organization'.

It was during the planning of my project that I got in contact with Sparekassen Nordjylland (Sbn Bank) in Denmark (see Chapter 5). The bank has developed the concept of Ethical Accounting together with Danish researchers at the Copenhagen Business School. They have been a great inspiration and help in starting the Ethical Accounting Process at Wøyen Mølle and elsewhere in Norway. Although we already had started the dialogue on ethics and shared values within our organization, we had not found a good method to structure and systematize our efforts. Neither had we found a way to involve our external stakeholders and to identify and respond to their value-based expectations. In other words, we lacked both a framework and an operational approach to value-based management.

Furthermore, although the leader at Wøyen Mølle was very interested in my study of the ethical accounting process in Denmark, there were many questions to be answered before a decision could be made to instigate the process at Wøyen Mølle. In retrospect, I am convinced that the most important party – both in planning and in implementing an Ethical Accounting Process – is the organization's top management. It takes quite a lot of courage and dedication to invite so many external stakeholders to participate in an ongoing dialogue about the values and obligations of the organization. Management must be willing and prepared to accept public feedback on how well the organization promotes stakeholder values and expectations.

My first task was therefore to discuss with the leader of Wøyen Mølle the underlying theory, the process and most of all the possible consequences of starting such a process. Some of the questions we dealt with include the following:

- What is the aim of such an Ethical Accounting Process?
- What might be as problematic?
- Is the organization too small – with only 24 employees?
- What will it cost – in time and money?
- Is there a need for motivating the employees?
- Who are the most important stakeholders?
- How can we make them understand what this is about?
- Will the organization be able to implement and maintain the dialogue culture?
- How can we balance the needs and claims of the different stakeholders?
- How can we insure the anonymity of the respondents?

- Would I, as a former leader of the organization, be able to maintain both the respect of the employees and my own integrity if I were to lead the project?
- What human resources will the organization have to put into the project, now – and in the future? And what qualifications are needed to be a leader of the process?

The energy and interest of Wøyen Mølle's leader was both personal and professional. The process could continue.

WHY PRODUCE AN ETHICAL ACCOUNTING STATEMENT?

I have already briefly mentioned some of our major considerations. However, before the organization actually dove into the process, the leader established a group who would pave the way. I was appointed to lead the group and the ensuing project.

These are the reasons why the group – and then the organization as a whole – decided to implement an Ethical Accounting Statement:

- We had for a long time looked for a systematic and well-founded method which could help us to implement the concepts of value-based management in a 'learning organization'.
- We wanted to develop a stronger consciousness of, sensitivity to and competance in responding to ethical questions within the organization.
- We wanted to reflect on and document whether Wøyen Mølle lived up to the core values and norms we had agreed to promote. We asked ourselves: 'Do we do what we believe and say we do? Do we practise what we preach?'
- We wanted to engage our major stakeholders in an ongoing interaction and dialogue about their expectations with due respect for their fundamental values. We would assess to what extent their values were perceived as being fulfilled through our conduct and activities.
- We wanted to try out the Ethical Accounting Process as a new way to promote organizational and personal development.
- Finally, in all modesty, by going in for Ethical Accounting, we hoped to exert influence on the development of ethical consciousness in society at large, and in public and private organizations in particular.

CARRYING OUT THE PROCESS AT WØYEN MØLLE

After the leader had decided to implement the Ethical Accounting Process, we considered it to be very important that employees were thoroughly informed of the why's and wherefor's – that they understood the motivation and the methodology. This meant giving employees the chance to discuss the implications and consequences for both themselves individually as well as for the organization as a whole.

This was accomplished through several half- and whole-day seminars where we discussed the practical task at hand, the possible consequenses and the philosophy behind ethical accounting. One of the seminar days was called: 'A trip through the Ethical Accounting Process in One Day.' Even though the cycle of a normal Ethical Accounting Process takes one year, this mini tour through each of the steps in the process was said, by employees, to give a concrete understanding of what it all was about.

I think it is very important to emphasize the importance of giving time to these inner talks. They permit the development of a deeper insight into Ethical Accounting and contribute to a broad acceptance of starting the process. It became clear to us that employees should be given a chance to develop ownership of the concept before the external stakeholders were invited to participate in the process. A quotation from Robert F Kennedy was an inspiring guidance for both the internal and the external dialogues about values and expectations: 'Some people see things as they are and ask, "WHY?" I dream of things as they could be and ask "why not?"' We were ready to start.

Important Stakeholders

It was not difficult to agree on the four most important groups of stakeholders:

*   the participants in the different programmes – about 150 people;
*   the employers who take the participants into their firms – about 100 firms;
*   the employees at Wøyen Mølle – 24 people;
*   public authorities – this is a heterogeneous group that consists of Social Services, the school system, the employment office, the health authority and the police – about 170 persons.

The total number of people included – about 450 – spanned the four stakeholder groups that Wøyen Mølle is in contact with. A representative selection of these were invited to participate in what we called value-circles. We established seven such value-circles, with six to twelve people in each.

Dialogues on Shared Values

The chosen representatives of each of the stakeholder groups were invited to take part in their respective value-circle. The members of each circle met at Wøyen Mølle for one day to discuss the project and to reach consensus about the shared values which were important for them as a stakeholder group in their interaction with Wøyen Mølle.

The other task the value-circles faced was to implement each value so that it could serve as the basis for measuring how well Wøyen Mølle lives up to it. This was achieved by defining, for each value, several statements about how the values were expected to be carried out in practice. When the partici-pants in a circle concluded that the statements were necessary and sufficient for defining a value, the statements could then serve as the content of the value in a questionnaire.

Together with a process consultant from Wøyen Mølle, my job was to lead the process in each of the value-circles – to inspire everybody to take part in the discussion and to see to it that each group came to an agreement about both values and the associated statements. Another important task was to assure that all the participants in the circles understood both the intention and the different steps of the Ethical Accounting Process. It became obvious that the information we sent out with the invitation to the value-circles had not been clear enough. A few of the participants actually thought they were invited to a seminar to discuss religious questions!

We also realized that we had to allocate time to become familiar with a new working vocabulary such as organizational ethics and value-based management. Such experiences taught us how difficult it is, and how much patience is required, to establish meaningful dialogue about organizational and personal values. When we came to an agreement that, in an organizational context, ethics implies something about how we manage, something about our corporate soul, and what is valuable for our further co-operation, it seemed a bit easier to understand both the intention and the whole process.

The following are examples of some of the values and statements that the four stakeholder groups came to an agreement about. The *employers* in the region emphasized *development, commitment, openness* and *confidence* in their co-operation with Wøyen Mølle. The way they wanted to see this manifested in practice was expressed in a series of statements, such as: 'Wøyen Mølle is realistic in its demands of the participants about doing a good job.' 'Wøyen Mølle motivates the participants to improve their qualifications.' 'You as a manager are satisfied with the information you receive about a participant before he or she starts in your firm.'

The *participants* emphasized the values *security, human respect, co-operation* and *development* in their interplay with Wøyen Mølle. Concrete expressions which evaluated the extent to which Wøyen Mølle promotes these values were: 'You get the education you need to do your job well with the new employer.' 'You feel that you have the same rights as the other employees in the firm you join.' 'You get personal contact with your consultant when you need it.' 'You get adequate information about the possibilities for rehabilitation.'

The *public authorities* choose the values *quality, comprehensive thinking and understanding, creativity and flexibility, commitment and direct communication.* Statements expressing the content of these values were, for example: 'The professional methods of Wøyen Mølle are inspiring.' 'Wøyen Mølle takes good initiatives which improve the climate of cooperating.' 'Wøyen Mølle is looking for ways of solving the participants' problems.' 'Wøyen Mølle welcomes criticism.'

The last stakeholder group, the *employees* at Wøyen Mølle, emphasized several values in their interplay with their own organization: *creativity, development and co-operation, quality, security and commitment, human respect, appreciation and humbleness.* Here are some statements on how they expected to see these values realized: 'Conflicts are solved directly by those involved.' 'You have time to prepare the tasks you are responsible for carrying out.' 'Your working conditions contribute to a feeling of security.' 'Humour and pleasure characterize your workplace.'

During the conversations in the different value-circles we gathered considerable information about how the external stakeholders looked upon the organization. We were allowed to pass this information on to the employees, and they immediately saw things that they could change without much effort to meet the expectations of the external stakeholders. The following exemplifies this – and at the same time provides a small, but good example of a how to develop a 'learning organization'. The representatives of the stakeholder-group participants declared that a way to show them respect was if their adviser at Wøyen Mølle came to visit them at an agreed time, instead of when it was convenient for the adviser. The new practice was started immediately.

The values and the associated statements were now formulated into a questionnaire for each stakeholder group. The respondents could choose between the following replies to a statement: 'strongly agree', 'slightly agree', 'slightly disagree', 'strongly disagree' and 'unanswered'. The next step in the process could now start.

Carrying out the Questionnaire

Wøyen Mølle is a rather small organization to carry out such a process. I am especially thinking of the guarantee to respondents of anonymity and the importance of a broad representation. Therefore we decided to contact a high percentage of the members of the stakeholder groups. All the employees at Wøyen Mølle and about 50 per cent of the external stakeholders, chosen at random, were interviewed. We employed two independent interviewers to do the interviewing. All the interviews were made via phone and each interview took about five minutes. The interviewers finished the interviews after two hectic weeks. Over 96 per cent of those contacted participated.

I think that the high participation rate can be ascribed to the interest the stakeholders take in the organization, the high degree of confidence they have in Wøyen Mølle, and the quality of the information which was distributed prior to the interviews.

Interpretation and Publishing of the Ethical Accounting Statement

The project group, which was originally established to pave the way for the process together with the process consultant, performed the interpretation of the stakeholders' responses. It seemed like going into a jungle of information on many levels. Once again we received valuable advice from those responsible for the Ethical Accounting Process in Sbn Bank in Denmark.

As we had a rather small number of respondents in spite of the high percentage of respondents, we decided to look at those who answered 'strongly agree' and 'slightly agree' as one group, and likewise with the 'slightly and strongly disagree' answers. The results of the questionnaire interviews, together with the interpretation of the responses, were published as Wøyen Mølle's (and Norway's) first Ethical Accounting statement. However, before it was published, all employees were involved in the interpretation of their responses. We found it important to make them familiar with the results and to celebrate that we had discussed things internally before we invited the external stakeholders to a dialogue.

There were indeed many aspects of the culture to be proud of, but the feedback also unearthed problems that required both creativity and hard work to solve. Here are a few examples of the confirming answers that we were rather proud of.

- *Participants*: 'You feel that you are needed where you work.' (97 per cent)
- *Employers*: 'Wøyen Mølle meets the participants with realistic demands.' (84 per cent)
- *Public authorities*: 'Wøyen Mølle gives high priority to the participants.' (95 per cent)
- *Employees*: 'You have freedom with responsibility in your job.' (100 per cent)

Some answers were a challenge for us.

- *Participants*: 'You are satisfied with the information you got about Wøyen Mølle before you started.' (59 per cent)
- *Employers*: 'You are satisfied with the information you got about the participant before he started in your firm.' (50 per cent)
- *Public authorities*: 'Wøyen Mølle takes the initiative in establishing cooperation.' (62 per cent)
- *Employees*: 'Wøyen Mølle promotes the professional and social well-being of the organization as a whole.' (39 per cent)

As can be seen from these examples, fairly large percentages of the stakeholders expressed dissatisfaction with important aspects of Wøyen Mølle's actions. Such dissatisfaction was also expressed in connection with other questions. When the results were discussed with the employees at Wøyen Mølle before the Ethical Accounting Statement was published, many of them saw things they could improve immediately. Nevertheless, we agreed that we had to wait for the dialogue with the other stakeholder groups to see, in more detail, what they wanted the organization to focus on. So, even if some of the results were unpleasant, both for the management and the employees, we were now ready to open up to the public!

Dialogues with External Stakeholders

After we published our first Ethical Accounting Statement and sent it to all 450 stakeholders, to the politicians of the local government, to the administration of the county, and to many others, we invited representatives of the stakeholder groups to the so-called 'dialogue circles'.

Each circle discussed the results of their own stakeholder group. Where did the members of the circle feel that their group's values and expectations were fulfilled – and where did they feel that improvement was needed? To stimulate suggestions for improvement, we used the future workshop-model. This method goes through three stages which activate the members of a dialogue circle to:

Arbeidsgivere
Hovedresultater i utdrag

Wøyen Mølle har et aktivt
samarbeid med 60 arbeids-
givere innen privat og offentlig
sektor. I tillegg har vi til enhver
tid en "jobb-bank" på ca. 25
ulike arbeidsplasser.
Arbeidsgiverne har deltakere fra
Arbeidstrening og MAIS. 30
arbeidsgivere har deltatt i
denne undersøkelsen.

Denne interessentgruppen kom
fram til følgende tre fellesverdier
de synes det er viktig Wøyen
Mølle møter dem med:

> Utvikling
> Engasjement
> Åpenhet og tillit

Kvalifisering og motivering av
deltakerne skal være en rød
tråd gjennom året.
Arbeidgiverne er opptatt av
utvikling og engasjement i
samarbeidet med Wøyen Mølle.
Flere av svarene viser imidlertid
at det har vært en nedgang i
positive vurderinger under disse
verdiene.

En merkbar nedgang i de
positive svarene om
arbeidsgiver er kjent med
arbeidstakers utviklingsplaner og
ressurser er en skikkelig
tankevekker for oss.
Arbeidstakers utvikling og
kvalifisering avhenger av at
disse resultatene fra

Utsagn som gir oss nye gleder
i 1995

• Du mener at arbeidstaker
 har rett til å delta på
 eksterne kurs i
 arbeidstiden   84%
• Du motiverer
 arbeidstaker
 til å kvalifisere seg   87%
• Du har tillit til Wøyen
 Mølles arbeid for å
 få unge ut i jobb/skole   93%

arbeidsgiver forbedres
betraktelig. Dette krever en tett
dialog mellom arbeidskonsulent,
deltaker og arbeidsgiver.

Det er gledelig å se at så mange
arbeidsgivere mener at eksterne
kurs i arbeidstiden er en
rettighet som arbeidstaker har.
Dette understøtter at 80% av
arbeidsgiverne sier de selv
motiverer arbeidstaker til å
kvalifisere seg.

Wøyen Mølle oppfatter det også
som en betydningsfull
tillitserklæring å få nesten topp-
karakter fra arbeidsgiverne når
det gjelder arbeidet vi gjør for
å få de unge ut i jobb. Årets
tilbakemeldinger viser at de

Utsagn vi gledet oss over i	1994	Res. 1995
• Wøyen Mølle stiller realistiske krav til arbeidstakeren om å stå i jobb	84%	70%
• Du ser det som viktig at arbeidstaker får delta på interne kurs i din bedrift/skole	82%	90%
• Du er godt kjent med arbeidstakers utviklingsplaner	84%	60%
• Du har kjennskap til arbeidstakers ressurser	84%	67%
• Du er fornøyd med den kjennskap du fikk til Wøyen Mølles mål og metode før arbeidstaker begynte hos deg	79%	80%
• Arbeidstaker får reell lønn for den jobben han/hun gjør	92%	87%
• Det er klare forventninger til samarbeidet mellom deg som arbeidsgiver og Wøyen Mølle	97%	86%

Figure 10.1: *Wøyen Mølle's Ethical Accounting Statement*

- discuss their criticism of the present situation;
- bring their fantasies and wild ideas of how things could be;
- come to an agreement on the realistic and needed improvements that should be proposed to the leader of the organization.

Although there were no real conflicts in the dialogue circles when reaching agreement as to which improvements were most important, on occasion, the conversation tended to be rather tense. This was particularly the case in the employees' dialogue circle.

It was interesting, but perhaps not astonishing, that the proposals from the dialogue circles did not focus on quite the same challenges as we in the project group had done in our interpretation of the results. Here are some of the suggestions for improving the value-based relationships between the stakeholders and the organization:

- *Participants*: 'Better information is needed about qualification require- ments and possibilities of acquiring the necessary competancies as well as about conditions in the labour market. Education must be differenti- ated according to the wishes and needs of the participants.'
- *Employers*: 'Make a well-structured and binding contract for the co- operation between the participant, Wøyen Mølle and us. Better discussions are required with the participants on their future plans and possibilities.'
- *Public authorities*: 'Establish a closer structure for co-operation and infor- mation. Improve the relationship between the schools and Wøyen Mølle.'
- *Employees*: 'Improve education on the philosophy and methods of Wøyen Mølle, especially for new employees. Establish more secure working conditions.'

All the proposals, which appear at first glance to be very broad and general, included specific strategies on how to put them into practice. It was particu- larly interesting to note that the external stakeholders, and especially the employers, commited themselves to take part in and to be co-responsible for the activities suggested.

The Corporate Meeting

The proposals from each of the dialogue circles, in order of determined priority, were sent to the leader of Wøyen Mølle. After a discussion with her management group about time, money and the resources available for the coming year, she extended an invitation to the so-called corporate meeting. Here representatives of the stakeholders from each dialogue circle were invited to participate in the discussion of the proposed improvements. This was also a good occasion for the different stakeholders to get a more complete impression of the organization in general and of the value-based suggestions for improvements from the other stakeholders in particular.

At this meeting, the leader had to decide which proposals could be approved and which could not. And she had to state her reasons for her decisions! What actually happened at this first corporate meeting was that the leader agreed to put all the first-priority suggestions into action, although one of them (establish more secure working conditions for the employees) would be a difficult matter to solve because it has to do with changing temporary jobs into permanent ones.

This first corporate meeting really gave us the feeling that we now had come closer to the inner meaning of The Ethical Accounting Process: we were beginning to develop the values of the organization in a close dialogue with our interested parties, and 'ideally speaking, an action is ethical if all parties affected by it can accept it.' All the stakeholder representatives at this first corporate meeting agreed that they now understood both the intention behind, and the possibilities within, in the process much better than in the beginning. One of the employers brought up the idea to invite several smaller firms and organizations to a discussion on value-based management and the Ethical Accounting Statement. Another suggested that the Ethical Accounting Statement would be interesting for all firms and organizations which were reorganizing or adapting themselves to new conditions. And the public authorities said, 'This kind of process is needed throughout the public sector.'

An Ethical Budget: Committed Plans for the Next Year

The accepted proposals for improvements were now considered within the organization. Many of the proposals could be put into action immediately, while others had to be co-ordinated with Wøyen Mølle's plans and financial budget for the following year. So, it remains to be seen if next year's Ethical Accounting Statement will show that the improvements suggested by representatives of the stakeholder groups really met the needs and expectations of the stakeholders. I am sure we still have to work harder, and that we will have to find new solutions, roads to follow and doors to open to come closer to 'the corporate soul' in an ongoing dialogue culture.

And what do I see now, one year after, when Wøyen Mølle's second Ethical Accounting Statement is about to be published ? The aim and intention of the Ethical Accounting Process is to establish and develop a dialogue culture, a learning organization and an ethical conciousness on all levels. I feel and see that this is slowly being realized at Wøyen Mølle.

These are some of the differences the Ethical Accounting Statement has contributed to Wøyen Mølle so far:

- I see a catalogue being made with the ideas from the dialogue circles. It states how and when proposals will be implemented and who is responsible for them.
- This will bring both new creativity and life into the organization, and will contribute to learning and development when – little by little – the proposals are put into practice.
- I hear an ethical conciousness in discussions at all levels.
- I hear it, in particular, in public pronouncements on the organization's obligations.
- I see it in a more open attitude at meetings.
- The Ethical Accounting Statement is used to find out what really matters, instead of simply discussing details.

- Decisions and new plans and ideas are being discussed with the Ethical Accounting Statement in mind: 'will we practise what we preach?'
- The employees are claiming and taking ownership of their values – and it is likely that they will act responsibly in accord with these values in practical situations.
- Little by little I think that Wøyen Mølle is getting good ambassadors outside the organization, because working on the Ethical Accounting Statement increases confidence in the organization.
- I also think that the Ethical Accounting Statement gives the organization an early warning system through dialogue with the stakeholders.

Clearly, small changes and short steps are required, including the courage to affect the motivations of others, both as a person and as an organization.

11

Constructing the Social Balance: Consumer Cooperative, Italy

Alessandra Vaccari[1]
(Consultant, Strategie & Organizzione)

Social accounting is not widespread in the Italian business community, and it is only recently that organizations have felt the need to communicate openly on the social impact of their activities. The Italian cooperative movement, however, has considerable experience in social accounting. Almost all of the cooperatives associated with the umbrella organization, The National League of Cooperatives, publish a Social Balance called the Cooperative Social Balance, together with their annual financial accounts.

The Basevi Law (1948) is the key legislation for cooperatives and defines the principle of mutualism and the role of the National League of Cooperatives. It is based on Article 45 in the Italian Constitutional Charter which states, 'The Italian constitution must promote and defend the cooperation and its mutualistic role'. More recent legislation (L 59/92) requires all cooperative companies to specify 'the criteria used in fulfilling their social mission' in their annual balance.

The case study discussed below describes the use of social accounting by one particular part of the Italian cooperative movement, the Consumer Coop. The Consumer Coop consists of approximately 320 consumer cooperatives, grouped under the Coop tradename and coordinated by the National Association of Consumer Coops (NACC). The NACC lies at the heart of the political and strategy-making process of the Italian consumer cooperative movement, and is therefore central to its overall development and identity. The NACC continues to play a critical role in the development of social accounting within the movement.

The Coop's social accounting experience is highly significant in the Italian context due to the sheer size of the exercise. Furthermore, the case study allows direct *comparisons* to be made between the experiences in social accounting of the different Coops. The 16 largest Italian consumer cooperatives (all selling under the tradename Coop) have been involved in social accounting. Together, these cooperatives account for 80 per cent of the Coop's total turnover of over UK£4 billion (1994) and are leaders in the general distribution sector, with a current national market share of 6 per cent.

WHAT IS THE COOP?

The Coop has grown, developed and is managed within the broad tradition of the cooperative movement and is specifically a *consumer* cooperative. Its underlying aim is to accumulate assets to satisfy the interests of its member and non-member consumers. The Coop's profits and reserves must be used to achieve this basic purpose. More generally, it is intended that members participate in the company as consumers, and also by actively expressing their views on the management of the organization. To achieve this end, the board of directors is elected by, and represents, the Coop's members.

The Coop is an association of 320 consumer cooperatives spread throughout Italy. As Table 11.1 shows, the number of Coop consumer/members is almost three million. The Coop network comprises approximately 1165 separate outlets employing in total, close to 30,000 people. The Coop's sales turnover was UK£4.5 billion in 1994, the majority of which was generated by the 16 largest cooperatives operating under the Coop trade name.

Table 11.1: *Italian Coop Key Indicators 1994*

	Larger	Smaller	Total
Associated cooperatives	16	304	320
Outlets	610	555	1165
Sales Area (square metre: 000)	599	25	724
Members (,000)	2557	350	2907
Employees	25,632	4080	29,712
Sales (billion pounds sterling)	3.9	0.6	4.5

Source: NACC financial department

The Coop's network of outlets includes hypermarkets, integrated supermarkets, food supermarkets and mini-markets. During the 1980s, there was a substantial growth of large, integrated supermarkets (1000–2000 square metres) allowing for increased consumer choice and the introduction of non-food departments. The 1990s has seen the advent of hypermarkets located in shopping centres, typically 5000–6000 thousand square metres, providing a vast assortment of food and non-food products on a single floor, and with a sales policy providing discounted, high-quality products.

The distinctive identity of the Coop rests in its values and specific approach as defined in the Coop *statutory* aims and the members' requirements, which find expression in its organizational and entrepreneurial strategy and management decisions. The success of the Coop in society and the market strictly depends on the coherence between, on the one hand, its ethical, solidarity-related, civic and constitutional objectives and, on the other, its organizational and entrepreneurial response processes. This unique and distinctive concept of success and failure is the principal motivation for the development of its social accounting practice.

The Coop exists to serve the interests of its members by ensuring quality and genuineness, by safeguarding against fraud, and by providing reliable and adequate information, more efficient services and greater sensitivity to environmental conditions. Thus the Coop has sought to:

• Develop the Coop brand, so as to guarantee high-quality standards and the provision of appropriate and accurate information.
• Establish a commercial policy aimed at improving service, broadening the product range and guaranteeing low prices.
• Develop social and cultural initiatives aimed at achieving more knowledgeable and more environment-conscious consumer behavior. An example of this is the Young Consumer Days initiative targeted at state schools with the aim of making young people aware of health issues, and training them in food information and environmental protection.

Over the last few years the Coop has made a point of adjusting and updating the contents of its consumer protection and environmental protection policy by committing itself to, for example, the reduction of phosphates in detergents and to the responsible use of plastic. Other environmental protection initiatives have involved the promotion of eco-compatible packaging, plastic recycling, the installation of 'ecological islands' for the separate collection of batteries, glass, cardboard, and plastic, the use of environment-friendly materials, and research into energy-saving technology.

In 1994, more than UK£3.2 million was spent on product-quality control, amounting to a total of 100,000 tests on 400 Coop brand products. In 1994, in addition to maintaining quality control on existing products, considerable efforts were dedicated to the development of new high-quality products. Products are carefully monitored throughout the production and processing phases, from the initial source to the retail outlet, through an intensive analysis programme which, in 1994, included more than 7000 tests.

The Coop carries out consumer education in schools through specific 'social centres for consumer education, documentation and orientation'. These are highly specialized structures suitably equipped to provide accurate and up-to-date information on food. The Coop has also provided critical input on a new law on pesticides. Its proposal emphasizes that the law should focus on regulating the sale and use of pesticides in agriculture. This should be overseen by a governmental agency with scientific, technical and control tasks.

Although some of these initiatives and objectives are shared by other supermarkets, the Coop has, in many instances, pioneered the approach in the Italian context that the overall aim of the initiatives is to improve social and ethical performance rather than market share. The Coop has a long history of value-based initiatives; indeed, old members magazines include suggestions to save money and to respect the environment. The core values and the institutional function of the Coop has remained unchanged: the mission is only, and can only be, updated to reflect changing social needs.

WHY THE COOP TURNED TO SOCIAL ACCOUNTING

More than six years ago, the Coop initiated a series of discussions about the need to give an account of its social performance in relation to its mission. It was at this time that the Coop had grown from an ensemble of small outlets to being the biggest consumer organization in Italy and the market leader in the field. It was at this peak of economic development that the Coop felt the need to re-analyze its social roots and update its values and social mission. The discussions about its social performance were predominantly internal, stimulated in the main by university academics exploring the use of social accounting as an instrument to develop a new identity both inside and outside the organization.

A major factor motivating Coop managers to implement social accounting is the perceived need to increase the legitimacy of the cooperative movement. In recent years the efficiency, social values and non-profit status of the cooperative movement have been challenged, causing management difficulties and embarrassments. Since much of the controversy was a result of misunderstandings, the Social Balance was seen as a communication tool serving to disseminate objective and accurate information. Therefore, the need to give an account of the relationship that exists between a company's values and mission, and the actions that it carries out on a daily basis, has underpinned the Coop's decision to develop its social accounting practice. From this perspective, the 'social accounts' of most mainstream companies focus on performance in relation to the interests of shareholders in maximizing profit, or focus on the financial market value of invested capital. This is, after all, a central mission of the company. The fundamental difference with the Coop is reflected in the different emphasis placed on social accounting. The Coop Social Balance quantifies the effectiveness of the Coop in fulfilling its institutional function to act in the interest of its member-consumers, to maximize the social benefit to all its stakeholders while being a non-profit organization, and at the same time demonstrates its ability to compete effectively in the market.

For the Coop, then, the Social Balance is a means of giving an account of its actions and performance to all its stakeholders in relation to its mission and values. However, this is not the end of the story. The Social Balance also provides an instrument that allows members and different parts of society to participate in the Coop. The Coop management plays a key role in the process of social accounting. The process provides a means for the management to combine efficiency and social strategy, values and actions, into an integrated approach that reflects the holistic Coop identity, and also its specific entrepreneurial and social culture.

Social accounting for the Coop has therefore involved reviewing the meaning of stakeholder involvement. The process of social accounting, and of course the Social Balances themselves, have provided one means of clarifying the identity of the consumer cooperatives, demonstrating how to strengthen that identity, and ensuring transparency in relationships with the various stakeholders – which include, in particular, members, consumers, staff, the cooperative movement, human society (local community, university, etc), and the market (suppliers, competitors).

BOX 11.1: KEY REASONS FOR SOCIAL ACCOUNTING

- Inform consumer members to what extent the social performance corresponds to the mission.
- Fullfill the commitment of transparency of all actions.
- Ordinary financial accounts do not give an inclusive account of the Coop's results and do not measure the consistency between the social performance and the Coop mission.
- Promote participation by members and other sectors of society in the activities and decision-making of the Coop.

These motivations are further reinforced by certain key aspects of the Italian socio-economic situation:

- the need for the Italian economy to consider more seriously its rules and market values;
- the need to recognize and promote the role and function of co-operative firms within the home economy;
- the need to disseminate examples of good practice and methods appropriate to an ethical and egalitarian concept of the market.

HOW THE COOP'S SOCIAL BALANCE IS BUILT

The period during which the Coop has implemented social accounting has been one of growth, characterized by an expanding sales turnover and an increase in the number of hypermarkets and members. The principles of social accounting are listed below:

- *Systematic*: the Social Balance is drawn up periodically to report an estimated final balance. The Balance is prepared using the same method each time.
- *Verifiable*: there is a code of procedures which allows reliable, controlled and certified information.
- *Comparable*: the results of the Social Balance are compared annually and, in some cases, compared with other cooperatives and similar companies.
- *Participative*: the Coop's Social Balance is prepared and used by many people. It is an inclusive approach to accounting made up of contributions of many people.

For the Coop, social accounting is a *process* involving the definitions of the following:

- mission;
- Social Balance and final Balance plan;
- social information support system;

- communication plan;
- auditing process.

The Social Balance was designed to address three specific objectives:

- the Social Balance as a communication instrument;
- the Social Balance as a control of performance in relation to the mission;
- the Social Balance as a formative base for the social strategy.

We will consider each of these objectives in turn.

THE SOCIAL BALANCE AS A COMMUNICATION INSTRUMENT

The first stage of the Social Balance is to identify and communicate in an analytical manner the social activities of the Coop. These include '*activities (and associated costs) not directly joined to the activity characteristics of the company*' (source: Coop social balance project paper, NACC, 1992). These include, for example, charitable donations, volunteer efforts, family benefits, etc.

The Social Balance defines activities in terms of their costs and benefits. The social costs and activities that give rise to social benefits are selected from the general financial accounts for one period and grouped into five categories:

- members;
- consumers;
- employees;
- civil society;
- co-operative movement.

Defining activities in terms of their costs and benefits was seen as a relatively well-defined way to identify and communicate information about activities to stakeholders, as well as to define those activities in a way that was relevant to management decision-making processes.

THE SOCIAL BALANCE AS A CONTROL OF PERFORMANCE IN RELATION TO THE MISSION

This approach did not give any sense of what was being achieved in relation to the Coop mission. What remained, therefore, was to find a means of determining whether costs and activities corresponded to the aims of the Coop.

An analysis of financial costs was simply not sufficient for this purpose. This is because existing financial accounts do not show when the aims of the mission are being attained. This shift takes place when it is realized that it 'is not a luxury to give an account of the relationship between the statutory and the obtained management objectives' (source: introduction, social balance project paper, NACC, 1993).

From a procedural point of view, progress is judged by the degree to which it is possible to *explain all the data of the balance and not only the customary expenses* and, therefore, to understand the social impact of all activities. The method involves:

- an elaboration of the mission statement;
- an elaboration of information and indicators to demonstrate the consistency between the mission statement and practice;
- an elaboration of the mechanisms used to inform the members and the other stakeholders.

THE SOCIAL BALANCE AS A FORMATIVE BASE FOR THE SOCIAL STRATEGY

In the course of experimentation it has been recognized that the Coop Social Balance can be used as a good working basis for developing the social strategy or, in other words, for redefining the relationships existing with and between different Coop stakeholders.

The process of building the Social Balance involves an analysis of the mission statement. It was insufficient to formalize a mission based on statute; instead, top management needed to redefine policy and strategy in relation to each of the most important stakeholders. In addition, stakeholders themselves were able to redefine their engagement with the Coop on the basis of the new strategy. This approach is unique as there is no separation between the social strategy and the overall organizational strategy of the Coop. The Coop becomes a manager of social relationships as well as a manager of resources.

BUILDING THE SOCIAL BALANCE

The basic steps include:

1 *Building Capacity Commitment*: develop appropriate management processes and commitment (see above).
2 *Statute or mission*: specify the mission and assess the different stakeholders' expectations.
3 *Social Balance plan*: for each element of the mission, identify indicators that allow for an assessment of the consistency between the mission and practice.
4 *National aggregated Social Balance*: each year, the aggregated social costs and related benefits for the 16 largest cooperatives are disclosed in the National Social Balance.
5 *Information system*: construct the information system and procedures for collecting and identifying relevant quantitative and qualitative information.
6 *Communication plan*: distribute the balance to stakeholders.

BUILDING CAPACITY COMMITMENT

Building the Social Balance is not a short term activity, nor is it an activity confined to a particular aspect of the organization. It takes an average of five to six months from the initiation of the process to the production and distribution of the Balance. Furthermore, the Coop needed about three years of work (three editions) to really understand the meaning and correct use of social accounting. A similar timeframe would probably be experienced by other organizations.

For this reason, a key starting point is the institutionalisation of the process through an appropriate management structure of responsibilities and authorities. In each consumer co-operative which produces a Social Balance, a working group is set up, most commonly including the president or director general, the members and consumers director (normally the project manager), the director of communication, the personnel director, the administrative director or director of planning, and the director of information systems, or people representing and having responsibility for these functions.

During experimentation phases, it is usual for the overall responsibility to lie with the social director. However, should Social Accounting become a recurrent and formalized practice, line managers should not have exclusive control over the process, and the service centre for the whole organization, for example the director of planning or administration, or alternatively by the general director or the president's staff, should assume responsibility.

This shift in responsibility from line to staff is seen as a substantial step towards legitimizing the Social Accounts as a standard instrument of management. It means that the Social Balance is not interpreted as a functional and technical instrument for external communication and marketing but as an interfunctional way to define social strategy. Thus the organizational centre for the development of the process is the director of planning. An active presence by the director of planning allows for a more integrated approach to constructing and evaluating social objectives. This is most likely when the traditions of making annual or longer-term plans already exist. Furthermore, the capacity or *elasticity* of the internal information system to generate qualitatively and quantitatively suitable information is greatest when the function is under the supervision of the director of planning – it is normally this person who best understands the capacities of the information system and is able to direct it towards the needs of the social accounting process.

SPECIFICATION OF THE MISSION AND ASSESSING STAKEHOLDER EXPECTATIONS

The second step in the construction of the Social Balance is the specification of the mission, taking the statutory objectives as a starting point. The statutes of Coop Estense are listed below:

• The cooperative pursues the social function of defending consumer members and non members, and providing goods in the best possible conditions.

- The Coop provides services and undertakes suitable initiatives with the aim of safeguarding their [consumers'] interests, protecting their well-being and increasing their knowledge and education so as to ensure complete freedom of choice and the avoidance of wastefullness and harmful behaviour by the consumers in the use of goods, services, and natural resources.
- The active and democratic participation in the life of the cooperative is encouraged in accordance with the objective of self-management through suitable forms of organization, the promotion of and participation in cultural, recreational and mutualistic services and activities.
- The Coop aims to stimulate a spirit of providence and savings amongst members.
- This will contribute to the promotion and development of cooperation for mutualistic purposes.
- The Coop encourages the promotion of joint actions with other cooperatives, bodies and companies in order to contribute to the continuous improvement of the distribution system, so as to develop direct relationships between production and distribution.

Source: Giuridic Statute of Coop Estense (company bylaw), 1993.

Some of the specific aims and objectives, therefore, that might emerge in the case being examined would include:

- Offering the maximum quality and the best service at the lowest possible prices on the market;
- protecting and representing the rights of the consumer, defending their economic interests, protecting the environment;
- representing the interests and securities of the members and guaranteeing their democratic participation in the life of the co-operative;
- protecting the bargaining power of the members by means of investment in the co-operative; and
- achieving maximum integration in the local area through varied local social activities.

The translation of statutes into specific aims and objectives against which performance can be measured is underpinned by an appreciation of stakeholders' expectations. The analysis of stakeholder expectations is based on an examination of research reports (when these are available) and, more generally, on an awareness of the relationship between the Coop and each of its stakeholder groups. This awareness is built up through the long tradition of relationships between the Coop and the community, especially at a local level. There is a system of consolidated relationships at both a local and national level which gives rise to a series of indicators which, when combined with other data obtained in an *ad hoc* fashion, provides a useful overview of stakeholders' expectations.

Stakeholder Expectations

* *Consumer members*: Every year the Coop holds about 1000 meetings with its members to discuss subjects such as: service, price and quality. Furthermore, research is carried out periodically to determine the level of satisfaction.
* *Saver members*: These are members who have deposited their savings with the Coop. Meetings are held with these members to discuss the service, interest rates and the Coop's use of the money loaned. Research on this group is also carried out periodically.
* *Elected members*: These are the members elected to local committees (either at a shop level or at an area level). These members have frequent meetings with the management concerning investments, the closing or opening of outlets, and the organization of activities concerning consumer education.
* *Non-member consumers*: The Coop storeholder conducts intense consumer monitoring at local and national levels. For example, every year the Coop commissions an investigation of the socio-cultural trends of society and the Italian consumer, with a specific in depth study of the trends of the Coop consumers.
* *Cooperative movement*: The consumer cooperatives grouped under the trademark Coop belong to the largest national league of Italian cooperatives (two other smaller cooperative leagues exist in Italy).
* *Employees and management*: Specific surveys and research are periodically carried out on issues such as the business climate, and the expectations and satisfaction of the personnel.
* *Trade unions*: Group meetings and discussions are held. Specific surveys are not commonly held.

THE SOCIAL BALANCE PLAN

A Social Balance Plan is prepared by the Coop project team on the basis of every point of the mission statement. The plan has to be validated by the board of directors and by the members. The Social Balance Plan is composed of quantitative and qualitative indicators. It serves as a basis for comparison with the previous year and between the 16 Coops. The choice of indicators is based on several key principles:

* measurability (it has to be quantifiable);
* significant (it has to be meaningful for the stakeholders);
* comparability;
* cooperative specific.

Each of these points is discussed thoroughly and agreed upon by the top management and the board of directors.

The information to be included in the Social Balance is reclassified into three categories as listed below:

Internal Indicators

The internal indicators are developed by the top management and are based on the objectives that they have set themselves. They are compared with the budget (starting from the second year of publication) and the results of the previous year only. Some examples of these internal indicators are set out below:

* number of new members;
* number of people involved in the social activities;
* number of members present at the annual general meeting (AGM);
* number of tests on products; see Table 12.2;
* number of initiatives organized; see Table 12.3.

Table 11.2: *Tests on non-Coop products, 1994*[2]

Type of Test	Number
Suppliers checked	428
Products analyzed	700
Site inspection	28
Written reports	315
Meetings with supplier	44
Total	13,210

Benchmark Indicators

Benchmark indicators are those which can be compared with other companies in the same sector. These include:

* prices;
* investment in service improvement in shops and shop facilities;
* investment *pro capita*;
* percentage of young people on the staff.

Although at present it is only prices that are compared, in subsequent years other criteria will be included.

External Indicators

These are quantatative indicators that are selected on the basis of surveys carried out on the stakeholders. For example:

* percentage of Coop employees who state that they are satisfied with their pay, training, career, and safety at work;
* percentage of Coop consumers who state that they are satisfied with the after-sales service, opening hours, prices, courtesy of staff and product quality.

Table 11.3: *Education, Information and Consumer Protection Initiatives Organized by Area Members of Coop Estense, 1994*

Place	Activity	No. of People Involved
Carpi	A safe home; a public meeting on the safety of domestic appliances	100
Novi	Your diet using the computer	50
Mirandola	Health on a plate – series of meetings on food for the elderly	170
Modena	A gardening course	40
Ferrara	A look at food – national exhibition on consumption in Italy over the last 100 years	6300
Bondeno	Your diet using the computer	80
Ferrara	The fish is on the table – a theoretical and practical course on cooking fish	54
Argenta and Voghiera	Meetings on food organized in collaboration with the Public Health Authority and aimed at the elderly	150
Sassuolo	At school in the supermarket – a consumer education workshop	200
	It's worth eating well – survey on school children	200
Castelfranco E.	At school in the supermarket – a consumer-education workshop for middle school	100
Castelnuovo	At school in the supermarket – a consumer-education workshop for middle school	75
Vignola	At school in the supermarket – a consumer-education workshop for middle school	50
Carpi	At the Coop, and the marketing school – consumer-education workshop for upper middle schools	42
Modena	Tin opener	1450
Codigoro	Adventure school – national exhibition on safety at school and for sport	800
Comacchio	Adventure school – national exhibition on safety at school and for sport	1340
Ferrara	Food Project with De Pisis schools	65
Total		11,266

THE NATIONAL AGGREGATED SOCIAL BALANCE

Since 1992 a national aggregated Social Balance has been drawn up annually for the 16 largest Italian consumer cooperatives coordinated by the National Association of Consumer Cooperatives. Emphasizing the assignment of profits and the growth of indivisible reserves is typical of a consumer cooperative. For the Coop, the indivisible reserve is not just a financial performance indicator, it is also a social indicator because it is a reserve destined to become 'next generation benefits'. It is not owned by the Cooperative but by the public, and should the Cooperative close down, it is used for public benefit.

Table 11.4: *The National Social Balance*

	1992 lire (millions)[3]	1993 lire (millions)
Profit – indivisible reserves	328,507	424,602
Development promotion fund	10,745	13,491
Subtotal	339,252	437,953
Members' costs	91,818	94,346
Consumers' costs	15,192	13,551
Employees' costs	9667	13,740
Civil society costs	8739	7586
Total	464,668	567,176

A more detailed breakdown of these figures is provided in Table 11.5 below.

The case study described here illustrates a very complex social accounting project involving 16 individual companies. The compilation of a national aggregated Social Balance has involved a great deal of consensus building. This has only been possible due to the fact that the companies share the same basic core values and have a well-defined social function.

The data for the national aggregated Social Balance is collected in the form of a questionnaire that is completed by the individual co-operatives after they have published their individual Social Balance; it is passed to the NACC for compilation. In 1996 this data will be collected automatically using Social Information System software.

THE SOCIAL INFORMATION SYSTEM

A Social Information System (SIS) has been set up to systemize the procedures used by the 16 cooperatives to collect information for compilation in the national Social Balance. This will be used for the first time in 1996. The SIS is managed both centrally (for collection, preparation and reporting functions) and at an individual cooperative level (for local planning, information-gathering and control).

Table 11.5: *Coop Italia Social Balance*

Description of costs	1992 lire (millions)	1993 lire (millions)
Members' costs		
Representation and participation costs	28.000	26.401
Discounts for members	57.472	60.340
Social communication (eg Coop magazine)	6.324	7.605
	91.818	**94.346**
Consumers' costs		
Product quality and safety costs	7.472	8.072
Consumer education and training initiatives	5.030	3.649
Information and research	772	772
Environmental protection	1.918	1.057
	15.192	**13.551**
Employees' costs		
Training and maintenance of a high-quality work environment	9.667	13.740
	9.667	**13.740**
Civil society		
Eg: support for Multiple Sclerosis research	4.000	4.000
Local cultural improvement initiatives	3.887	3.182
Support for developing countries	852	404
	8.739	**7.586**
Co-operative movement		
Profits – indivisible reserves	328.507	424.462
Development promotion fund	10.745	13.491
	339.252	**437.953**
Total	**464.668**	**567.176**

COMMUNICATION

Dissemination of the Social Balance is considered to be a very important element in the entire process of social accounting. Without getting this right, the entire exercise can be a waste of energy and resources. It is here that key stakeholders come to understand what the Coop has (and has not) achieved, obtain the means to know what they would like to encourage the Coop to do, and in subsequent years see if the Coop has carried out their recommendations. The dissemination strategy of the 16 cooperatives working under the Coop trademark is as follows:

*   *Members*: The Social Balance is distributed to all the members who participate in the local meetings, to prepare for the AGM, and also to the delegates of the AGM. The balance is also distributed to the elected members in the leading bodies of the members' committee, and to the board of directors.

- *Member-Consumers*: All Coop member-consumers receive information about the Social Balance by means of an internal information magazine. Two cooperatives also inform their own member-consumers via brochures that give a succinct picture of social performance. One cooperative exhibits the full results of the Social Balance.
- *Employees*: Half of the 16 Coops only circulate the Social Balance among the middle managers, whereas others also circulate it to the retail outlet managers. One cooperative distributes the report to all of its employees.
- *Opinion leaders*: Almost all the cooperatives distribute the Social Balance to union organizations, environmental and voluntary associations, as well as to banks, public institutions and the media. The document is also distributed to schools and colleges that have collaborated with organizing consumer-education initiatives. One of the 16 Coops distributes a complete version of the Social Balance to accountancy colleges.
- *The cooperative movement*: The Social Balance is circulated to the major players in the cooperative movement.

THE EFFECTIVENESS OF THE COOP'S SOCIAL ACCOUNTS

The 16 members of the Coop who have, to date, participated in developing the method and practice of social accounting have sought to demonstrate the relevance of their values and perspectives to the modern world, and in particular to the world of business. To achieve this it is not enough to simply disseminate the Social Balance; the process must appear to be *demonstrably useful* to key stakeholders. For members in particular, the Social Balance is a critical tool which increases the transparency of all the activities in relation to member expectations.

AGM attendance is, on average, 100,000 people, many of whom are consumer-members interested in the well-being of 'their' firm. The Social Balance provides a clear basis for responding to the many pragmatic questions raised on issues such as prices, quality and freshness of the goods, opening times, and competence of the Coop's personnel. A reliance on financial data alone would not provide sufficent information for the host of enquiries.

Apart from the normal members, the Social Balance also provides useful information for elected members. The Balance provides a logical and objective interpretation of the Coop's own mandate by establishing aims and objectives, and weighing performance against agreed indicators and targets. In addition to individual members, staff and management, the Coop's Social Balance is also relevant to other organizations, not least the *cooperative movement* itself. For example, the National League of Italian Cooperatives (the representative association of the whole cooperative movement, not just of the consumer cooperatives) has recently announced that all affiliated organizations have to prepare a Social Balance. In addition, the Coop social accounting process, and its formalized expression in a Social Balance, has aroused much interest in organizations beyond the cooperative movement: in particular, suppliers and competitors.

To date, however, many players, including the academic community, have regarded the Social Balance as a marketing device rather than as a method of accounting for social commitments taken on by the Coop. This perception is changing and the Coop 'case' is now often treated in universities as a subject for graduate study, and requests for information increase daily. In addition, the ethical business community is interested in developing ethical business codes based on the code of ethics that the Coop has developed as part of its social accounting process.

CONDITIONS FOR EFFECTIVENESS

The method underlying the Social Balance serves to identify social costs and benefits arising from the Coop's activities; it offers a means for assessing social performance against the mission, as well as offering a basis for developing strategy. The ultimate aim is for the Coop to improve its social performance.

It is important to consider whether a Social Balance can be applied to any situation, or whether particular conditions exist that facilitate or hinder its introduction? Experience so far suggests that there are certain preconditions which, in general, act to reduce the effectiveness of the Social Balance, and certain others that tend to increase effectiveness.

The Nature of the Market

The Coop has a great deal of interaction with its consumers; its consumer base is very conscious of brand image, and is actively encouraged to engage with the company through membership as well as purchases. Logically, this close relationship with consumers should increase the effectiveness of the Coop's social accounting process. The Coop relies on a strong commitment from key stakeholders for its success, and social accounting ensures active participation by these groups in key management decisions.

On the other hand, the more a company feels part of a real or imaginary enclave (social or entrepreneurial) that seems to assure its survival, the more it is convinced that its own future depends on the existence of such an enclave, and the less it wants to modify its own social and communication strategy.

The Existence of an Authority

There is a need for an overarching body that has specific responsibility for promoting the correct application of the Social Balance, maintaining consistency, and making comparisons between the social performance of different companies. Thus far the NACC has played this role, although plans for another authority are now being actively considered.

The State of the Economy

In a healthy economy, where stakeholders are thriving, the social accounting process will be more effective. This is because the stakeholders will have the means to take an active interest in the social performance of business.

Predisposition of Top Management Towards Innovation and Change

By far the most important factor determining the effectiveness of the social accounting process, or indeed whether it occurs at all, is the predisposition and commitment of top management towards innovation and change.

FUTURE DEVELOPMENTS

A key future objective is to set up an authority who will check that the Coop achieves its objectives. This authority will check and certify the genuineness and validity of the statistics and information contained in the Coop's Social Balances. Although at present this function is carried out by the NACC, by law the authorities responsible for monitoring the Coop's social impact are both The National League of Cooperatives and the members themselves. The NACC board has entrusted to a work force made up of Coop members the task of developing the Social Balance to its full potential; this role includes maintenance of high standards that are reliable and practical. The work force is in the process of devising a standard Social Balance model.

The Coop has been preparing Social Balances for three years. Key goals for the future of social accounting include the following:

- to foster consistency in social accounting processes and controls;
- to increase the involvement of stakeholders, in particular members, in building the mission statement;
- to introduce new phases into the social accounting process – for example, a certification system (at present a form of self-certification is carried out via the NACC);
- to continue to raise awareness of social accounting within the Italian co-operative movement and worldwide.

The Coop social accounting experience can usefully be evaluated under three dimensions:

- as a case study of a specific sector: the cooperative;
- as a case study involving the use of the Social Balance method; and
- as a case study illustrating and comparing the experiences of 16 separate companies.

The Coop experience has shown that it is possible for a large organization to adhere to its original aims and principles even when it is, or has become, a market leader. Indeed, it is by its very commitment to stakeholders and adherence to its ethical values that the Coop has been able to become a market leader.

ENDNOTES

1   The author is particularly grateful to Claudia Gonella and Simon Zadek for their work in improving the English, presentation, and overall quality of the paper.
2   Goods tested: fish and meat, sausages, salami and German sausage, fresh pasta, eggs, luxury foods, wine, fruit and vegetables.
3   UK£1 is roughly equivalent to 2200 lire.

12

Ranking Disclosure: VanCity Savings & Credit Union, Canada

Cathy Brisbois
(VanCity Savings & Credit Union)

This chapter documents VanCity's move toward improving and extending its reporting of its operations, financial performance, and corporate social role activities. The process of increasing the credit union's disclosure level and accountability started in October 1992, with the planning of the 1992 annual report. At VanCity, research and discussion about social accounting continue today through the organization's Annual Report working group which reports both to VanCity's executive management group and the audit committee of the board.

THE ORGANIZATION

Vancouver City Savings & Credit Union, known locally as VanCity, is Canada's largest credit union and one of the largest in the world. With over C$4 billion in assets and 210,000 members, or customers, VanCity provides a complete range of financial products and services to compete with banks and trust companies. Founded in 1946, the credit union is locally owned and operated by its members.

VanCity's head office is located in Vancouver in the province of British Columbia. Membership is open to all Vancouver lower mainland residents who purchase C$50 in membership shares. Serving one in eight lower mainland residents, VanCity invests its funds locally – no offshore assets are held.

In 1989, VanCity developed a socially responsible real-estate development subsidiary called VanCity Enterprises Ltd. Its mandate is to provide affordable housing through innovative development strategies involving community groups, churches, local governments, and the private sector. That same year, VanCity also created the VanCity Community Foundation. Guided by its own board and operating at arm's length from the credit union, the foundation fosters long-term community economic development through non-profit enterprise, employment initiatives, and alternative housing. While VanCity is regulated provincially, in 1991, VanCity purchased Citizens Trust, a federally chartered trust company with six offices locally and one in Calgary, Alberta.

THE 1992 VANCITY ANNUAL REPORT

In the autumn of 1992, the decision was made to refine the 1992 VanCity annual report to provide information on VanCity's corporate social role. Although VanCity must legally report its financial earnings annually, no mandatory reporting requirements existed for the credit union's social reporting. Nor do any requirements exist today.

VanCity's annual report is read widely and is viewed as the most important document that reflects the organization's objectives. Consequently, the report was considered the right vehicle to provide social information. Why did VanCity decide to provide greater disclosure in the 1992 report? A comprehensive approach had been developed by Leo Paul Lauzon at the University of Quebec at Montreal (UQM), in co-operation with the Society of Management Accountants of Canada (SMA), to report corporate information that was more comprehensive and socially responsible.

The SMA approach maintains that, since large organizations have such a wide-ranging impact on almost all aspects of our society, they have a moral and legal obligation to report on how they have managed their resources in both financial and social terms. The overall objective of the approach is to encourage organizations to expand disclosure to include more detailed financial and social accounting. This approach was developed in 1990. By 1992, the project was analyzing and researching approximately 750 Canadian companies annually to determine the level of disclosure provided and to assign a ranking. Both social and financial information was considered. The analysis evaluated 170 variables pertaining to social information and 261 variables for financial information. Work was conducted year-round involving 12 months of continuous effort at UQM by a staff of ten, plus a senior researcher. The approach also provided a format or framework that encouraged the reporting of information in a more detailed, comprehensive and socially responsible nature.

According to the SMA approach, the social and financial information contained in VanCity's 1991 annual report had been rated for level of disclosure. Out of 147 Canadian financial institutions, VanCity's 1991 annual report placed sixtieth overall. In terms of social information, VanCity ranked forty-seventh, and in the category of financial information, the credit union ranked sixty-fourth.

In comparison, the Royal Bank, Canada's largest bank, had been ranked much higher than VanCity in its disclosure of social information. As a relatively small, locally owned financial institution, with no offshore assets and a long history of strong community reinvestment and support, VanCity had expected to excel in this area. The rating of VanCity's social information as inferior to the 'big banks', especially the Royal Bank, surprised and disappointed both VanCity's executive and the board.

At VanCity, annual board planning sessions typically include presentations on emerging issues. For the May 1992 board planning session, the executive management group recommended that Mr Lauzon present his ideas on the UQM/SMA approach to increasing corporate disclosure. After Mr Lauzon's presentation, VanCity's board and executive agreed to tailor the 1992 annual report to meet the recommendations which encouraged increased disclosure according to the SMA approach. The consensus of

VanCity's board and executive management group was that the credit union could do considerably better with its 1992 annual report. VanCity was capable of providing a much more comprehensive review of its operations. And, as a member-owned, locally based financial organization with a strong history of community support, VanCity had an obligation to fully report on its socially responsible community initiatives. The SMA approach appeared to be a natural fit for a credit union such as VanCity.

The objective review of VanCity's social and financial information by UQM and comparative ranking also generated a competitive impetus for VanCity to further develop the disclosure level of its reporting mechanism. To discuss the application of the SMA approach to VanCity's operations, a VanCity manager visited the University of Quebec in October 1992. From December 1992 to March 1993, the 1992 annual report was compiled. The process involved meeting with several VanCity divisional vice-presidents to access the type of information that was required. The finished product included a section called Social Accounting which reported on the following areas: members (customers), staff, community and ecological responsibility.

The amount of information contained in each area was weighted according to the credit union's immediate responsibilities and accountability. Accordingly, the members section was most comprehensive, with information presented in the following categories:

- products and services;
- branch development;
- technology;
- competition;
- multicultural marketing;
- credit union structure;
- government relations.

Information about the VanCity Community Foundation, VanCity's equity policy, and VanCity's environmental policy was also included, as well as a glossary of terms, pertaining mostly to financial information contained in the annual report.

RESULTS OF VANCITY'S 1992 ANNUAL REPORT

The SMA approach is designed to increase disclosure about all areas of a company's operations. Accordingly, VanCity provided detailed, comprehensive information in all three areas of responsibility: members, staff and the community.

According to the annual social audit review by UQM, conducted on behalf of the SMA, VanCity's 1992 annual report ranked eighth out of 134 Canadian financial institutions in the category of large organizations. The report progressed by 30 points for social and financial information combined, scoring 54 points in the 1992 report, compared with just 24 points in the 1991 report. VanCity's 1992 annual report was recognized with an award for the 'Most Improved Social and Financial Information.'

Table 12.1: *Disclosure Ranking of VanCity's Annual report - Canadian Financial Institutions (Large Organizations)*

	1991 Annual Report	1992 Annual Report
Social information	47th	4th
Financial information	64th	32nd
Overall	60th	8th
Number of Canadian financial institutions	147	134

Source: UQM/SMA

Specific changes to VanCity's 1992 report corresponded to the SMA framework that is designed to increase the level of a company's disclosure, including more detailed information on human resources such as employee training, recruitment, promotion, fair employment practices, as well as various relevant statistics.

Table 12.2: *Promotions, Transfers, Recruitment - 1992 Annual Report*

	Employment Opportunities	Filled Internally	External Recruits
Non-Management	427	238 (56%)	189 (44%)
Management	51	48 (94%)	3 (6%)

Table 12.3: *Training Information - 1992 Annual Report*

Number of Courses	Number of Participants	Average Number of Training Days Per Employee	Course Expenditures*
213	1,933	8	$712,000

* Excludes training salaries

Table 12.4: *VanCity's Full-Time Workforce (Breakdown by Gender) - 1992 Annual Report*

Number of Assistant Managers	Number of Managers	Number of Executives*	Total Workforce
31 (79%) female	22 (57%) female	4 (21%) female	569 (79%) female
8 (21%) male	17 (43%) male	15 (79%) male	150 (21%) male
39 (100%)	39 (100%)	19 (100%)	719

*Includes regional managers

The level of disclosure was also increased to present:

- more detailed description of contributions to the community: financing of programmes related to the arts; donations to employment initiatives in ethnic communities; and support for economic development via the VanCity Community Foundation;
- discussion of the environment: recycled paper programme; policy and objectives to reduce consumption of natural resources; and aid to ecological groups by financing a television programme on the Earth Summit.

For many years, VanCity's annual report has included a message from the chair. Based on the SMA approach, the message in the 1992 annual report was also revised to provide more details about VanCity's corporate giving. Changes included disclosure of the:

- actual corporate donation amount, stated as a percentage of net earnings, after income taxes and dividends;
- number of community initiatives that VanCity supported;
- corporate donations programme by referring the reader to the Social Accounting, section under the category of community.

Readership of the annual report includes VanCity members, customers, peers, non-profits, and government agencies. Each year, VanCity conducts an annual report readership survey, which for the 1992 annual report survey involved issuing 682 annual report questionnaires to two readership groups.

The first group consisted of 167 VanCity members who attended the 1993 annual general meeting, at which the 1992 annual report is distributed. The second group consisted primarily of the non-members, mentioned above, with the addition of VanCity members who had not attended the annual general meeting. The survey yielded a 14 per cent response rate overall, with a 19 per cent response rate from those who attended the meeting and a 12 per cent response rate from the primarily non-member group.

Highlights of the readership survey results included:

- The Social Accounting section of the annual report was ranked as 'extremely important' by 38 per cent of members versus 17 per cent of non-members. Over two-thirds ranked this section as a '3' out of '5' in terms of usefulness, with '1' being 'not useful at all' and '5' being 'very useful'.
- 'All' or 'most' of the information in the Social Accounting section was new to approximately 37 per cent of both members and non-members.
- Almost 47 per cent of members and 41 per cent of non-members reported that the information in the Social Accounting section affected their perception of VanCity as a financial institution.

The SMA approach also encourages a detailed level of financial reporting. A new five-year financial retrospective containing 31 different data items was added to the 1992 annual report, while the financial information reported in the financial statements was not expanded significantly.

To provide more in-depth financial detail, especially for the past five years as recommended by the SMA approach, a comprehensive review of VanCity's audit procedures and planning would be required. VanCity's board and executive management group felt that it would prove too costly to recreate the past financial information required. However, changes to VanCity's financial data collection process were recommended and implemented in January 1993. The objective was to provide more detailed financial information beginning with the 1994 annual report.

THE 1993 VANCITY ANNUAL REPORT

While VanCity's 1992 annual report had provided much more disclosure than the 1991 report, there were some concerns. Information that appeared in the new section called Social Accounting might be considered selective or lacking in impartiality. So, although disclosure level had increased significantly, impartiality might have been compromised somewhat since the disclosed material had been reviewed and approved by senior management and the board. And, according to the 1992 annual report readership survey, although the report was very well received, some criticism surfaced about the material being self-serving and self-congratulatory.

In 1993, the audit committee of the board met with VanCity's financial auditors to assess whether they had ideas to contribute to the development of a socially responsible accounting model. While there was interest in this subject, there was not the required expertise. Consequently, VanCity staff continued to research socially responsible reporting models. At this time, VanCity focused on increasing the level of disclosure provided through the annual report and, in particular, on extending its reporting information about VanCity's corporate social role activities. While there was interest in providing as much quantifiable information as possible, little confidence existed about the level of consensus around various methodologies, such as social balance sheets. There was also concern over the difficulties of establishing financial measures for what are, in some cases, qualitative or subjective perceptions of an organization's impact – different versions of the 'truth' by stakeholders with very different interests and perceptions. Furthermore, while there was interest in involving stakeholders, VanCity wanted to ensure their role would be clear and meaningful. There was also a sense that VanCity's 'house' would need to be put in order in terms of VanCity's corporate social role, the development of clear social performance objectives that integrate both financial and social goals, and the clarification and formalization of existing policies relevant to this role. Lastly, VanCity wanted to ensure that decisions around reporting were achievable in the long term – that staff resources were available.

In view of the above concerns and following research on various socially responsible reporting models, VanCity adopted the Measurement by Objective approach. This model lays out objectives as well as policies, and programmes implemented to meet the overall objectives. Where results differ significantly from stated objectives, an explanation of the variance is provided. Objectives for the following year are also reported, which increases the accountability significantly, because it lowers the discretion of disclosure. The Measurement by Objectives model has been followed by Canada Trust, a leading Canadian trust company that has been praised for the clarity of its annual report and also for its degree of financial disclosure. The recommendation for the 1993 annual report, which was approved by VanCity's board and executive management group, was to report in the areas prescribed by the SMA approach using the Measurement by Objectives format.

VanCity decided to utilize the Measurement by Objectives format based on VanCity's 1993 strategic business plan. For competitive business reasons, actual numerical targets and results would not appear; instead, percentage changes would be stated. The Measurement by Objectives format would lay out VanCity's objectives, according to its business plan, and the actions undertaken to achieve them. As VanCity prepares quarterly progress reports on its business plan, compilation of the results and presentation of the information would be relatively straightforward.

An example of the format is as follows:

- 1993 Objective: Make VanCity's services more accessible to the Indo-Canadian and Asian communities.
- Performance: Total business received through VanCity's business development managers serving the local Asian and Indo-Canadian communities has increased 21 per cent over 1992. In addition to English and French, a Cantonese language option was installed in automated teller machines (ATMs) at the Richmond and Chinatown community branches and the Maple Ridge community branch drive-through ATM.
- 1994 Objective: At all VanCity branch ATMs, offer the two most frequently spoken languages within each branch's serving area, in addition to the standard English and French language options. Provide Cantonese, Punjabi, French languages on the 24-Hour Service Line (telephone banking service).

The rationale for adopting the Measurement by Objectives model included:

- The report must be credible. VanCity realized that freedom from bias is required to eliminate the risk of self-serving and distorted social reporting. Many observers already perceive that presently reported social information is carefully selected to avoid bad impressions and tends to exaggerate the social benefits generated by the corporation. VanCity sought freedom from bias by ensuring the information presented is verifiable and is complete. While an organization cannot report on everything, it was understood that critical information should not be omitted.
- The report must be understandable. VanCity recognized that reports are worthless if they cannot be understood. Quantifying information aids understanding and is desirable when it can be achieved with reliability.
- The information-gathering process should not require excessive staff time or be expensive.
- The information gathered should be useful, not only for external reporting, but also as information for VanCity's management.
- The report should conform with standards upheld by a professional body, or an emerging consensus on reporting, or public expectations.

Rather than contain 'social information' in a special section of the annual report, such as the Social Accounting section of the 1992 annual report, the decision was also made to adopt a socially responsible approach to presenting the information in the 1993 annual report. Accordingly, a new section called 'Review of Operations' was added to the 1993 VanCity annual report. The new section contained information about members, staff, community, including coverage of the environment, and government relations and competition. Information about VanCity's subsidiaries – Citizens Trust and VanCity Enterprises Ltd – was also presented in the Measurement by Objectives format.

Specific information contained within the Members and Staff sections included:

Members Section:
- products and services;
- branch development;
- technology;
- multicultural marketing;
- credit union development.

Staff Section:
- benefits/compensation;
- training;
- equity.

The review of operations section also contained strategic business information and financial details relating to VanCity.

In employing the Measurement by Objectives model, each objective from VanCity's 1993 business plan was stated, detailed performance of the objective was recorded, and the 1994 objective corresponding to each initiative was also reported. Numerical information was included, where possible, to provide greater disclosure. Figures for both 1993 and 1992 were provided and projections for 1994 were stated. Numerical information was expanded and presented in chart or table format, including information such as: volume of incoming telephone calls; mutual fund sales; detailed training information, including number of courses, number of participants, average number of training days; information regarding employee promotions, transfers, and recruitment ; work force breakdown by gender; and financial information about grants to environment groups.

Information for the 1993 annual report was compiled beginning in November 1993, and the final report was printed in March 1994. While the type of information included in this new section entitled review of operations continued to be based on the SMA model that had been used for the 1992 annual report, VanCity's 1993 business plan determined what corporate objectives would be disclosed in the annual report. Information for the report was compiled using quarterly updates to the 1993 VanCity business plan. These updates are submitted by all senior managers. The report really progressed in late January 1994, once the 1993 year-end results were filed by all divisional vice-presidents.

Information about Citizens Trust and VanCity Enterprises Ltd, two of the credit union's subsidiaries, was also reported according to the Measurement by Objectives model, while details about the VanCity Community Foundation were presented in narrative style since the foundation operates on a different fiscal year-end. VanCity also focused its efforts on improving disclosure in other sections of the report. Accordingly, both the 1993 message from the chair and board of directors' report provided more detailed information than the 1992 annual report.

Other information, about VanCity's corporate social role activities relating primarily to corporate and environmental donations, was included in side bars – text that ran one or two paragraphs in length, accompanied by a photo – inserted throughout the report. Due to the report's space constraints, just nine side bars were included in the 1993 report. An example of a side bar from the 1993 report is listed below:

Better Environmentally Sound Transportation (BEST)

Reusing, recycling and decreasing air pollution are goals of this organization's community bike shop, which trains people to repair discarded bicycles. The shop then makes the bikes available to low income citizens requiring transport. VanCity supported the local shop with a C$15,000 EnviroFund grant. Along with promoting a clean form of transportation, the shop offers valuable training and mechanical skill enhancement to staff and customers, particularly women, who typically lack experience in buying and maintaining bicycles.

Like the 1992 annual report, a five-year financial retrospective containing 31 items was also included in the 1993 annual report. No additional financial disclosure was provided beyond regulatory requirements for financial institutions.

THE 1994 VANCITY ANNUAL REPORT

The 1994 annual report format continued with the Measurement by Objectives model based on VanCity's 1994 strategic business plan, reporting detailed, comprehensive information about all areas of VanCity's operations as recommended by the SMA approach.

Planning for the 1994 annual report began in November 1994, while information was compiled beginning in December. Information-gathering for the review of operations section was relatively easy, as this was the second consecutive year of compiling this type of information. The source of the information were the quarterly reports or instalments to VanCity's business plan, which are submitted by divisional vice-presidents. As in the previous year, some information-gathering was delayed until mid January 1995, pending 1994 year-end final results. For continuity and comparability, the same tables and charts that appeared in the 1993 annual report were included in the 1994 report. The 1994 annual report was completed and printed in March 1995.

Improvements to the 1994 annual report focused on comprehensive changes to the financial information section. By December 1994, the changes to VanCity's financial data collection process, which were implemented in January 1993, had enabled VanCity to increase financial disclosure and provide more detailed financial analysis. A new six-page section entitled 'Financial Review' was added to the 1994 annual report. Financial disclosure was increased considerably with the inclusion of ten tables that appeared in this new section. Most tables provided figures and analysis for five consecutive years, starting with 1990 and running to year-end 1994.

The format for the financial review section evolved throughout production – from December 1994 to early February 1995 – as the annual report was being compiled. Incompatibility between the computer systems of VanCity's accounting department and the advertizing agency producing the annual report resulted in a slow-moving production process, since figures had to be entered, edited, then re-entered. And, as usual, there is always much discussion about the numbers by both the internal accounting staff and external auditors before final sign-off.

The initiative to present this type of information had been brought forward by the senior vice-president responsible for accounting and approved by VanCity's senior management group and its board.

RESULTS OF VANCITY'S 1994 ANNUAL REPORT

In keeping with the co-operative, democratic nature of a credit union, VanCity is committed to providing this level of financial disclosure in the financial review section of the report. Changes in VanCity's financial data collection system and the development of a more comprehensive financial information section will make compilation and production much easier for the 1995 annual report and subsequent reports.

FUTURE DIRECTION OF THE ANNUAL REPORT

The 1994 annual report contains a commitment to report on the following information in the 1995 report:

- affordable housing initiatives;
- community economic development lending;
- voluntarism;
- job creation;
- technical assistance;
- environmental impact;
- work placement and training;
- employment environment.

In addition, VanCity ethics guidelines – mission statement, management philosophy, and employees' standards of business conduct – will be included in the 1995 annual report.

The 1995 annual report will continue with the Measurement by Objectives model based on VanCity's business plan, reporting an increased level of disclosure about VanCity's operations in accordance with the SMA model.

While the 1993 and 1994 annual reports have continued to provide increased disclosure about the credit union, VanCity realizes that the current approach lacks external validation and a 'reality check' from the organization's stakeholder groups. VanCity's Board has much interest in continuing to examine models that report on organizational activities and performance in a socially responsible manner. In particular, interest has been expressed in two areas: social audits, and quantifying social performance/information.

Accordingly, an Annual Report Working Group evolved in March 1995 to research these areas. Staff include a vice-president, the controller, an environmental consultant, one staff member closely involved with VanCity's corporate social-role activities, and two staff members who produce the annual report. The group reports to the Executive and the audit committee of the board. VanCity's chair and vice-chair are also consulted, as both have strong interests in this area. To date, work in progress has centred on:

- a review of the annual reports of several American socially responsible companies;
- attendance by VanCity's current chair at the Social Venture Network conference in Tuscany, Italy, in April, 1995;
- a review of social audit resource information from the New Economics Foundation in England;
- discussions with representatives of socially responsible companies in the UK by VanCity's current vice-chair;
- attendance by a member of the Annual Report Working Group at the Society for Business Ethics annual meeting in Vancouver;
- discussions with the Society of Management Accountants of Canada regarding quantifiable social information;
- discussions with Professor Max Clarkson, founding director of the Centre for Corporate Social Performance and Ethics and professor emeritus and former dean of the Faculty of Management at the University of Toronto, about the risk-based model of stakeholder theory;
- attendance at the annual American Business for Social Responsibility (BSR) conference in San Francisco in the autumn, 1995 by two members of the Annual Report Working Group;
- preparation of a social audit policy framework to guide VanCity's approach to social accounting;
- a presentation to the executive management group and the audit committee of the board recommending that VanCity undertake a social audit for the 1997 fiscal year and subsequent approval from the board for this initiative.

Throughout 1996, staff from VanCity's Annual Report Working Group and members from areas most closely involved with corporate social-role activities will develop a cohesive policy framework to define VanCity's corporate social role. This work will be integrated into VanCity's five-year business plan, which involves all areas of the organization and is being recast during 1996. The development of VanCity's social audit process can be described as a 'go slow; get it right' approach that will fully reflect VanCity's corporate social role values and its experience in this area to date.

Later in 1996, measurement criteria for the 1997 social audit will be set. These measurements will be implemented throughout the organization for year-end 1996 to enable collection of data that will be used in compiling the 1997 social audit. VanCity's 1997 social audit will be available in March 1998.

13

The Practice of Silent Accounting

Rob Gray
(Centre for Environmental and Social Accountancy Research, University of Dundee)

Social accounting refers, principally, to the practice of collating and reporting information about an organization's activities on such matters as employment conditions, racial and sexual equality, health and safety, relations with local and international communities, protection of consumers, and impact on the natural environment. It covers four broad ranges of activity – summarized in Figure 13.1.

In this chapter, I will be using the term social accounting to refer specifically to information which is collated by the organization *itself* for use by either the management of the organization or for a wider social constituency, such as employees or the local community.[1] More particularly, I shall concentrate upon the external social accounting or, more properly, 'Corporate Social Reporting' (CSR). CSR relates to social accounting information which is collated by the company (or other organization) and then released into the public domain.

Social accounting – especially by large companies – has been around, in one form or another, for over 100 years. However, with the enormous growth in organizational size since World War II has come an increasing awareness that large companies could no longer be effectively controlled by markets, shareholders or even governments (see, for example, Lindblom, 1984). One manifestation of this was the rise in calls in the 1960s for companies (in particular) to acknowledge a wider social responsibility. These calls, in turn, led to an increased concern with new mechanisms for the social accountability of organizations. Corporate social accounting is one such mechanism.

Companies' motivations for disclosing such data are varied and complex. Such information may very well be part of a company's public relations strategy and, at times, indistinguishable from advertizing. However, the development of such CSR does have implications for corporate accountability and, potentially, for corporate democracy – whether or not the organization in question wishes this to be so. It is this potential for corporate social accountability which makes the phenomenon worthy of note.

Figure 13.1: *Different Approaches to Social Accounting*

Report for the Consumption of....	Report Compiled by... Internal Participants	External Participants
Internal Participants	• Social accounts; • Programme evaluation; • Attitudes audit; • Performance indicators; • Compliance audit; • Environmental audit and accounting.	Quango Reports, eg: • Health and Safety; • Her Majesty's Inspectorate of Pollution (HMIP); • Environmental Protection Agency (EPA) • Water pollution regulators; • Environmental consultants; • Waste and energy audits.
External Participants	• Social accounts; • Social reports; narrative; quantitative; qualitative; financial; • Compliance audit; • Mission statements; • Environmental performance report;	• Social Audit Ltd; • Counter Information Services; • New Consumer; • Consumers Association; • Friends of the Earth; • Greenpeace; • Journalists; • Ethical investment/EIRIS; • 'Social audits'.

Source: adapted from R H Gray *Trends in Corporate Social and Environmental Accounting* (British Institute of Management, London) 1991b p3.

A BRIEF BACKGROUND TO CSR

For convenience, we can perhaps think of CSR over the last 20 or 30 years as falling into three categories: the high profile, more sophisticated *experiments* undertaken by a small number of companies; the more widespread, but less systematic, development of *voluntary disclosure*; and finally, the inexorable increase in *mandatory* (eg *legally required*) *social disclosure*.

Experimentation with CSR has produced a scattering of interesting attempts to produce substantial, systematic accounts of the social and environmental dimensions of an organization's activity. The heyday of this experimentation was the early 1970s in the US. Companies published attempts at: financially quantified 'social income statements and balance sheets'; statements of compliance with standards and legislation; performance indicator reports; and combinations of qualitative and quantitative data about many aspects of corporate social responsibility. Although such experiments have continued from time to time in various countries, they are nearly always isolated examples. None of the experiments entered reporting orthodoxy. More recently, we see the experimentation with environmental accounts and the recent growth in social audits. Much as we need such experimentation – to define both the 'art of the possible' and the limits of current best practice – history tells us that they are likely to remain marginal until national governments and the accounting professions finally recognize *their* responsibilities for – and the necessity of – legislation and guidance on social accountability reporting. This is especially well illustrated by the experience of general voluntary social and environmental disclosure that companies have undertaken over the years.

Voluntary CSR by the larger companies throughout the industrialized, capitalist world is immensely variable – but has grown steadily over the last two decades. As subjects become more important, the volume of voluntary disclosure related to that topic grows. It then declines again as companies perceive that the subject is attracting less widespread interest – a seemingly inevitable consequence of voluntary reporting. So, in the UK for example, during the early 1970s, broad social responsibility was the key issue which then gave way to an increased concern for employees. This in turn was replaced by a slight increase in community involvement, pension-related matters, health and safety issues and employee share-ownership schemes in the 1980s. The 1990s, more obviously, were the years of the environment.

The general trend in voluntary reporting is a steady increase in the volume of information provided. The annual report of a large British company would, on average, have contained about half a page of voluntary social and environmental information throughout the late 1970s and early to mid 1980s. By the mid 1990s this had risen to over four pages of information. Throughout, this information would have been dominated by employee-related issues, but as the years advanced, community and then environmental issues began to catch up. Although there is less systematic data about CSR in other countries, this seems to be the general pattern.

This rise in voluntary disclosure by companies has been accompanied by a rise in *mandatory CSR*. The data which companies have to disclose by regulation, (including company law), varies between countries. For example the UK Companies Acts require a company to disclose its charitable donations and lay down fairly extensive requirements on the data which must be reported about employees. France requires companies to produce a *bilan social* which, while it emphasizes employee-related issues certainly goes beyond this to a wider set of social issues. In the US, companies must disclose environmental information, especially that relating to land contamination and other environmental issues with direct financial consequences.

THE SILENT SOCIAL ACCOUNT

Any reasonably sized company has many channels through which it discloses information. Company brochures, product packaging, newsletters to staff, advertizing and special reports (on, for example, the environment) are all important sources of information about companies. But probably the most important channel is the company's annual report. This is governed, to a degree at least, by company law and contains the financial statements and, typically, a directors' report and a chairman's statement. The Annual Report goes to all shareholders and is generally available to the public. A great deal of time, money and effort goes into its production. The company is not just concerned with the information which the report contains but also with the format and presentation of that information. In many regards, it is the public flagship of the organization and conveys a great deal about the company and how it sees itself. A typical large British company will publish a glossy, professionally produced annual report of over 50 pages. Scattered around that Report will be the elements of the voluntary and mandated social and environmental information which we have discussed above. The range is shown in Figure 13.2.

In different parts of the financial statements, in the directors' report, in the chairman's statement and elsewhere in the annual report will be small nuggets of social and environmental data. For the large companies, as we have seen, these nuggets will amount to over four pages of data. These pages represent a significant step on the road to the sort of fuller social account which the literature on CSR explores.

And yet, no company has ever, to my knowledge, put these four pages together to produce a fairly substantial social report. Why is this? The obvious answers (for example, companies may never have thought of it) may be too glib. However, there has not, so far as I know, been any research undertaken which asks this question. As a first step, therefore, it seems apposite to see what such a 'silent account' might look like.

Figure 13.2: *Typical Areas Covered by CSR in UK Company Annual Reports*

Voluntary	Required/Mandatory
• Environmental protection	• Charitable donations
• Energy saving	• Employment data
• Consumer protection	• Pension fund adequacy
• Product safety	• Consultation with employees
• Community involvement	• Employee share ownership schemes
• Value-added statement	• Employment of the disabled
• Health and safety	• Contingent liabilities and provisions
• Racial and sexual equality	for health and safety or
• Redundancies	environmental remediation
• Employee training	
• Mission statement/statement of social responsibility	

Source: adapted from R H Gray *Trends in Corporate Social and Environmental Accounting* (British Institute of Management, London) 1991b p3.

AN ILLUSTRATION OF THE SILENT SOCIAL ACCOUNT

The final section of this chapter contains a social account reconstructed from the 1994 annual report of Glaxo Holdings plc. To illustrate what a reconstructed social account might look like for a conventional British company, it seemed appropriate to avoid both very small companies (whose social disclosures would be minimal) and the UK's notable leading disclosers such as ICI or British Petroleum, (partly on practical grounds – their social account would be very long – and partly because such companies would not be typical of UK companies). Within these parameters, the choice of Glaxo is entirely arbitrary. Glaxo is a very large pharmaceutical company and is not known for innovative voluntary social disclosure, but neither is it a company which historically restricts itself to the very minimum of mandatory disclosure.

The resulting eight-page report is a compilation of elements from all parts of the annual report and is, inevitably, somewhat disjointed in places. The social account follows the basic format so frequently spoken of in the social accounting literature – sections cover: mission and policy; directors and employees; community; environment; and customers. In addition, the recent developments from the Cadbury report on corporate governance are a highly pertinent element of social disclosure and accountability and have also been included.

The reconstruction of the company's social account is arresting in a number of ways. Perhaps most importantly, we reconstruct a social reality of the company (Hines, 1988) by bringing together a substantial amount of socially related data which, as a result, has far more impact as a social statement than it does when scattered around other aspects of the annual report. The information, I believe, then suggests a greater substance to the social – as opposed to the economic – dimensions of the company. It also achieves a sort of information-synergy in that the impression created by the whole is greater than that of its component parts which are traditionally dispersed throughout the report.

Equally important, the reconstruction of the social account enables us to, *first*, identify which, if any, broad areas of activity (employees, community, environment and customers) are ignored by the company and, *second*, to highlight areas of missing data within the broad areas. So, for example, in the case of the Glaxo social account, we can see their very cursory treatment of the environment (although further data is available on this area); the absence, in the employee section, of any health and safety information; and the crucial issue of the company's relationship with lesser-developed country communities, which is only hinted at in the comment on transfer pricing.

This reconstructed social acount is not, therefore, intended to illustrate best practice but, rather, to illustrate what could be made of conventional practice. This, in turn, could form a template for corporate social disclosure against which companies' reporting could be systematically judged, and provide a basis for the development of more systematic and substantial development of company social disclosure.

THE PRACTICALITIES OF A FIRST STEP?

As I mentioned earlier, as far as I am aware, this is the first time anybody has reconstructed a company social account from existing company social data. (This is in stark contrast to the reconstruction of social accounts of a broader nature using externally generated data – see, for example, Medawar, 1976; Gray, Owen and Maunders, 1987; Gray, Owen and Adams, 1996). It is a relatively simple exercise whose implications deserve, I think, further exploration. For parties external to the company, (typically non-governmental organizations and researchers), the process could be interesting as either a means of monitoring company social disclosure at a more detailed and specific level than is traditionally the case, or as an attempt to publicize the social accountability issues arising within large companies. For the company itself, the direct information costs of producing such a social account are negligible – the data already exists and it is simply a matter of rearranging it. The *indirect* costs would be two-fold: there would be legal and auditing costs (see below) and there would probably be increased attention to the company's social behaviour. It is not clear whether this increased attention would be beneficial to the company. The benefits of the development of social accounting would probably accrue to society and to the development of social accountability – not issues on which companies are traditionally enthusiastic.

The legal and auditing costs would need attention. That is, the data for this social account is drawn from both the statutory and non-statutory parts of the annual report. The Companies Acts currently determine what information should be included in the statutory financial statements and what information must be attested to by the financial auditor. One can well imagine that the rearrangement of this social information would raise howls of objection from the traditionally reactionary accounting profession. At the same time, it is well established that voluntary initiatives in the reporting field are generally unsuccessful. Although a significant proportion of the very largest companies follow the initiatives, this only accounts for a small minority of all companies and even this minority's interest in the initiatives wanes after a few years.

The reconstruction of a company social account is a matter to which the accounting profession and the government could so easily give attention – a small change to the Companies Acts and to current accounting standards could deliver a regular, if somewhat basic, social account for all UK companies at virtually no direct cost. Both the accounting profession and the UK government have flirted with social and environmental reporting for over 20 years. Here is a simple and practicable way forward that would provide an initial – if token – step that would demonstrate some real commitment to their, so far empty, statements of support for the improved social account-ability of the corporate sector.

DEVELOPING A BASIS FOR REAL ACCOUNTABILITY

Would a company, however, actually want to do this? It has enough to do without looking for more work. And why should a company wash its dirty laundry in public and thereby give ammunition to social activitists and pressure groups? It may well be that this is exactly how companies do feel about such things. Nevertheless, it would be rather nice to hear our largest, most influential companies saying this. The sheer size and power of corporations is frequently legitimized through the maintenance of an image of corporate social responsibility. A socially benign company will not mind proving the case. On the other hand, society probably has a right to know which companies have no real intentions of adopting a more open and socially responsible attitude. It may well affect government attitudes and the behaviour of employees, shareholders and customers.

Taking this resultant, embryonic (silent) social account further would, however, require careful thought and time. The social accounting data currently reported is ad hoc, partisan and incomplete. To make the account more systematic would involve, first, a more systematic analysis of the company's social dimensions (a combination of what is happening with environmental reporting through the environmental audit plus a stakeholder analysis of the sort reported throughout this book) and then, second, designing the information systems – the social bookkeeping – to produce the information required (as, again, companies are doing with environmental information systems). (For more information on social bookkeeping, see Dey, Evans and Gray, 1995). For many large companies, the bones of such a social bookkeeping already exist. The personnel information system, the environmental information systems, the established processes of reporting on health and safety and racial and sexual equality, and other extant information systems established to provide information for legal reporting purposes and/or for management control, already exist and are used as the basis of the company's current CSR. It is a matter of systematically extending these to produce reliable, consistent and complete data on the wider web of issues that will constitute a full social account.

Precisely what such a full social account should look like is, however, still a matter of some debate and experimentation. It is probable that there will be no *single* form of social accounting which will suffice for all situations. The form of social accounting discussed here is designed to continue the trends in corporate social accounting observed over the last 20 years or so. It is a form which is clearly modelled on conventional accounting thinking and sees the company as the sole reporting entity. It contrasts somewhat with the more recent approaches to social accounting taken by NEF, Traidcraft, Shared Earth and others (explored throughout this book), which tend to be a combination of internal and external participant inputs and which emphasize the voices of the stakeholders rather than the voice of the company. While these two approaches are predominantly complementary, they are not identical. Resolving the theoretical issues that arise from these different approaches – and resolving the (far from trivial) practical, political and economic implications of each – is the principal challenge for the nascent social accounting movement in the coming years. But finding a resolution is more important than *how* we achieve this because the establishment of some real basis of social accountability and transparency for large organizations has never been more important.

It is important to note that this social account is based entirely on the *Annual Report and Accounts 1994* of Glaxo Holdings plc. Annual reports are public domain documents. Material from the *Glaxo Annual Report* has been extracted and rearranged to form this social account. Because of this process, it is possible that material may have been taken out of context and, therefore, the name of Glaxo has been removed from the social account in order to recognize that – though this is based on Glaxo's words – it is not a Glaxo document.

THE SOCIAL ACCOUNTS OF XO PLC

Mission and Policy Statements

XO plc is an integrated research-based group of companies whose corporate purpose is to create, discover, develop, manufacture and market throughout the world safe, effective medicines of the highest quality which will bring benefit to patients through improved longevity and quality of life, and to society in general through economic value.

Corporate Governance Statement

The company pursues its corporate purpose with the objective of enhancing shareholder value over time. Fundamental to the fulfilment of corporate responsibilities and the achievement of financial objectives is an effective system of corporate governance.

Board and Committee Structure

The board of XO Holdings plc is responsible for the group's system of corporate governance and is ultimately accountable for its activities throughout the world. the board comprises executive and non-executive directors. The role of non-executive directors is to bring independent judgement to board deliberations and decisions.

The offices of chairman and chief executive are held separately. The chief executive is also deputy chairman and a non-executive director holds the position of vice-chairman. On 30 June 1994 the chairman relinquished all executive responsibilities. Since then he has fulfilled his role in a non-executive capacity and will retire at the annual general meeting on 18 November 1994. His successor will be appointed non-executive chairman.

The board meets regularly throughout the year. It has a formal schedule of matters reserved to it for decision but otherwise delegates specific responsibilities to committees as described below.

The group executive committee is responsible for the executive management of the group. It is chaired by the deputy chairman and comprises the executive directors, the chief executive of XO Inc, the group head of research and the director of group development. The committee meets monthly and its minutes are placed on the agenda of the board.

The group audit committee reviews the half-year and full-year results and the annual report and accounts prior to submission to the board and considers any matters raised by the auditors. The committee comprises the non-executive directors and is chaired by the vice-chairman; it meets three times a year with certain executive directors and the auditors in attendance.

The senior emoluments committee approves the remuneration of the executive directors and is responsible for the policy and operation of the XO plc group share-option schemes. The committee comprises the non-executive directors and is chaired by the vice-chairman.

The group appeals committee carries out the boards' policy on charitable and community contributions. The committee meets quarterly.

Pension Schemes

The company and a number of its overseas subsidiary undertakings have established pension schemes for the administration of staff retirement benefits. In the UK the company and its UK subsidiary undertakings participate in and contribute to pension schemes which are administered separately from the group by formally constituted trustee companies. A number of the company's executive and non-executive directors, together with a number of outside directors, serve on the boards of the trustee companies.

> 'The country's economy depends on the drive and efficiency of its companies. Thus the effectiveness with which the boards discharge their responsibilities determines Britain's competitive position. They must be free to drive their companies forward, but exercise that freedom within a framework of effective accountability. This is the essence of any system of good corporate governance.'
>
> (Cadbury Report)

Accountability and Control

XO plc operates and attaches importance to clear principles and procedures designed to achieve the accountability and control appropriate to a science-based business operating multinationally in a highly regulated business sector. The main precepts of this corporate ethos are: concentration on, and expertise in, a single industry sector; central direction, resource allocation and risk management of the key functional activities of product strategy, research and development; manufacture and financial practice; formally constituted subsidiary undertakings in all significant world markets, with operating and financial responsibility clearly delegated to local boards; and lines of management responsibility from general managers of subsidiary undertakings to executive directors of XO Holdings plc.

These principles are designed to provide an environment of central leadership and local operating autonomy as the framework for the exercise of accountability and control by the board, its committees and executive management. Essential features of the company's system of internal control comprise: focus on key business objectives; integrated group-wide financial approval and reporting procedures; central promulgation of functional policy and monitoring of compliance (including on-site audit of product quality, manufacturing standards, environmental care, health and safety, and insurable risk; and a newly formed internal audit department which assists in the monitoring of financial practice across the group); and central ratification of appointments to the boards of subsidiary undertakings.

Remuneration of Directors (Extract)

Remuneration Policy

The company seeks to provide rewards and incentives for the remuneration of directors that reflect the performance, and align with the objectives, of the company. The company is a global business that trades multinationally; its shares are listed on the principal international capital markets. Directors are appointed to the board, from different national backgrounds, to bring to the management and direction of the company the skills and experience appropriate to the needs of an international business; they are remunerated on terms competitive with international market rates that recognize their responsibilities to shareholders for the performance of the company.

Non-executive directors receive fees for their services to the board and other emoluments for services to board committees and in certain cases to the Boards of certain subsidiary undertakings and to the boards of the UK Pension Funds' Corporate Trustees. Further detail is provided in the Remuneration Policy on how remuneration is established, including additional details on salary and benefits; performance-linked payments; post-retirement benefits and share options.

Table 13.1: *Remuneration of Directors in Aggregate (£000)*

	1994	1993
Fees	156	147
Salary benefits and other emoluments	5643	5903
Performance-related payments	1868	1676
Contributions to pension schemes	1898	1541
Funding of past service pension deficit	–	4700

Table 13.2: *Remuneration of the Chairman (£000)*

	1994	1993
Salary benefits and other emoluments	1053	1033
Performance-related payments	436	410
Contributions to pension schemes	696	487
Funding of past service pension deficit	–	3,200

On 30 June 1994 the chairman relinquished executive responsibilities and on that date his contract of employment with the company was terminated by mutual consent. No compensation is due to him. The Senior Emoluments Committee has exercised its discretion to permit his continued participation in the performance-linked plan in respect of periods to 30 June 1994; payments to him will be disclosed as payments to a former director when paid.

The emoluments, excluding pension scheme contributions and including performance-related payments, of the directors of the company, including the chairman and overseas directors are listed in Table 13.3.

Employment Report

Staff Policies

In these times of change within the pharmaceutical industry, the quality, commitment and effectiveness of XO plc's staff are crucial for continued success. The group continues to invest in its employees, to provide as much scope as possible to develop their skills and individual contribution, and to create a working environment which emphasizes trust, teamwork and continuous improvement. Staff policies and programmes take their direction from a broad framework of corporate values that encourages employees to become involved in their companies and which seeks to reward and develop all staff according to their contribution and capability.

Employee communications are a high priority; company newspapers and journals and the annual *Report for Staff* in booklet and video form represent some of the methods used to ensure that all staff are properly informed. Employment policies do not discriminate between employees or potential employees on the grounds of colour, race, ethnic and national origin, sex, marital status, religious beliefs or disability. In the UK, for example, if an employee become disabled while in employment and, as a result, is unable to perform normal duties, every effort is made to offer suitable alternative employment and assistance with retraining.

In the UK, the company is committed to the Opportunity 2000 Campaign which seeks to remove traditional barriers to women's progress in the business environment.

The XO group share-option schemes enable employees to share in the success of the company. On 30 June 1994 the group employed 47,378 staff.

Pension and Post-Retirement Costs

Group undertakings operate pension scheme which cover the group's material obligations to provide pensions to retired employees. These schemes have been developed in accordance with local practices in the countries concerned. The principal schemes are of the defined benefit type where retirement benefits are based on pensionable remuneration and length of service. The group also operates a number of defined contribution schemes in which retirement benefits are determined by the value of funds arising from contributions paid in respect of each employee. In the majority of cases the

Table 13.3: Emoluments of the Company Directors

Not Exceeding £000	Exceeding £000	1994 Number	1993 Number	Not Exceeding £000	Exceeding £000	1994 Number	1993 Number	Not Exceeding £000	Exceeding £000	1994 Number	1993 Number
20	25	1	–	255	260	–	1	695	700	1	–
25	30	–	4	300	305	1	–	710	715	1	–
30	35	2	–	345	350	1	–	720	725	–	1
35	40	1	1	425	430	1	1	740	745	–	1
45	50	1	–	450	455	1	–	810	815	1	–
50	55	–	1	510	515	–	–	930	935	1	–
55	60	1	–	565	570	1	1	1320	1325	–	1
60	65	–	1	570	575	–	1	1440	1445	–	1
75	80	1	–	590	595	1	1	1485	1490	1	–
80	85	–	1	630	635	–	1				
90	95	–	1	680	685	1	–				

Table 13.4: *Average Number of People Employed by XO plc (including Directors)*

	1994	1993
Manufacturing	17,688	13,515
Research and development	7,476	7,133
Selling, general and administrative	20,025	19,376
Total:	47,189	40,024

Table 13.5: *Aggregate Employment Costs (£ million)*

	1994	1993
Wages and salaries	1064	969
Social security costs	132	120
Pension and post-retirement costs	104	98
Total staff costs:	1300	1187

Table 13.6: *Average Number of Group Employees (000s)*

	1994	1993	1992	1991	1990	1989	1988
United Kingdom	12.0	12.2	12.0	12.4	12.3	11.4	11.0
Overseas	35.2	27.9	25.1	23.2	20.9	17.3	15.4
Total:	47.2	41.1	37.1	35.6	33.2	28.7	26.4

contributions to defined benefit schemes are generally held in separately administered trusts or are insured. In certain cases, overseas group undertakings hold assets with the specific purpose of matching the liabilities of unfunded schemes, both in terms of maturity and value.

The cost of contributions to, and provision for, the various pension arrangement is listed in Table 13.7.

The funds of the UK-defined benefit schemes are administered by trustee companies and are kept separate from those of the group's. Independent actuaries prepare valuations of the schemes at least every three years and, in accordance with their recommendations, annual contributions are paid to the schemes so as to secure the benefits set out in the rules. On 31 March 1992, the date of the last actuarial valuation of the UK-funded defined-benefit schemes, the market value of the assets was UK£626 million.

Table 13.7: *Pension and Post-Retirement Costs*

	1994 (£ million)	1993 (£ million)
UK-funded defined-benefit schemes	49	55
UK-unfunded defined-benefit schemes	5	-
UK-funded defined-contribution schemes	3	3
Overseas-funded defined-benefit schemes	26	21
Overseas-unfunded defined-benefit schemes	8	7
Overseas-defined contribution schemes	13	12
Total:	104	98

Expression of Appreciation

It has been a privilege to serve XO for 29 years and a source of pride to see how the skill, initiative and commitment of our staff and employees throughout the world have brought the group to the highest rank of the industry. On behalf of the Board, I wish to express my sincere appreciation to them, both for this achievement and for another successful financial year (Chairman).

Community Report

Charitable and Community Support

XO Holdings plc made charitable donations amounting to UK£6.5 million during the year and its UK subsidiary undertakings made other contributions in support of the community amounting to UK£0.9 million. The combined total of UK£7.4 million was equivalent to 4.4 per cent of that share of group pretax profit proportional to the UK contribution to group turnover.

XO's approach to charitable contributions in the UK places particular emphasis on support for initiatives which improve healthcare provision and scientific and medical education. A wide variety of contributions has been made, including £1.2m to the National Society for Epilepsy to make possible the establishment of the world's first Magnetic Resonance Imaging Unit dedicated solely to epilepsy diagnosis and research; UK£1.2 million to endow, with the British Lung Foundation, a new chair in respiratory science at a UK university; and over UK£500,000 to fund projects to help homeless people, including the establishment of the UK's first refuge for children under the age of 16, run by the charity Centrepoint.

The group's programme of support for healthcare in the developing world featured a substantial donation to the UK based charity MERLIN (Medical Emergency Relief International) to allow it to respond quickly with medical assistance to natural and man-made disasters around the world. With this assistance, MERLIN has helped people in Afghanistan, Burma, Siberia and Rwanda.

XO has also maintained its support for the environment and the arts. Major initiatives in the UK have included assisting the Natural History Museum in London to establish a membership scheme, which will allow many more people to appreciate the work of one of the foremost institutions working in the environmental field, and the sponsorship of an exhibition of the works of Modigliani at the Royal Academy of Arts, which was attended by over 130,000 visitors.

XO Inc made charitable and community gifts totalling US$12.8 million during the year and group companies in other countries, including Singapore and Canada, also made significant contributions.

Political Contributions

The company contributed UK£72,000 for political purposes in the UK during the year, comprising UK£60,000 to the Conservative Party Central Office and UK£12,000 to the Centre for Policy Studies.

Litigation (Extract)

XO has commenced proceedings against two companies, one of which has counterclaimed for unspecified damages alleging that XO's litigation has infringed US anti-trust legislation.

Taxation (Extract)

The most significant open issues relate to international transfer pricing.

Environmental Report

Environment

XO's commitment to continuous improvement in its environmental performance was further demonstrated during the year and is backed up by the provision of substantial capital and revenue expenditure: an outstanding example was the major investment in the development of a CFC-free propellent for use in respiratory treatments.

Environmental improvements can also offer financial benefits. One of the first chief executive's awards for outstanding achievements by group companies in the field of health, safety and the environment was made to XOB Ltd for a programme at Ulverston, which significantly reduced losses of solvents used in the manufacturing process. As well as cutting the emission of solvents to the atmosphere, the initiative has reduced annual expenditure by Ulverston on the purchase of solvents by some UK£370,000.

XO sets worldwide environment and safety standards and takes action to ensure that they are achieved. The group's adherence to good environmental practices has been recognized in various parts of the world. XO is also keenly aware of the importance of conservation and biodiversity, and has published a policy on the acquisition of natural product source samples which makes clear that it neither seeks nor supports the collection of endangered species.

Capital expenditure amounted to UK£183 million in 1993/94, of which some UK£40 million was for equipment and facilities for the launch of a wide range of new respiratory products which make use of CFC-free propellent technology.

Animals and Research

It is XO's long-standing policy to minimize the use of animals in the development of new medicines; alternative methods are used wherever feasible and the group is actively engaged in, and supports, research to develop alternative methods. Essential animal experiments are rigorously monitored to ensure that statutory requirements are met and that best practice is followed.

Customer Protection and Product Safety

Innovation For Customers (Extract)

As one of the world's largest pharmaceutical companies, XO is very much part of the process of change. We fully recognize the nature of that change and the need to reappraise our strategies and policies. Yet we see nothing in the rapidly evolving environment to deflect us from our basic mission – to bring innovative medicines to the market. There is no doubt in our minds that patients and society will continue to expect improved healthcare and that private enterprise research and development can deliver it. There is a need to ensure that new treatments are not only innovative but bring value which can be demonstrated clearly to governments and healthcare providers.

Development Programmes

Compounds moving out of research programmes into development undergo stringent evaluation to demonstrate not only their safety and effectiveness, but also to assess whether they offer real benefits to patients and significant clinical advantages over currently available medicines. Consequently, XO continually reassesses its research pipeline in order to reach its overall objectives.

Further Information

In addition to the annual and interim reports, the company produces publications which are available to shareholders on request. These include *XO in the Community*, *Key Facts* and *XO and the Environment*. Copies may be obtained from the group secretariat at the registered office address shown at the end of the annual report.

REFERENCES

Dey C, R Evans & R H Gray (1995) 'Towards social information systems and bookkeeping: A note on developing the mechanisms for social accounting and audit' *Journal of Applied Accounting Research* 2(3) December pp36–69

R H Gray, D L Owen & C Adams (1996) *Accounting and Accountability: changes and challenges in corporate social and environmental reporting* Prentice Hall International, Hemel Hempstead

R H Gray, D L Owen & K T Maunders (1987) *Corporate Social Reporting: Accounting and accountability* Prentice Hall, Hemel Hempstead

R D Hines (1988) 'Financial accounting: In communicating reality, we construct reality' *Accounting, Organizations and Society* 13(3) pp251–261

C E Lindblom (1984) 'The accountability of the private enterprise: Private – no: Enterprise – yes' in T Tinker (ed) *Social Accounting for Corporations* Manchester University Press, Manchester

C Medawar (1976) 'The social audit: a political view' *Accounting, Organizations and Society* 1(4) pp389–394

ENDNOTES

1   Terminology on social accounting, social audits, social reporting and so on is far from exact. The literature of social accounting has tended to use the terms social accounting, reporting and disclosure interchange-ably to refer to this self-reporting by organizations The term social audit has been generally taken in the past to mean information collated and reported by a third party, independent of the organization to which the information relates Independent attestation (the conventional use of the term audit) of social accounts has been fairly rare, (but see Gray, Owen and Maunders, 1987; and Gray, Owen and Adams, 1996 for examples and for more detail on this).

Key Contact Names and Addresses

Ben & Jerry's Homemade, Inc
PO Box 240, 15 Kimball Avenue
South Burlington, VT 05403, US
Email: alan@benjerry.com
Contact Person: Alan Parker

Centre for Advancement of Public Policy
1735 S Street NW, Washington, DC, 20009, US
Email: restes@american.edu
Contact Person: Professor Ralph Estes

Centre for Environmental and Social Accountancy Research
University of Dundee, Dundee, DD1 4HN, UK
Email: r.h.gray@dundee.ac.uk
Contact Person: Professor Rob Gray

Co-op Italia/ Strategie and Organizzazione (SMAER)
Via Ronco 1, 40013 Castelmaggiore (BO), Italy
Contact Person: Alessandra Vaccari

Copenhagen Business School
Department of Management, Politics & Philosophy
Copenhagen Business School, Blaagaardsgade 23B
DK–2200 Copenhagen N, Denmark
Email: pruzan@cbs.dk
Contact Person: Professor Peter Pruzan

Council of Economic Priorities
30 Irving Place, New York, NY 10003, US
Email: cep@echonyc.com
Contact Person: Alice Tepper-Marlin

European Institute for Business Ethics
Nijenrode University, Straatweg 25
BG Breukelen, Netherlands
Email: Hummels@hobbit.nijenrode.nl
Contact Person: Harry Hummels

Institute of Social and Ethical AccountAbility
112–116 Whitechapel Road, London E1 1JE, UK
Email: secretariat@accountability.org.uk
Contact Person: Claudia Gonella

Municipality of Aarhus
Aarhus Kommune, Aeldresektoren, Telefontorvet 4
DK–8000 Aarhus C, Denmark
Contact Person: Carl-Johan Skousgaard

New Economics Foundation
Vine Court, 112–116 Whitechapel Road
London E1 1JE, UK
Email: neweconomics@gn.apc.org
Contact Person: Simon Zadek

Sbn Bank
PO Box 162, DK–9100 Aalborg, Denmark
Contact Person: Keld Gammelgaard

The Body Shop International
Watersmead, Littlehampton, West Sussex, BN17 6LS, UK
Email: maria_sillanpaa@bodyshop.co.uk
Contact People: David Wheeler/Maria Sillanpää

Traidcraft
Kingsway, Gateshead, Tyne and Wear, NE11 ONE, UK
Email: tcexchange@gn.apc.org
Contact Person: Richard Evans

VanCity Savings and Credit Union
PO Box 2120 STN Terminal, Vancouver BC
V6B 5R8, Canada
Email: Priscilla_Boucher@vancity.com
Contact Person: Priscilla Boucher

Wøyen Mølle
Vangkroken 20, N–1313 Vøyenenga, Norway

Contributors

Cathy Brisbois has worked for VanCity since 1987. As manager of publications and marketing communication, she is responsible for producing VanCity's annual report. Cathy is also a member of VanCity's Social Audit Committee, Annual Report Working Group, and Corporate Social Role Task Force. Last November, Cathy was a panellist at the annual Business for Social Responsibility Conference in New York, presenting on VanCity's approach to its social report and social audit framework.

Tom Christensen has a university degree in Business Administration, 1975; he has since worked with two Danish consultancy firms which specialize in advising municipalities and counties concerning management and organization. He has also 12 years of experience from jobs as a manager in a public economic department and a public social department. Is now the president of EKL Consult in Aalborg. EKL is the Danish abbreviation for ethics, quality and management. The firm specializes in quality development and ethical accounting statements in the public sector.

Richard Evans studied with the Open University and Newcastle University and gained a Master's Degree in Business Administration in 1989. He worked from 1966–1979, mostly in the European foundry industry, in sales and technical support before joining the Intermediate Technology Development Group in 1979. He became a director of Traidcraft plc in 1980, and its first marketing director in 1985. In 1991 the *Journal of Business Ethics* published his paper 'Business ethics and changes in society'. In 1992, Traidcraft decided to extend its public reporting to include its social impact and ethical performance. The Social Accounting methodology he developed with NEF was published in *Auditing the Market* in 1993, and the method has been used subsequently by the Body Shop, Allied Dunbar, Ben and Jerry's Homemade Inc. and others. Now director of social accounting at Traidcraft Exchange, he leads a consultancy for companies developing social and ethical accounting systems.

Professor Rob Gray is Mathew Professor of Accounting and Information Systems in the Department of Accountancy and Business Finance at the University of Dundee. He qualified as a chartered accountant with KPMG Peat Marwick, is editor of the *British Accounting Review*, Director of the Centre for Social and Environmental Accounting Research, a Fellow of the Royal Society of Arts and author of over 90 books, monographs and articles. These include *Corporate Social Reporting* and *The Greening of Accountancy*.

Lise Nørgaard works as a consultant on leadership and organizational development in Norway. She received her education from the Universities of Copenhagen and Oslo (pedagogy, criminology and physical education). She has just completed a two-year state scholarship to investigate value-based leadership and ethical accounting in a Norwegian context. Based upon the experiences of working on an ethical accounting statement at Wøyen Mølle, she is now involved in helping a number of Norwegian organizations develop ethical accounting and value-based leadership. She also leads management training courses at universities in Norway for senior managers in health and welfare institutions.

Alan Parker is director of shareholder relations and social accounting at Ben and Jerry's Homemade, Inc. He has worked in the dairy industry in Vermont for 20 years in various management, sales, marketing, finance and communications capacities. His current responsibilities at Ben and Jerry's include all contacts with the financial community: shareholders, prospective investors, portfolio managers and securities analysts. In addition, he manages projects related to the company's social mission, such as the annual Social Report and attendant SEAAR methods, and developing company policies as they relate to agricultural issues. As this book goes to press, he is forming a consulting firm (SAAR Associates) whose business goal is to undertake social audits for businesses and non-profit organizations.

Peter Pruzan is Professor of Systems Science at the Department of Management, Politics & Philosophy, Copenhagen Business School. He has degrees from Princeton University (BSc), Harvard University (MBA), Case-Western Reserve University (PhD) and the University of Copenhagen (Dr Polit). He has been the president of a successful small business and has authored roughly 100 books and articles on operations' research, planning, systems science and organizational ethics. At present he is leading a research project sponsered by the Danish government on ethics, value-based management and ethical accounting and is in the process of establishing a new five-year educational programme for the Copenhagen Business School: Philosophy & Economics. His personal goal in these endeavours is to integrate concepts of human values and spirituality within the teaching and practice of management and economics.

Maria Sillanpaa is the Team Leader, Ethical Auditing in the Ethical Audit Department of The Body Shop International. In 1993 The Body Shop commissioned Maria to initiate a research project into social auditing and to propose a potential way forwards for the company. Since 1994 Maria has been a full-time member of the ethical audit team and is now responsible for the implementation and further development of social auditing within the group. She is currently working on a PhD in Corporate Social Responsibility. Her previous academic work and publications have focused on the linkages between social responsibility and strategic management.

Carl-Johan Skovsgaard was born in 1946 and holds a university degree in political science. His first job was as a lecturer at the Institute of Political Science, University of Aarhus, Denmark. Following that, he worked as a city clerk, managing director in the municipality of Bjerringbro and at present is head of the Senior Citizen Department, municipality of Aarhus. Has published a number of books and articles including contributions to Kenneth Newton (ed) *Urban Political Economy*, David McKay (ed) *Planning and Politics in Western Europe* and Terry Clark (ed) *Urban Innovations as Response to Fiscal Strain*.

Alessandra Vaccari is a partner of Smaer, a consultant society owned by the Italian co-operative movement, where she has worked since 1987. Since 1990 she has been following the social account project and carried it out in almost 40 co-operative companies, in different activity sectors. She has been managing the Co-op project since 1992. Alessandra is a graduate in Work Psychology at the University of Padova. She has also contributed to several Italian books and has written articles in Italian journals; moreover, she has collaborated with Italian academic researchers to prepare social account cases.

Dr David Wheeler is Head of Stakeholder Policy of The Body Shop International. Before joining The Body Shop in late 1991, David worked as a full-time adviser to the Shadow Secretary of State for Environmental Protection. In his four years with The Body Shop, David has overseen the publication of four comprehensive environmental statements and has established an auditing team comprising five areas of internal ethical practice. In 1996 The Body Shop published its first integrated ethical audit report, including statements of performance on environmental and animal protection and social issues. David has promoted campaigns for mandatory environmental disclosure in industry for the highest possible standards for European Community Eco-labels, and for maximum responsibility for retailers in post-consumer waste reduction, re-use and recycling. Throughout his career, he has published papers and articles in a wide variety of medical, academic and popular journals.

Dr Simon Zadek is currently Research Director of the New Economics Foundation, a London-based non-profit dedicated to promoting approaches to economics and business that support key principles of social justice and environmental sustainability. Previous to this, he was co-founder and partner of Maendeleo, an economic management consultancy dedicated to similar principles and practice, worked for a major international management consultancy, and lived and worked in St Lucia as a government economic planner. Simon has degrees from the University of Bristol, the London School of Economics, and Brunel University, and has published on many aspects of economics, business, and ethics, including his first book, *An Economics of Utopia: the Democratisation of Scarcity*. He is currently co-editing a book entitled *Mediating Sustainability: Sustainable Agriculture Practice-to-Policy in Latin America*.

Annotated Bibliography

Adams, J Carruthers, and S Hamil (1991) *Changing Corporate Values: A Guide to Social and Environmental Policy and Practice in Britain's Top Companies* Kogan Page, London

A good example of published corporate social and environmental screening and ratings, in this case by the British non-governmental organization *New Consumer.* Coverage of 128 companies acrosss all the major retail sectors and brand names.

D H Blake, W C Frederick, *et al* (1976) *Social Auditing: Evaluating the Impact of Corporate Programs* Prager Publishers, Inc, New York

This book begins with a general introduction to social auditing by identifying its purpose and perspective and revealing the problems of this field. The process of social auditing is outlined and strategic considerations, as well as techniques for obtaining information and their links, are discussed. In addition to this, methods of reporting social information are described and two case studies are added. In the final section social auditing is examined as a practical management tool and social audit models are given.

Business in the Community (1996) *Business in the Community* supplement to *The Financial Times*, 5 December, London

Provides an overview of some of the best pactice community responsibility activities by major corporations. Coverage of recent developments in social and ethical accounting and auditing, including the development of the Institute of Social and Ethical AccountAbility.

N Denzin and Y Lincoln (1994) *Handbook of Qualitative Research* Sage, Thousand Oaks

Probably the most comprehensive book on qualitative research methods in print today. This extensive review of theoretical and case study material offers crucial information to the reader interested in the practicalities of selecting approaches to stakeholder dialogue in social and ethical accounting and auditing that is both rigorous and appropriate to the particular context and needs.

R Estes (1996) *Tyranny of the Bottom Line: Why Corporations Make Good People Do Bad Things* Berrett-Koehler, San Francisco

Beginning with a general reflection about different ways of business, it reveals the reasons for the dominion of the corpocracy as well as the perversion of its purpose, and shows the consequences of unaccountability for its stakeholders. An alternative solution is given and the approaches to achieve this are shown. An annex is provided detailing what the author thinks should be included in a social report.

R Evans (1991) 'Business Ethics and Changes in Society' in *Journal of Business Ethics*, Volume 10 pp871–876

This article considers the role of business in its social and environmental context and points out that business as such cannot be separated from its ethical context. It argues for a 'total ethic' concept analagous to the zero defects concept in management. This ethic should both include and form the foundation of the organization's mission and values. The characteristics of this mission statement should be determined by all stakeholders, not just those with financial interests.

G Goyder (1961) *The Responsible Company* Blackwell, Oxford

One of the earlier generation of books covering corporate social and ethical accounting and auditing, prepared in an environment of nationalization of industries taking place in Britain in the 1950s and 1960s. Despite this different climate, the author outlines the reasons for doing it in a manner that is entirely relevant today.

R Gray (1987) *Corporate Social Reporting: Accounting and Accountability* Prentice-Hall, Hertfordshire

This book offers a detailed discussion of social accounting, corporate social responsibility and related issues as it stood in the mid 1980s. It begins with an introduction to social accountability and discusses developments internationally and in the UK. The author provides a review of accounting theories and explores linkages to corporate social responsibility.

R Gray, R Kouhy et al (1994) *Corporate Social Reporting by UK Companies: A Longitudinal Study, A Tale of Two Samples, The Construction of a Research Database and An Exploration of the Political Economy Thesis* Centre for Social and Environmental Accounting Research, Dundee, August 1994

This paper reports on the Social and Environmental Reporting Database Project at the University of Dundee. Using a detailed form of content analysis which develops and refines earlier work by Gutherie, social and environmental disclosures are captured and analyzed. The analysis is used both inductively, to infer explanations of changes in reporting, and deductively, to attempt to test the quality of various interactive theories of external reporting, most notably political economic theory, as a description and predictor of changes in voluntary reporting. The paper concludes with a recognition of the need for more systematic research into social and environmental accounting and disclosure.

R Gray, D Owen, and C Adams (1996) *Accounting and Accountability: Changes and Challenges in Corporate Social and Environmental Reporting* Prentice Hall, London

Addressing the underlying themes of accountability remains the main role of corporate social and environmental reporting. In advocating corporate social reporting as a practical and ethical alternative to conventional accounting practice, the text presents a candid perspective on recent changes and the challenges that come with them.

Institute of Social and Ethical Accountability/New Economics Foundation (1997) *Sixth Environment Foundation Windsor Roundtable on Social and Ethical Accounting and Auditing: Summary of Proceedings* Institute of Social and Ethical AccountAbility, London

A high-level international meeting of companies, non-governmental organizations and representatives of key professions met in early December 1996 under the umbrellas of the Environment Foundation, the New Economics Foundation and the Institute of Social and Ethical AccountAbility to take a hard look at the emerging practice of social and ethical accounting, auditing, and reporting. This report summarizes the proceedings.

D Korten (1996) *When Corporations Rule the World* Earthscan, London

An incisive challenge to the potential for corporations to deliver against social and environmental concerns within the prevailing structures of globalized competition. Included is a detailed analysis of the role of the financial community in constraining the ability of companies to deviate from narrow financial objectives.

R Levett (1996) 'From Eco-Management and Audit (EMAS) to Sustainability Management and Audit (SMAS)' in *Local Environment*, October

The local authority version of the Eco-Management and Audit Scheme (LA-EMAS) can already be used as a tool for managing towards sustainability. But it can also be used in a much less ambitious way. This article suggests how social issues, a concern over environmental carrying capacities, and stakeholder involvement raise interesting questions which should be considered in the run-up to the review of the EMAS regulation in 1998.

E Mayo (1996) *Social Auditing in the Voluntary Sector* City University, London

One of the most recent reports on social and ethical accounting and auditing for non-governmental organizations which draws particularly on experiences in the Philippines, South Africa, and the UK. Complementary to the *Workbook for Trainers and Practitioners* (Pearce et al) described below.

C Medawar (1992) *Power and Dependence: Social Audit on the Safety of Medicines* Social Audit Ltd, London

As the title implies, this book is about safety of medicines in the context of power and dependence. It reveals the power of the pharmaceutical industry and the secretive and unresponsive behaviour of government to consumer needs. In addition to this, the author discusses alternative ways of medicine and therapy and postulates a social audit on the safety of medicine.

J Nelson (1996) *Business as Partners in Development: Creating Wealth for Countries, Companies, and Communities* The Prince of Wales Business Leaders Forum in collaboration with The World Bank and The United Nations Development Programme, The Prince of Wales Business Leaders Forum, London

Comprehensive report of international examples of good practice business activities in the community, ranging from the activities of mainstream companies to the emerging paradigm of social enterprise. Includes essay on contemporary developments in social and ethical accounting and auditing.

New Economics Foundation/Catholic Institute Relations (1997) *Open Trading: Options for Effective Monitoring of Corporate Codes* NEF/CIIR, London

Report produced on behalf of a grouping of non-governmental organizations involved in negotiations to introduce monitoring and external verification against agreed labour codes for Southern suppliers to retail multinationals. Includes numerous case studies of existing monitoring and verification systems, as well as recommendations for future developments in the field.

J Pearce, P Raynard and S Zadek (1996) *Social Auditing for Small Organizations: A Workbook for Trainers and Practitioners* New Economics Foundation, London

A practical guide to social auditing for organizations that cannot afford, or do not want to expend resources on, extensive procedures and systems. Workbook takes the user through an eight-step approach that can be followed by employees/managers, or facilitated by an outside trainer or auditor. Workbook is the core of a 'learning network' that encourages and enables the user to share experiences with others around the world.

J Pretty, G Irene, J Thompson and I Scoones (1995) *Participatory Learning and Action: A Trainer's Guide* International Institute for Environment and Development, London

Based on work by researchers, policy makers, trainers, and community organizations, this book summarises experiences and methods in 'participatory learning'. This book is useful reading for those involved in undertaking or assessing social and ethical accounting and auditing which includes stakeholder dialogue with communities and community organizations.

P Pruzan and O Thyssen (1990) 'Conflict and consensus: Ethics as shared value horizon for strategic planning' *Human Systems Management* 9: 134–152.

The concept of organizational ethics is developed within a framework of self-organizing enterprises. This leads to a conception of corporate dialogue-culture and to a series of recommendation concerning the implementation of an ethical perspective on leadership. The article presents Ethical Accounting to a non-Scandinavian audience for the first time.

P Pruzan and O Thyssen (1994) 'The Renaissance of Ethics and the Ethical Accounting Statement', in *Educational Technology*, January 1994: 23–28

This paper postulate a renaissance of ethics as a complex of more fundamental tensions and relates concepts of shared values, morals, and organizational ethics to notions of value-based leadership and ethical accounting. The authors analyze the current approach to ethical accounting by discussing its limits and perspectives.

P Pruzan and S Zadek (1997, forthcoming) 'Socially responsible and accountable enterprise' *Journal of Human Values*

Also to be available in modified form in a book published by the 1996 Copenhagen Seminar for Social Progress. Treats five questions: 1) What underlies the growth of concern for socially responsible business? 2) What are the theoretical underpinnings of this new perspective on enterprise? 3) How can the theory lead to measurable accountability? 4) What is the status of social and ethical assessment? 5) How are such accounting methods being applied in practice?

Royal Society for the Encouragement of Arts Manufacture & Commerce (1996) *Tomorrow's Company: The Role of Business in a Changing World* RSA, London

Report of an extended enquiry by companies and other organizations into the likely terms on which companies will operate in the future. There is a focus on the development of long-term perspectives that take social and environmental issues more fully into account as a basis for successful business. Strong emphasis on the need to develop appropriate frameworks for measuring and reporting on social and environmental performance.

SustainAbility/United Nations Environment Programme (1996) *Engaging Stakeholders* SustainAbility/UNEP, London

Two-volume study of progress in corporate environmental reporting, with a particular emphasis on the increasing incidence of stakeholder consultation as an integral part of the environmental accounting and reporting process. Extention of five-stage model for reporting to encompass social as well as environmental reporting – this begins to detail, therefore, what 'sustainability auditing' might look like.

US Department of Commerce (1979) *Corporate Social Reporting in the United States and Western Europe: Report of the Task Force on Corporate Social Performance* US Department of Commerce, Washington, DC

This report summarises a period of considerable practical experience in corporate social and ethical accounting and auditing. With many examples of what companies were doing during the 1970s and why, this report is arguably the most comprehensive document covering that critical period. Also very useful bibliography.

D Wheeler and Maria Sillanpää (1997) *The Stakeholder Corporation: A Blueprint for Maximising Stakeholder Value* Pitman, London

This book offers the most detailed analysis to date of current approaches to building an inclusive company, with a particular focus on the case of The Body Shop.

S Zadek and P Raynard (1995) 'Accounting Works: A Comparative Review of Contemporary Approaches to Social and Ethical Accounting' in *Accounting Forum*, Volume 19, Nos. 2/3, pp164–175

This paper defines, describes and compares three core methods of social and ethical accounting (social audit, ethical accounting statement, social assessment). The paper focuses on social auditing and sets out the key features and highlights the underlying principles.

Annex 1
Social and Ethical Accounting and Auditing: Key Elements

Principle	Key Elements
1 Inclusivity	*Level of Stakeholder Consultation:* Accounting process design Stakeholder mission values incorporation Stakeholder objectives/aims incorporation Indicators selection design Impact/outcome
2 Comparability	*Forms of Comparability:* Mandatory compliance Non-mandatory compliance Inter-industry/company Organization score over time Social and ethical norms/benchmarks Targets
3 Completeness	*Stakeholder coverage* Stakeholder identification/acknowledgement Short term Long term (retrospective) Long term (forward commitments) Feedback on previous disclosure *Sustainability Linkages* Linkage/incorporation of financial data Linkage/incorporation of environmental data
4 Evolutionary	Regular Timeliness Development of breadth over time Development of depth over time Responsiveness of scope to feedback Responsiveness of scope to 'pinch points' ('hot spots')
5 Management Policies and Systems	Overall social and ethical policy statement Stakeholder-specific social policies Management systems Responsibility and accountability guidelines Internal auditing procedures and practice

	Social and ethical review
	Management reports
	Board reports
6 Disclosure	Publication of social statement (summary of social/ethical accounts)
	Completeness
	Intelligibility
	Usability
	Accessibility (includes cost of access to stakeholders)
7 External Verification	Third party
	Published verifier's report
	Coverage of verification
	Audit review panel
	Verifier qualification/accreditation
8 Continuous Improvement	Targets/commitments
	Stakeholder perspectives over time
	Reporting on stakeholder feedback
	Benchmarks

Index